ALSO BY
JOHN DARRELL SHERWOOD

Officers in Flight Suits:
The Story of Air Force Fighter Pilots in the Korean War

FAST

AMERICA'S JET PILOTS AND
THE VIETNAM EXPERIENCE

MOVERS

JOHN DARRELL SHERWOOD

THE FREE PRESS

NEW YORK   LONDON   SYDNEY   SINGAPORE

*f*P

THE FREE PRESS
A Division of Simon & Schuster Inc.
1230 Avenue of the Americas
New York, NY 10020

Printed in the United States of America
10 9 8 7 6 5 4 3 2 1

Library of Congress Cataloging-in-Publication Data
Sherwood, John Darrell.
    Fast Movers : America's jet pilots and the Vietnam experience /
John Darrell Sherwood.
        p.   cm.
    Includes bibliographical references and index.
    1. Vietnamese Conflict, 1961–1975—Aerial operations,
American.   2. Air pilots, Military—United States Biography.
3. United States. Air Force—History—Vietnamese Conflict,
1961–1975.   I. Title.
DS558'8.S54   2000
959.704'348—dc21   99-27744   CIP

ISBN 0-684-84784-1 (alk. paper)

This book is dedicated to the memory of Carl Richter, Roger Wilson, Mike Estocin, Bob Lodge, and all the other fast movers who flew and fought in America's longest war but did not return.

Major U.S. and North Vietnamese Airbases During the Vietnam War

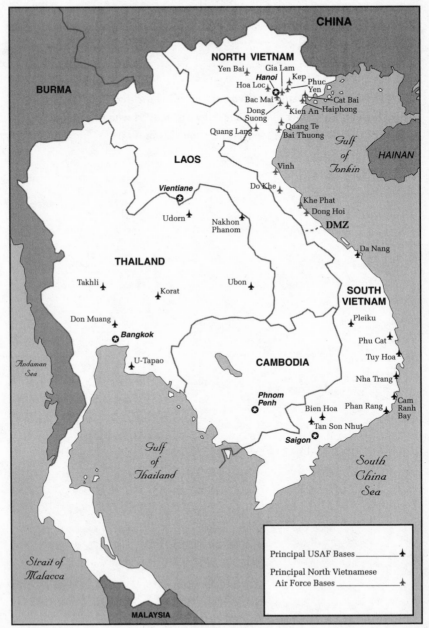

CHINA

NORTH VIETNAM

Yen Bai Gia Lam
Hanoi Kep Phuc
Hoa Loc Yen
Bac Mai Cat Bai
Kien An Haiphong
Dong
Suong Quang Te
Bai Thuong
Quang Lang

BURMA

LAOS

Vientiane

Udorn

Nakhon
Phanom

THAILAND

Takhli

Korat

Ubon

Don Muang

Bangkok

U-Tapao

CAMBODIA

*Phnom
Penh*

Bien Hoa
Tan Son Nhut
Saigon

Gulf
of
Tonkin

HAINAN

Vinh

Do Khe

Khe Phat
Dong Hoi

DMZ

Da Nang

SOUTH
VIETNAM

Pleiku

Phu Cat

Tuy Hoa

Nha Trang

Phan Rang Cam
Ranh
Bay

Andaman
Sea

Gulf
of
Thailand

South
China
Sea

Strait of
Malacca

MALAYSIA

Principal USAF Bases _____

Principal North Vietnamese
Air Force Bases _____

CONTENTS

DRAMATIS PERSONAE

Robin Olds World War II ace and commander of the 8th Tactical Fighter Wing at Ubon, 9/66–9/67. The top MiG killer of the Vietnam War until May 1972, with four kills to his credit.

Ed Rasimus A young F-105 Thunderchief pilot who served at Korat, Thailand in 1966. Rasimus flew some of the most difficult Rolling Thunder missions of the war.

Roger Sheets Navy Air Wing 15 commander during the spring of 1972. His unit participated in many significant missions, including the mining of Haiphong Harbor.

William "Charlie" Carr, Jr. A Marine navigator who flew with Roger Sheets in the A-6 Intruder during the mining of Haiphong Harbor as well as the Bai Thuong airfield attack. Carr was a member of VMA (AW)-224, the Marine A-6 unit attached to the aircraft carrier *Coral Sea* in 1972.

Phil Schuyler An A-6 pilot and Navy liaison officer with VMA (AW)-224, Schuyler often flew as Sheets' wingman.

Bill Angus A young Marine navigator in VMA (AW)-224 who ended up as a POW in Hanoi.

Ted Sienicki   An Air Force F-4 backseater and a POW in Hanoi in 1972.

Roger Lerseth   A Navy A-6 navigator who suffered significant injuries during his 1972 shootdown.

Jim Latham   An Air Force F-4 pilot who flew the fast FAC mission in 1972, and eventually wound up in Hanoi as a POW.

John "Pirate" Nichols, III   The Navy's all-time record holder for number of hours flown in an F-8, Nichols was also a MiG killer in Vietnam.

Richard S. "Steve" Ritchie   The Air Force's first ace in Vietnam, Ritchie is also the only Air Force pilot to make ace—the rest were navigators.

Charles "Chuck" DeBellevue   Ritchie's backseater and the top ace of the war, with six kills to his credit.

Clar & M. "Patty" Schneider: An Air Force intelligence officer with the 432nd Wing at Udorn, Thailand, 1972 who helped prepare intelligence for the Locher rescue. Locher and Schnieder eventually married after the war.

Roger Locher   An F-4 backseater with the 432nd Wing who survived twenty-three days behind enemy lines after being shot down over North Vietnam in 1972.

PROLOGUE

The Only War We Had

The American air war over Vietnam, Laos, and Cambodia spanned twenty-five years, and included a wide variety of pilots, planes, missions, and bases. By the war's end in 1975, more than half of the money America spent on it had gone to Air Force, Army, and Navy air operations. The United States dropped over eight million tons of bombs on the Southeast Asian countryside, and lost over 8,500 aircraft, both fixed-wing and helicopters. For all this investment, air power, though occasionally influential, did not enable America to win the war.

Although much has been written about the tactics and strategies of the air war, few books examine the individuals who fought it. *Fast Movers* will attempt to fill this void by revealing the hidden, personal side of the air war as seen by its primary combatants: the "fast movers," the men who flew jet fighters and attack aircraft. The product of nearly three hundred interviews and extensive documentary research, *Fast Movers* explores the lives and wartime experiences of some of the most famous men of the air war, pilots such as Colonel Robin Olds and Captain Steve Ritchie, as well as a host of unknown but equally intriguing aviators.

The United States Air Force dates its involvement in Vietnam to the summer of 1950, when it sent advisors to help France maintain and operate U.S.-manufactured aircraft in the war with the Viet Minh. After the Viet Minh victory and the partition of the country into North and

South Vietnam in 1954, America continued sending air advisors to South Vietnam. By the end of 1961, six South Vietnamese squadrons were ready for combat, supported by an American combat-training detachment known as Farm Gate. By the end of 1962, more than 3,000 Air Force advisors were serving in Vietnam. American pilots not only flew close air support and reconnaissance missions but also transported South Vietnamese troops around the country and defoliated jungle areas with C-123 "Ranch Hand" aircraft. During the latter program, which lasted over ten years, the Air Force sprayed 19.22 million gallons of herbicides and defoliants over nearly six million acres of South Vietnamese jungle and farmland.

The alleged August 1964 attacks on two American destroyers in the Gulf of Tonkin ushered in a new phase of the air war in Southeast Asia. Then-president Lyndon Johnson called these incidents "open aggression on the high seas" and received broad authorization from Congress to widen the war in Vietnam, beginning with retaliatory naval air strikes against naval facilities and oil storage facilities in North Vietnam. Near the end of 1964, Johnson initiated Operation Barrel Roll, a series of interdiction missions flown along the Communist supply routes developing in the Laotian panhandle. After the Viet Cong attacked the U.S. air base at Pleiku in February 1965, Johnson retaliated with raids against targets just north of the Demilitarized Zone (DMZ). Initially known as Flaming Dart, these reprisal missions evolved into a sustained air campaign, Operation Rolling Thunder, beginning in March 1965.

Operation Rolling Thunder was the longest air campaign in American military history. Between 2 March 1965 and 31 October 1968, Navy, Air Force, and Marine aviation flew one million sorties and dropped one-half million tons of bombs on North Vietnam. Rolling Thunder had several objectives. One was to persuade Hanoi to abandon its support of the South's insurgency; another was to raise the morale of the military and political elites in South Vietnam; and a third was interdiction—strikes against logistics targets such as bridges, roads, and railroads, designed to reduce Hanoi's ability to support the war in the South.

The majority of Rolling Thunder missions were carried out by U.S. Air Force tactical fighters based in Thailand and U.S. Navy fighter and attack squadrons based on carriers in the Gulf of Tonkin (called "Yankee Station"). Pilots and air crew members of these units suffered a disproportionately high share of the armed services' combat losses. Of the 532 pris-

oners of war (POWs) returned by North Vietnam in 1973, 501 were aviators downed over the North, most of them during Rolling Thunder.

The campaign was marked by a basic dispute between senior
American military leaders, who argued for a brief, intense campaign to
isolate North Vietnam from external supply sources and destroy its production and transportation systems, and President Johnson and his
defense secretary, Robert McNamara, who chose to alternate escalation
with bombing halts in the hope of compelling the North Vietnamese to
negotiate. During the three years of the campaign, Johnson and
McNamara ordered a total of seven such pauses. They also insisted on
unprecedented civilian tactical control, dictating the numbers and types of
aircraft, kinds of ordnance, and even the flight paths to be flown. Targets
were chosen by Johnson, McNamara, Secretary of State Dean Rusk, and
presidential assistant for national security affairs McGeorge Bundy (and
his successor Walt Rostow) during Tuesday lunch meetings.

Rolling Thunder strikes were initially limited to southern North
Vietnam, just north of the Demilitarized Zone (DMZ). The "bomb line," a
line just below the city of Vinh, formed the northern boundary of the
strike zone, beyond which attacks were forbidden. As the campaign
dragged on, the bomb line moved progressively further north, reaching to
thirty miles south and west of Hanoi by September 1965, and by July 1966
encompassing all of North Vietnam except the prohibited areas of Hanoi
and Haiphong, as well as a buffer zone along North Vietnam's border with
the People's Republic of China.

By November of 1965, this system of bomb lines and zones was for-
malized into six interdiction areas called Route Packages, or "Packs." Most
American aircraft losses occurred in Pack 6, the area near Hanoi and
Haiphong. Status within the pilot corps became defined by the number of
missions one had flown in that zone. Eighth Tactical Wing Commander
Robin Olds, for example, boasted of having flown 58 Pack 6 missions—
more than were flown by any other Air Force wing commander in
Southeast Asia.

The North Vietnamese used the prohibited areas in and around
Hanoi and Haiphong as sanctuaries in which to base surface-to-air missiles (SAMs) and Soviet-manufactured MiG fighters. During Rolling
Thunder, 919 U.S. aircraft fell victim to SAMs, MiGs, and anti-aircraft
guns of various caliber. The North, employing an air-denial strategy, used
high-altitude SAMs to compel American aircraft to fly low, thereby bringing

them within range of their anti-aircraft guns. MiGs were used very sparingly; usually, they made just one pass at a strike package before retreating home.

Throughout the campaign, American pilots clamored to "go downtown" (i.e., bomb military targets in Hanoi), but President Johnson, his advisors, and the Joint Chiefs of Staff turned down these requests. The Johnson Administration believed that the threat of more intensive destruction implicit in limited, incremental bombing would have a greater impact on Hanoi's willingness to negotiate than would an all-out terror offensive. They also believed that this gradualist approach would forestall possible Chinese intervention.

Rolling Thunder's climax came between August and October 1967 when Johnson, bowing to military pressure, ordered attacks on critical petroleum storage, electrical power generation, and transportation targets in Hanoi and Haiphong. Despite the success of these attacks, Rolling Thunder failed to accomplish its major objectives. The bombing caused an estimated $600 million worth of damage in North Vietnam and killed over 52,000 North Vietnamese civilians,[1] but it did not prevent the Communist forces from launching the Tet offensive early in 1968, nor did it bring North Vietnam's leaders to the negotiating table. It also cost the United States 919 aircraft and over $2 billion. Frustrated by the failure of air power to bring about a peace settlement, President Johnson scaled back the Rolling Thunder campaign after the Tet offensive, and eventually halted all offensive air operations against North Vietnam on 31 October 1968.[2]

Between the fall of 1968 and President Richard Nixon's resumption of offensive air operations against North Vietnam during the spring of 1972, air-strategy planners shifted the focus of the bombing campaign from North Vietnam to the supply traffic moving down the loose network of trails in Laos known as the Ho Chi Minh Trail. This logistics network eventually became the major target of the post-Rolling Thunder Air Force interdiction strategy known as Commando Hunt. What made Commando Hunt different from earlier efforts was its extensive use of aerial dropped sensors. Commando Hunt covered large stretches of the Ho Chi Minh Trail with acoustical and seismic sensors, with the greatest concentrations being located at the strategic passes into Vietnam: the Nape, Mu Gia, Ban Karai, and Ban Raving passes. The system, code-named Igloo White, consisted of three principal elements: sensors sowed by aircraft along the infiltration routes; the airborne relay aircraft that received and transmitted the signals; and the all-important nerve center of the system, the infiltration surveillance system at Nakhon Phanom, code-named Task Force Alpha. Analysts at Task Force Alpha analyzed sensor data as well as human intelligence from Special Forces teams operating in Laos under the code name Prairie Fire. This voluminous data, in turn, was fed into an IBM mainframe to produce daily interdiction-bombing orders. Each squadron received a fragment of that order, called a "frag." When the system functioned smoothly, the resulting intelligence became part of a targeting process that moved rapidly from an assessment officer manning a scope to another officer who directed the airborne command post and called in strikes on specific targets.

The centerpiece weapon of Commando Hunt was the AC-130 Specter Gunship. Sporting 20-mm Gatling guns and 40-mm Bofors cannons and equipped with low-light television, laser range-finders, and infrared detection systems to seek out hot spots associated with truck systems, the AC-130 boosted the statistical success of Commando Hunt operations. In 1968, for example, the Air Force claimed 7,332 trucks destroyed or damaged, compared to 3,291 the previous year. Another significant weapon in Commando Hunt was the B-52 heavy bomber. B-52 Arc Light strikes cratered road systems and caused landslides in the strategic mountain-pass areas on the border between Laos and Vietnam. Other aircraft (A-1s, F-4s, F-100s, C-130s) laid millions of small gravel mines along roads to hamper the efforts of North Vietnamese repair crews and to disable their vehicles.

For all its technological wizardry, Commando Hunt had little impact upon the Communists' ability to wage war. Every year of the campaign American forces, either alone or with their South Vietnamese allies, had to take drastic action on the ground to prevent them from launching a major offensive. The campaign in the A Shau Valley in 1969 by the U.S. Marines, the Cambodian incursions in the spring of 1970, and the South Vietnamese invasion of Laos in February and March of 1971 all demonstrate that Commando Hunt was not as successful as official Air Force figures led many to believe. But the most serious challenge to the effort was the massive North Vietnamese invasion of South Vietnam in the spring of 1972.

Linebacker I was President Richard Nixon's response to this invasion, known as the Easter offensive. Linebacker's goals were much clearer than those of Rolling Thunder: to halt the invasion of South Vietnam and force North Vietnam to resume peace negotiations. Consequently, unlike during Rolling Thunder, commanders were given wide latitude to achieve those goals. American air power was employed with full intensity from the outset; U.S. military commanders exercised full control of tactics and targeting within broad White House guidelines; laser-guided bombs (LGBs) were available in quantity; and categories of targets previously off limits were attacked.

During Linebacker I, tactical fighters from Thailand attacked transportation, power-generation, and petroleum targets. In particular, the new laser-guided bomb technology proved highly effective against bridges. By mid-October, with war materiél depleted, the North's transportation net in shambles, and the People's Army of Vietnam (PAVN) forces withdrawing, North Vietnam communicated its willingness to negotiate and Linebacker I was terminated.

Linebacker II, the subsequent Christmas bombings, was Nixon's iron-willed response to the diplomatic unwillingness of the North Vietnamese to come to a peace agreement acceptable to U.S. negotiators. For the first time in the war, B-52s attacked targets near Hanoi.[3] During the first three nights of the campaign, the bombers attacked in three plane formations at evenly spaced intervals using the same altitudes and ground tracks for their approaches. On the first night of the campaign, three B-52s were lost, and on the third night a staggering six planes went down in a 9-hour period. The loss of these aircraft produced discontent among crews stationed in Thailand and Guam, and Strategic Air Command planners in Omaha, Nebraska. For the next four nights the campaign was run at a reduced level while tactics were changed. The strikes on 26 December 1972 decided the entire air war over North Vietnam: 220 air force and navy aircraft hit a variety of targets all within a fifteen minute window. Only two B-52s went down that day, but the North Vietnamese air defense system was shattered. Their largest missile-assembly facility was destroyed, their ground-based radar early warning and intercept system (GCI) was degraded, and their MiG bases were rendered temporarily unusable. North Vietnam was virtually defenseless against further B-52 attacks, and Hanoi quickly proposed a resumption of peace talks in Paris on 8 January 1973. Although the air attacks continued for the next three days and 4 more B-52s went down before the bombing north of the 20th parallel stopped on 29 December, the air battle was essentially won on 26 December. If U.S. losses had proved unacceptable on the 26th, Nixon would have been compelled to cancel the attacks and no negotiated settlement on acceptable terms would have been achieved in Paris.

The general outlines and major difference of the two major strategic air campaigns of the Vietnam War, Rolling Thunder and Linebacker, are well known; less well understood is the fact that beneath the differences between the campaigns lay a common, un-Vietnam-like, fast-mover culture—a success-oriented culture based on airmanship and membership in an elite group. Far from despising the Vietnam war, most fast movers viewed it as the high point of their careers. The war challenged and affirmed their skills, but more importantly, it united them with a group of like-minded men who shared a common success ethic.

Rolling Thunder was the longest air campaign and the greatest failure of air power in the war. It is this campaign that most aviators think of when they discuss the futility of American air power in Vietnam. During the Gulf war 24 years later, Colonel John Warden, then the Air Force's chief strategist, constantly reminded coalition commander General H. Norman Schwarzkopf during briefings that "This is not your Rolling Thunder. This is real war, and one of the things we want to emphasize right from the beginning is that this is not Vietnam! This is doing it right. This is using airpower!"[4]

The men who flew during Rolling Thunder risked their lives in this futile campaign not because they believed in the cause but because they took pride in their service, their units, and their unique fast-mover culture. By stressing the importance and status of this culture, a World War II veteran named Robin Olds managed to take a unit that had been thoroughly discouraged by the poor management of its previous commander and turn it into one of the Air Force's top MiG-killing outfits. His story, therefore, opens this book.

From there the narrative turns to a very different example, which nonetheless also demonstrates the success of the fast-mover *Gemeinschaft* or collective culture. Ed Rasimus, a relatively unknown but earnest pilot, joined the Air Force because he loved the idea of flying. He never thought he would end up in Vietnam, however, and when he learned of his assignment to Southeast Asia he became almost paralyzed with dread. What is intriguing about Rasimus's story is that at any point in the process he could have extricated himself from combat status. Unlike members of the other combat arms, pilots are permitted to remove themselves from flight duty and combat at any time and often, after having done so, continue to serve in the military in ground jobs. As one naval aviator aptly put it, "An airman enjoys a luxury which the infantryman never knows. It's the easiest thing in the world to get grounded temporarily or removed from flight status entirely. And it needn't be anything so dramatic as marching into the CO's office and dropping your wings on the desk. All it took was the merest hint that flying had lost some of its appeal, a casual remark at the O Club, or a couple of aborted flights," and you were out.

Like Robin Olds, Ed Rasimus got through the experience of war bolstered by the stimulation of combat and a respect and love for the men with whom he flew. In particular, acceptance within the unit proved to be of paramount importance to Rasimus. To be accepted, a pilot did not have to believe in the war or support the Johnson or Nixon Administrations in a political sense. He did need to be patriotic and love the U.S. military. Even more important, he had to be willing to make his squadron and its well-being his number one priority in life. Careerism and self-interest were the ultimate taboos of this group; the supreme honor was to die for a squadron-mate, or better yet for some poor grunt on the ground. This is what Vietnam-era pilots mean when they refer to themselves as "professionals." "Professional" in their lexicon had nothing to do with their officer status, degrees, or pilot's rating; it had everything to do with their willingness to expose themselves to extreme danger and adversity, even death, to ensure the survival of their comrades and brothers in arms.

To illustrate that this fast-mover culture extended across campaigns and even across services, this narrative next turns to a group of Marine aviators. The collective culture of the Marines who flew off the aircraft carrier USS *Coral Sea* in 1972 was not markedly different from that of the Air Force units who flew similar missions out of Thailand and South Vietnam. Like their Air Force compatriots, the Marines took tremendous pride in their group—especially after the charismatic naval officer Roger Sheets took command of the *Coral Sea*'s air wing in the middle of its cruise. Different campaigns, a different service branch; yet, again, a charismatic leader made a big difference and inspired a fierce culture of success.

No single event during the war reveals the collective, cross-service nature of the fast-mover *Gemeinschaft* more vividly than the history of the Fourth Allied POW Wing. When taken prisoner the airmen generally conducted themselves with dignity and heroism. Though often perceived by other arms of the service as spoiled individualists who would fall apart when removed from the creature comforts of their bases and aircraft carriers, these pilots and navigators were as committed to the basic military tenets of organization, leadership, discipline, and unit cohesiveness as any other group of military professionals.

As the POW experience demonstrates, there was a paradoxical quality to the air war that makes its social history very difficult to characterize in general terms. Vietnam War pilots often behaved outrageously in base officers' Clubs but then demonstrated iron discipline while incarcerated or when flying missions. Some of America's best pilots were also notorious drinkers and womanizers. Leadership at the highest levels tended to be inadequate, but wing and squadron leaders often proved to be some of the finest air leaders America has ever sent to war. Pilots hated the war but loved flying individual missions.

No missions were more satisfying to pilots than those they flew against MiGs. MiG engagements allowed a pilot to pit his skill against another aviator just like himself. Admittedly, many kills were straightforward missile shots from the rear quarter, which required very little maneuvering. Nonetheless, some MiG engagements demanded every ounce of a pilot's stick and rudder skills. It also took a profound desire to hunt and kill. Not surprisingly, the war became personal for the MiG killers. Theirs was not simply a tour of duty but a quest for personal excellence. For some, this quest could lead to burnout or—worse—death or a bailout. But for the lucky few (like Steve Ritchie from North Carolina, discussed in chapter 6), a quest for personal excellence turned a small-town boy into a world-renowned ace.

But it was the camaraderie more than the killing that kept pilots going. The search-and-rescue missions (SARs) form perhaps the most powerful example of the strength of this bond. As pilot and historian Darrel D. Whitcomb aptly put it, in a "war without end or purpose, there was one mission with which every aircrew member could identify: the rescue of one's own."[5] SAR became a metaphor for the entire air war. The Linebacker II campaign, for example, in the end became nothing but a large-scale SAR effort to secure the release of American POWs in Hanoi—hence its great popularity with airmen. More than any previous American air war, Vietnam became a war fought for the airmen's buddies. The ultimate irony of the air war in Vietnam was that for all the bitterness and hatred they expressed for the overall war and for campaigns such as Rolling Thunder, these men also loved the war. They loved certain missions and certain unit commanders, but most of all they loved the men they fought beside.

CHAPTER 1

OLD LIONHEART

Robin Olds and the Eighth Tactical Fighter Wing, 1966–1967

Ubon, Thailand, October 1966

For the men of the Eighth Tactical Fighter Wing at Ubon, the summer of 1966 was a season of bitterness. Mired in the fruitless bombing campaign known as Rolling Thunder, the Eighth Wing pined to strike the North Vietnamese airfields, factories, and command-and-control facilities in Hanoi, but neither the political leadership in Washington nor the local Air Force commanders in Saigon and Ubon would hear of it.

To President Lyndon Johnson and his key advisors, the bombing of North Vietnam was primarily a political tool, its purpose being to convince the North Vietnamese to give up their support of the insurgency in the South. One accomplished this aim, reasoned Johnson, by attacking the North's supply routes to the South, not by waging total war against its urban and industrial areas. But for the U.S. military pilots this strategy proved exasperating. Rolling Thunder's limited portfolio of targets meant that the North Vietnamese military could easily predict where U.S. planes would attack and could concentrate their defenses accordingly, leaving other areas undefended.[1]

If that were not enough, the Eighth Wing's lackluster commander, Colonel Joe Wilson, compelled his pilots to fly standard routes and times, and to carry standard bombloads. Anxious to please his superiors in Saigon and Washington, Wilson believed that such standardization would result in a higher sortie rate for the Eighth Wing. Higher sortie rates, in turn, would allow Air Force Secretary Harold Brown to petition Secretary of Defense

Robert McNamara for more money for the Air Force. This program to increase sortie rates, called Rapid Roger, ran from August 1966 through February 1967, and greatly undermined morale at the Eighth Wing.

"It was shitty, it wasn't the way to efficiently win a war," recalled "slick-wing" Captain John Stone about Rapid Roger. (Junior pilots in the Air Force call themselves "slick wings" because their wing insignias didn't have a star above them like those of senior and command pilots.) The predictability of the missions annoyed Stone the most: "There were no tactics, everyone went the same route, the same time of day, the enemy knew we were coming." Another junior captain, Ralph Wetterhahn, complained that to achieve a rate of 1.25 sorties per aircraft per day Rapid Roger compelled the men of the Eighth to fly night missions—dangerous missions usually flown by specialized night squadrons. Moreover daytime sleeping, in un-air-conditioned quarters with no blackout curtains, meant that in the hot, humid, mosquito-ridden conditions of Thailand pilots simply could not get enough sleep.

The extra night sorties also strained the aircraft maintenance system to its breaking point.[2] Airman First Class Robert Clinton, a member of an Eighth Wing load crew, remembered maintenance teams working around the clock and breaking every safety rule in the book to keep up with the demands of Rapid Roger. "We would unload live bombs right on the taxiway and just roll them to the side rather than sending the planes to the ordnance-disarming area."[3]

Colonel Joe Wilson cared little for his maintenance crews and their problems. An administrator more comfortable in a starched tropical khaki uniform than in a flight suit, Wilson could not think very far beyond his career. When Wetterhahn lost four feet off his right engine tailpipe from flak, he got "his ass chewed out" by Wilson.[4] This from a commander who flew so rarely that his subordinate pilots even began to question whether he was flight qualified. How dare someone who never flew chastise a pilot for getting shot at in wartime? Did he not understand that "junior birdmen" like Wetterhahn and Stone were leading flights against some 4,400 guns, 150 surface-to-air missile (SAM) sites, and over 70 MiG fighter aircraft, with no guidance from above and with tactics designed not to save lives and put bombs on target, but to please civilian bureaucrats in the Pentagon and the White House? According to the pilots, Wilson did not; instead, he just sat in his office and "raised hell" when planes got shot down.[5]

There was a lot of hell to be dispensed. In July 1966 North Vietnamese defenses claimed 43 American aircraft, the highest monthly total since the start of Rolling Thunder in March 1965. During the first ten months of 1966 the MiGs alone forced 77 fighter-bombers to jettison their heavy bombs and flee before reaching their targets. More significantly, they shot down nine U.S. aircraft. American pilots, by comparison, only downed 24 MiGs during this period—a favorable kill ratio of 2.6 to 1, but one far lower than the 7 to 1 ratio achieved by the U.S. Air Force in Korea.[6]

Clearly something drastic needed to be done, and in late summer 1966, the Seventh Air Force Commander in Saigon, General William "Spike" Momyer, himself a former fighter pilot, began thinking about replacing Wilson with someone who would lead from the cockpit. Warrior colonels, however, were almost an extinct species in the USAF tactical-fighter community by the summer of 1996. Indeed, 40 percent of the pilots in the Air Force were over forty years old late in that year, and most of these men did not have good enough stamina or reflexes to perform well in a high-performance tactical fighter like the F-4.[7] Many older fighter pilots instead could be found performing crew duties in bombers and transports. Others worked in limited resource specialties such as development, engineering, and procurement, and could not be replaced.[8] Still others were leaving the Air Force to take lucrative jobs with civilian airlines; in the mid-1960s, the U.S. Air Force was losing over 1,400 pilots a year to the rapidly expanding commercial-aviation sector.[9]

There was, however, one iconoclastic colonel left at Shaw Air Force Base in South Carolina who had no aspirations to be an airline pilot, or even a general officer. This pilot embodied the best and the worst qualities of America's jet-pilot elite. On the one hand, he could inspire young men to kill by leading from the front—a rare skill that can never be overvalued, in a profession dedicated to violence and the force of arms—but he also drank too much, spoke his mind at every opportunity, loved using abusive language, occasionally interpreted orders loosely, and often failed to show appropriate deference towards his superiors. The man, in short, was a loose cannon, and General Momyer knew it. He didn't care. The Eighth Wing needed to be jump-started—and Colonel Robin Olds, with his cockpit style of leadership, might just do the trick.

Robin Olds' story stands out as one of the most interesting examples of true flight-suit leadership in modern air-power history. In 1967 the Eighth Wing did not possess a more talented group of pilots than any other F-4 wing in Vietnam. The 366th Wing, based at Da Nang in South Vietnam, for example, had just as many skilled pilots, but this unit only achieved 18 aerial victories during the war compared to the Eighth Wing's 38.5. What transformed the Eighth from an ordinary line outfit into the premier MiG-killing wing of the period was Robin Olds' leadership and the sheer force of his personality.

Olds' tremendous success as a combat leader stemmed from three elements in his personality: his loyalty to his men, his desire to share danger with his men, and his willingness to socialize and interact casually with his troops. Olds never asked someone else to do something that he wouldn't do himself. He also did his utmost to shield his men from policies and orders that he deemed nonsensical or downright dangerous. This last characteristic made him a controversial figure with his superiors and hurt his career in the long run. His tendency to fraternize with his men also hurt his reputation. The old pilot adage, "Live by the throttle, die by the bottle," certainly applied to Robin Olds. His love for drink bordered on alcoholism. However, given the *Zeitgeist* of the Vietnam War, where most U.S. servicemen didn't quite understand why they were there or what they were fighting for, seeing their charismatic leader shooting down MiGs in the air and later drinking with them at the bar helped created an *esprit de corps* difficult for non-combatants to understand. As one aviator put it:

> We weren't fighting to defend our country, no one was threatening our country. We weren't fighting to defend the South Vietnamese. On the contrary, we were disgusted by the pictures and stories of those long-haired, Honda-riding, drug-dealing, draft-dodging, duck-legged little bastards living their corrupt lives in Saigon, actually buying their way out of the draft, while our guys were being sent over to die for them. For what actual purpose we were over there, I don't know even today, 26 years later.[10]

Olds, in short, made his men want to fight for him and the unit rather than for the unpopular cause of the war. For his men, he transformed the war from a vague cause to a personal crusade.

A Tradition of Arms: Robin Olds's Childhood and Early Career

Shortly after Robin Olds retired from the Air Force in 1977, he was invited to give a speech at Davis-Monthan AFB in Arizona to a mixed audience of fighter pilots and Strategic Air Command (SAC) personnel. He began his speech by saying, "My name is Robin Olds and I want to identify myself to everybody in this room: Peace is *not* my profession!"[11] The SAC members of the audience turned red in the face. In front of them stood one of the most decorated officers from the Vietnam War making fun of their beloved motto, "Peace is our profession." Who *was* this warmonger, this Prussian, this relic? The answers to these questions lie in Olds' unique background.

Born in Hawaii in 1922, Robin Olds grew up steeped in the culture of American airpower. "The first sounds I remembered," he recalled, "were the cough of Liberty engines warming up at dawn and the slap of the ropes in the night wind against the flagpole on the parade ground."[12] During his childhood, he crossed paths with a veritable Who's Who of American aviation. His father, Major General Robert Olds, was General Billy Mitchell's aide during Mitchell's court-martial in 1925.[13] "General Tooey Spaatz [commander of the Eighth Air Force in World War II], then a major," remembered Robin, "lived nearby, and I used to chase his daughters to the front door and out the back." Robin's greatest childhood memory, his "ultimate thrill," was meeting Captain Eddie Rickenbacker, the World War I ace and Medal of Honor recipient who could lay claim to 26 confirmed aerial victories.[14]

Robin Olds, in short, grew up surrounded by a small but very famous group of pilots. To these men, and ultimately to Robin, the air service was not a paycheck, a stepping stone to the airlines, an opportunity to attend schools and gain training, or a bureaucracy dedicated to expanding its empire. Rather, it was a small priesthood of warriors dedicated to fighting and winning America's wars. The 1,200 officers in the U.S. Army Air Corps in the early 1930s served their country with almost no potential for promotion and at half pay because of the Depression. Throughout his life, Olds would take great umbrage at officers of any rank who did not possess this level of dedication to the service.

After high school in 1939, Robin Olds attempted to join the Royal Canadian Air Force to fight in World War II.

"How old are you son?" The recruiter asked him.

"Nineteen, Sir!"

"We need your parents' permission to recruit you."[15]

Robin then went home and petitioned his father to sign his recruitment papers. General Olds hit the roof. For him, there was only one acceptable route to military service—the United States Military Academy at West Point. West Point would guarantee Robin a regular commission, and with it accelerated promotions for the rest of his career.

Robin Olds entered West Point during a unique period in that institution's history. Due to the wartime emergency, cadets who started classes in 1940 would graduate a year early. Furthermore, those destined for the Army Air Corps would earn both their wings and their gold lieutenant's bars in a mere three years. Robin did his basic and advanced flight training at Stewart Field, just 17 miles north of the academy, played football, and passed all his academic courses. "It was a tough schedule but we didn't care," he explained. "All we wanted was a piece of the action before the war ended."

Olds has mixed memories about West Point. He enjoyed flying, his classmates, and playing football as an All-American offensive right tackle in 1942, but he despised the school's tactical officers (the men who taught nonacademic military courses such as drill and marksmanship). "The place was full of nonentity tac officers and other people who thought they were great because they were assigned to West Point. They weren't."[16] Olds wanted to be a fighter pilot; he learned very early in his career to judge people not on their intelligence, rank, or status but for their competence and valor in a combat situation. The staff at West Point disappointed him in this regard—very few had ever heard a shot fired in anger.

Another aspect of the place that left a bitter taste in Olds' mouth was its strong emphasis on alumni networking. When asked if he ever engaged in ring knocking (the practice of showing your class ring to gain special treatment from commanders), Olds recoiled. "Bullshit, no! That might be true with the infantry or the coast artillery or that bunch, but not in my business, which was raw goddamn fighter piloting. Hell, we had to *hide* the fact that we were West Pointers when I got out of the place because we were detested!"[17] The Army Air Forces during the World War II and Korean War period contained thousands of pilots who had gained their training directly after high school in the Aviation Cadet Program, and therefore had never attended college. In 1948, for example, only 37 percent of regular U.S. Air Force (for such it now was) officers possessed four-year college degrees.[18] In such an environment, a West Point ring could be a source of jealousy and resentment. Olds refused to take advantage of his West Point status simply to please others.

The Army Air Forces trained Olds to fly the P-38 fighter and dispatched him to RAF Wattisham in Suffolk, England to fly with the 479th Group. He flew with the 479th during its roughest month—June of 1944. During this month of the Normandy-invasion, young American pilots fresh from training were thrown up against some of Germany's top aces and paid dearly for their lack of experience. Fourteen pilots went down that month, including the group commander, Colonel K. L. Riddle.

On 11 August, the tide began to turn for 479th. In an attempt to improve the unit's performance, the Army Air Forces sent Colonel Hubert "Hub" Zemke, already an ace and an experienced group commander, to take over the unit. Before taking over the 479th Group, Zemke led the 56th Fighter Group, a unit credited with 665 air-to-air victories. By the end of the war, Zemke himself would have 17.5 confirmed kills, putting him in the top 25 of all World War II Army Air Forces fighter pilots. On his first day at Wattisham, Zemke sat the whole group down informally on the parade ground and gave them "the speech." From now on he said, "pilots would be expected to show discipline, devotion, and dedication, down to the lowest ranks."[19] Zemke repeated his mantra over and over again until things began to stick. This was the "Zemke way." To Robin Olds and the other young pilots at Wattisham that day, the "hard-bitten, gimlet-eyed" young ace embodied all that a combat leader should be. "He led us, inspired us, trained us, and sparked us," wrote Olds.[20]

Hub Zemke impressed Olds on both a professional and a personal level. Professionally, Hub could fly an airplane better than anyone in the group. Possessing keen situational awareness, Hub would often lead flight right to an attacking squadron of German fighters without once referring to a map during the entire six hour mission. As a leader, he turned the unit around by insisting on basic tactics and instilling discipline into his troops. Under him, pilots were not permitted to strafe a heavily defended target until heavy bombers had softened the defenses with 500-pound bombs.[21] Escort squadrons would provide top cover to prevent enemy fighters from bouncing the group, and wingmen would always support their leaders. But his most significant tactical innovation was the "Zemke Fan." First used on 12 May 1944, the Zemke Fan dramatically altered an Eighth Air Force policy, requiring escort fighters to stay with the bombers at all times. Zemke convinced Lieutenant General William Kepner, the head of the VIII Fighter Command, that if some fighters fanned out well ahead of the bomber force, many German fighters would be shot down while forming up to attack the bomber stream.[22]

On the ground, Zemke held classes on such subjects as fighter tactics, geography, and enemy air defenses. He relentlessly hammered basic concepts into the young minds of his jocks until they finally got it. Was he a disciplinarian? Most certainly—but one who could instill discipline with panache. When Zemke walked into Wattisham, he put a sign up on his office door that said, "Knock before you enter. I am a bastard too. Let's see you salute." Hub could be firm—but in the end he was a fighter pilot and a "hell of a nice guy."[23]

As Zemke gained confidence in an individual pilot, he would begin to allow him to act independently on the battlefield, so long as basic Hub principles were not violated. Robin Olds did just that in August 1944. Olds' assignment that day was to bomb the bridge at Châlons sur-Saône in the Burgundy region of France. He left RAF Wattisham before dawn and reached the bridge just as the sun began to poke over the lush vineyards between Dijon and Rhône-Alpes. He blazed over the bridge at 414 miles per hour and knocked one of its spans out with a 500-pound bomb. He made a 180° turn and had just begun to head home above a tree-lined road when two dark specks flashed across his canopy to the left. They were not dust but the silhouettes of two Focke-Wulf 190s—a highly maneuverable German air-superiority fighter.[23] Rather than retreat, Olds stayed low and surprised the two bogeys from the rear. "I Just pulled up behind them. The dumb shits didn't see me. I shot the wingman and when he blew up that got the leader's attention."[24] Olds and the leader then went around and around in a circle until finally Olds got a clean shot across the bow. The German pilot bailed out and his plane crashed in a field about a hundred yards away from him. In 1948, he would return to Châlons-sur-Saône with his wife to celebrate his first kills over a bottle of local wine at a restaurant near the foot of the bridge. The span still bore signs of his handiwork four years earlier.

With two relatively easy kills under his belt, Robin Olds became cocky and overconfident. Two weeks later, On 25 August 1944, this attitude nearly killed him. On this day Olds, now a flight leader, was leading a four-plane formation in a sweep to Berlin. Zemke's plan called for Olds and the other 64 pilots of the 479th to fly ahead of an American bombing force in an attempt to flush out fighter opposition. The flight would then escort the bombers through the most heavily defended areas near Berlin and then "beat the hell out of anything that flew, rolled, floated, or crawled in Germany."[25] The plan worked.

Several miles south of Muritzgee, Olds' flight ran straight into a huge swarm of 55 Messerschmitt 109s. The ME-109, Germany's most famous fighter of the war, had a maximum speed of 386 mph and carried a 20-mm cannon and two 13-mm machine guns. Olds' twin-engine P-38, by comparison, could reach a top speed of 414 mph and carried one 20-mm cannon and four .50-caliber machine guns, but it was less maneuverable than the agile 109. As Olds remembered it, the hair on his neck began to stand up, so he edged his flight way out to the left of the group. Finally, he spotted his prey.

Frightened, the pilots in his number three and four planes bugged out, leaving Olds and his wingman alone against this massive armada of Nazi fighter power. The ME-109s were in perfect position to wipe out the attacking Allied bomber force. "I remember vividly the exhilaration, the cotton-mouthed excitement," recalled Olds. "I knew all the others had fallen behind, so far behind they didn't have me in sight. I also knew the two of us were about to attack fifty-five enemy aircraft alone."[26]

As his first target grew larger and larger in his sights, Olds placed his finger on the trigger of his four .50-caliber machine guns, ready to squirt a stream of lead into the cockpit of the 109. Suddenly, his engines sputtered and quit. In all the excitement, he had forgotten to switch fuel tanks and his engines had run dry. Without taking his eyes off the target, he switched tanks. The engines erupted and came back to life, and Olds took his shot. "I don't know if anyone ever shot down an enemy aircraft while on a glide slope, but I did. I fired and he sparkled with hits, smoked, dove off on his right wing and promptly bailed out."[27] Olds then continued toward another bogey. He downed this second Messerschmitt with a lucky deflection shot, earning him his second kill for the day and fourth in the war.

Olds then pulled out of his dive at 15,000 feet with both his Allison engines at full boost. The force of this pullout sucked the canopy right off his aircraft. He was now 500 miles from home in enemy territory, low on gas, so cold he was teetering on the edge of hypothermia, and with limited maneuverability due to his open cockpit. If that weren't enough, an ME-109 pulled into Olds' rear quadrant and started to pepper him with its 20- and 13-millimeter gunfire. "I tried to break left and pulled desperately at the yoke.[28] The old P-38 wouldn't turn worth two cents with that canopy gone, and the bullets continued to come home."[29]

He continued to try to jink his aircraft to frustrate the ME-109's gunfire—but then the tables suddenly and miraculously turned. The ME-109 overestimated Olds' speed and overshot him. "Now I wasn't the crippled prey, I was the hawk. I rolled wings level, sighted, fired a long burst, and caught him square."[30] The ME-109 yawed up and then nosed down into a field, bursting into a ball of fire in sight of the Baltic Sea. He knew then he would survive "for it was a different day; a different day for the rest of my life."[31] Robin Olds was now an ace!

Before the war ended, Olds would get another seven kills in the air and destroy 11.5 enemy aircraft on the ground. He would also leave Europe a squadron commander and a major at the tender age of twenty-two.

Footloose and fancy free, Robin Olds took 45 days of leave after the war and headed to California to visit his stepmother in Beverly Hills. His plan was to spend a month with this delightful, wonderful woman whom he "loved to death," attend some parties, and meet "fabulous people."[32] Instead, he ended up on a collision course with reality. At one party he ran across a colonel named K. O. Desert. The next day Desert, who happened to run the local replacement depot, phoned Olds in an official capacity and told him, in no uncertain terms, that he was already a month late for his new post— as Ned Blake's assistant football coach at West Point.

Olds jumped into a P-38 and flew clear across the country to assume his new assignment. When he arrived, the academy adjutant immediately buttonholed him in the hall. "This tall, stick-skinny, beady-eyed, hawk-nosed son-of-a-bitch stopped me," recalled Olds. Olds saluted very smartly, but his dress and bearing were not good enough.[33] "Here I am a major," he thought, "with a whole bunch of DFCs [two] and Silver Stars [two] and Air Medals and all that stuff." What Olds failed to realize was that in a status-conscious environment like West Point, a Silver Star above the pocket of a twenty-two-year-old major could be more of a hindrance than an asset. It had taken Olds only two years in wartime to rise three ranks, but it would take him 22 years of peacetime service plus a 14-month tour in Vietnam to gain his next three. He simply could not respect officers who had never experienced the dangerous work of combat. This attitude would nearly derail his entire military career. But promotions never mattered to Robin Olds; throughout his career, the opportunity to fly fighters, fight wars, and command like-minded men meant everything.

For his next assignment, Olds flew the P-80 at March Field in Riverside, California for six months and then accepted a position with the Air Force's first jet aerobatic team. The team, led by a World War II ace named "Pappy" Herbst, barnstormed around the country showing off the Air Force's new jet, the P-80.

During one show near Palm Springs, Olds ran across the most gorgeous woman he had ever laid eyes on—the actress Ella Raines. Famous for her supporting role in *Tall in the Saddle* (1944) with John Wayne, Raines had just finished a new film called *The Senator Was Indiscreet* (1947), and glowed bright with stardom.[34] Fearless in the air, Major Olds didn't do too well on the ground that night. "I kept looking and thinking that girls didn't come that beautiful," Olds remembered, but he couldn't seem to get himself to approach the object of his affections and hold an extended conversation with her.[35] Instead, he invited her to attend an aerobatic show at March Field. A grandstand view of Olds' flying impressed Miss Raines, and soon the two were dating regularly. According to Robin Olds, he met Ella at the air show, but June G. McNaughton, Raines' cousin claims otherwise. According to Ms. McNaughton, Ella met Robin through Kenneth Trout, an Air Force officer who worked for Olds in England. "The air show was Robin's subtle way of blowing her socks off," wrote McNaughton in correspondence with the author, "a common Air Force courtship custom. I was visiting Ella in her Beverly Hills home once when she had a date with Robin. I remember him coming down the steps into her huge, high-ceilinged living room, and absolutely filling it up with his charismatic presence. She seemed so little next to him, but her expression was of amusement and complete control of the situation."[36]

Dinner at Ciro's, skiing at Tahoe, a trip to Lake Arrowhead, and two months later on 6 Feb 1947 the fighter ace and the movie star were married.[37] Pappy also got married that year, but his marriage did not have a happy ending. On 2 July 1947, the members of the aerobatic team got "falling down drunk" at a stag party for Herbst. On 3 July Pappy was married, and by 4 July he was dead. At a show in Del Mar, California Pappy didn't allow enough room for the team to complete a fancy landing pattern and pulled up a split second too late. Olds sensed the disaster a moment sooner than Herbst and pulled up just in time, missing the ground by only ten feet. "That was a pretty deep trauma, 'cause I loved the man," Olds lamented. "Smoothest pilot I ever flew with, but he screwed up."[38]

After Herbst died, Robin Olds became the leader of the team, but that position lasted only a few months. General Glenn O. Barcus, who would later command the Fifth Air Force in Korea, believed that the cocky young Olds set a bad example for the younger pilots and needed to be reined in. Olds consequently ended up in a paper-shuffling job at Twelfth Air Force headquarters at March AFB. Rather than trying to make amends with the powerful general, Olds again looked for a way to buck the chain of command and sneak away from the assignment. His position in the headquarters building facilitated his defiance. When he discovered that Britain's Royal Air Force (RAF) was looking for an exchange pilot, Olds put his own name at the top of the list.

In England, the RAF placed Olds in a Gloster Meteor[39] squadron at RAF Tangmere in Chichester in Sussex. By the end of the year, he had been promoted to squadron commander of RAF Number One Squadron. This was the first time a foreigner had ever commanded a regular RAF unit.

Robin Olds' stint in England no doubt improved Anglo-American relations, but it did not help his career. When he got back to March AFB in the fall of 1949, Robin found himself in charge of the 71st Squadron—a squadron destined not for glory over the skies of Korea, but rather for garrison duty with the Air Defense Command in a delightful place called Greater Pittsburgh Airport, Pennsylvania. At "Greater Armpit," as he affectionately calls the place, Olds not only commanded the 71st but was base commander as well; he found himself converting a reserve transport base into a regular Air Force fighter base while many of his friends were off in Korea shooting down MiGs. "My name headed every list to go over to Korea," claimed Olds, "but the group commander, Colonel Jack Bradley, said 'I ain't going and neither are you.'"[40]

Annoyed and discouraged, Olds got in his car and drove once again to Washington, DC—this time to submit his resignation papers at Headquarters, USAF. In the Pentagon General Freddie Smith, who later became vice chief of staff of the USAF, got word that Robin Olds was outprocessing, took him by the arm, and talked some sense into the impetuous major.

Olds wound up in General Smith's office, the Eastern Air Defense Force headquarters. "It was a very bad time for me personally," recalled Olds, "Very, very upsetting. But I learned a hell of lot and I worked with some wonderful damn fine people. We were all doing our best."[41] Robin would lick his wounds for ten years before getting another opportunity to serve his country in air combat. In the meantime, Smith at least managed to get Olds promoted to lieutenant colonel in 1951 and full colonel in 1953.

Smith also gave Olds a well-deserved sabbatical from staff assignments in 1955. He sent Olds to Landstuhl, Germany, to command a squadron of F-86s.[42] While assigned there, Olds spent much of his time in North Africa, helping to improve the Air Force gunnery range at Wheelus AFB near Tripoli in Libya. Wheelus became a fighter-pilot safe haven in the 1950s, a place where pilots could escape from staff officers (and meddling wives) and enjoy practice dogfights over the vast expanses of the North African desert. James Salter, a pilot during this period, wrote, "We traveled and lived in tents; we had our time-worn code, our duties, and nothing more: to fly, to sit in the shade of canvas and eat a white-bread sandwich with grimy hands, to fly again."[43]

For Olds, this flight-suit paradise would be interrupted by the great plague of the fighter pilot—hemorrhoids. Caused by the excessive G-forces to which he subjected his body, his hemorrhoids finally forced him out of the cockpit in Cazaux, France in 1957. After his third gunnery mission of the day, Robin was so weak from loss of blood that a crew chief had to pull him out of the bloody cockpit of his Sabre. For forty days and forty nights, Olds would undergo a battery of painful operations in London. As if to add insult to injury, the Air Force rewarded him at the end of his surgery with another tour in the "five-sided squirrel cage [the Pentagon]."[44]

Robin Olds spent the next five years in Washington, DC: first at Headquarters, USAF in 1958–1960, then with the Joint Chiefs of Staff from 1960 to 1963. While in the Pentagon, Olds managed as usual to make many more enemies than friends. During this period, SAC[45] generals dominated the entire Air Force staff establishment and they killed fighter-plane projects at every opportunity. Olds, ever the fighter pilot, tried to fight the bomber generals and lost. On one occasion his boss, the deputy chief of staff for operations and a bomber general, called him into his office.

"Olds," he said, "I'm tired of these studies that you keep sending in to me. You're not going to put on your leather jacket, your scarf, your helmet and goggles and go out and do battle with the Red Baron. You've got to get it into your head: we're never again going to fight a conventional war."[46]

To Olds, men like the general were "halter-blinded people from the Strategic Air Command who thought they had the world by the balls." With their nuclear weapons and their nifty slogan, "Peace Is Our Profession," many in SAC thought that conventional war was indeed obsolete. This attitude made Olds angrier with every passing year he spent in the Pentagon. "I was irate because my Air Force, that I loved with all my heart, was acting like a bunch of dumb shits."[47]

The irony of Olds' career is that success was hidden in what appeared to be failure. Olds' staff studies may have been controversial but they were brilliantly written. He spent hours in the Army Department library on the A ring of the Pentagon reading everything from military classics to theology. His paper, "A National Strategy for Space," became the "intellectual basis" for "Star Wars" in the 1980s. No one could accuse Robin Olds of being simply another dumb fighter pilot. The man possessed a keen analytical mind, keen enough for him to be selected to attend the National War College (NWC)[48] in 1964.

Study at NWC was a necessary prerequisite for selection to the rank of general officer, but that didn't mean much to Robin. For him, the assignment meant another year in Washington, DC—the land of the staff officer and the bureaucrat. "I went to the War College and listened to all these great guys from the State Department and all the other governmental agencies come in and lecture to us and tell us how to run the world, how to think like military people."[49] But Olds stuck with the program, earned his NWC certificate, and left Washington never to return. His next assignment would be a dream come true, a USAF tactical-fighter wing based in England.

The 81st Tactical Fighter Wing at RAF Bentwaters was one of the most prestigious wings in the Cold War Air Force. In the event of nuclear war, F-101 Voodoo fighters[50] from this unit would fly deep into Communist territory and obliterate airfields and SAM sites with nuclear bombs, thereby paving the way for more massive strikes by B-52 bombers against industrial centers. It was a deep-penetration one-way nuclear strike force: the sharpest point of America's nuclear spear.

Robin Olds arrived at Bentwaters a few weeks after the Kennedy assassination in 1963 and left in the fall of 1965. He brought Colonel Daniel "Chappie" James, Jr., who would later become America's first black four-star general, as his deputy commander. Olds met James in the Pentagon and the two officers immediately hit it off. Chappie James, a self-proclaimed connoisseur of "deep-dish olive pies" (martinis), enjoyed knocking down a few drinks with the always convivial Olds after a long day in the Pentagon. During these gatherings, James would serenade the ace with World War II fighter-pilot songs or tell him tasteless jokes. As their friendship blossomed, Olds quickly recognized that James had talents that he himself lacked. Whereas Olds preferred leading from the cockpit of a fighter, James' strength lay in managing ground operations. James could size up people, bureaucracy, and political factions in a hot minute, and could disarm them completely with his jovial wit and charm.[51] Olds, in short, chose James as his deputy to handle all the issues he hated—personnel, paperwork, housing issues, community relations, the press, and so forth. In this role James excelled. The 81st Wing won the Daedalion Trophy in 1963 for outstanding maintenance capability, the American ambassador's Anglo-American Community Relations Award for five consecutive years, and the National

Safety Council Award of Merit for four consecutive years. Much of the work that went into winning these awards was James' doing, not Olds', and Robin would reward Chappie for his administrative efforts by bringing him to Thailand as deputy commander of the Eighth Wing several years later. Although Olds would never admit it, teaming up with a black officer during a period when the Air Force was struggling to make strides in the area of racial integration also had its benefits: increased media coverage for his unit and more opportunities for Olds to showcase his achievements.

But beyond simply generating good PR, Olds earned his kudos at Bentwaters by working relentlessly to make his nuclear strike force the U.S. Air Force's best. To him, the unit served no purpose unless his men were willing and able to strike hard at the enemy with nuclear weapons. Robin worked relentlessly to achieve that goal. He would stay up all night with the men in the alert shacks, lead three missions a day, and serve on alert status more than any other pilot. He insists that he hated nuclear weapons, but he understood the underlying philosophy behind their existence and played his role in the Cold War nuclear standoff to the best of his abilities. Despite this achievement, the Air Force ultimately removed his name from the brigadier generals' promotion list.

Robin, in any event, did not want to be a general officer. During the 1960s, general officers could not command wings or fly combat sorties. For him, it was a supreme irony of ironies that the Air Force, whose very mission was to "fly and fight," might not allow him to perform these roles as a general officer. Thus, when he discovered that his name was on the generals' list, he quickly developed a scheme to sabotage his promotion prospects—while at the same time honing his unit's flying skills. With several members of the 81st, he formed the first and last USAF F-101 aerobatic team. The team performed Thunderbird-style stunts around Europe in a plane designed primarily for straight and level flying. The F-101Cs flown by the 81st Wing suffered from skin crack and corrosion problems—structural problems that were exacerbated by the high-G maneuvers typical of aerobatic flying.[52] Nevertheless, Olds believed in training the way the Air Force fights, and in combat a pilot often had to engage in high-G maneuvers to survive.

Unfortunately for him, his superior in London did not agree with this approach and actually pushed to have Olds court-martialed for his actions. General Gabriel Disosway, the head of USAF Europe, ultimately came up with a quick compromise. He fired Olds as the 81st's commander, tore up his citation for a Legion of Merit, and sent him packing to South Carolina for six months to "cool his heels."[53]

Robin Olds didn't cool for long. The war in Southeast Asia was heating up, and the rules began to change. The Air Force desperately needed proven combat leaders who could fly fast movers, and Olds soon received orders to report to Thailand as the commander of the Eighth Tactical Fighter Wing, nicknamed the "Wolf Pack."

Setting the Stage: The Technology of Air-to-Air Combat During the Vietnam War

Throughout the Vietnam War, the Air Force's workhorse air-to-air fighter was the McDonnell-Douglas F-4 Phantom. The Phantom in many ways embodied the American automobile culture of the late 1960s and early 1970s. It was big, loud, phallic, smoky, and loaded with gee-whiz technical features—in short, a Corvette with wings. Although not every feature worked on every mission, when things did work nothing in the North Vietnamese inventory could stand up to this mighty machine. For starters, the Phantom could cruise at a maximum sea-level speed of 816 miles per hour, over 115 mph faster than its rival, the MiG-21. Its powerful radar was a supreme technological breakthrough at the time.[54] It could guide radar-homing Sparrow missiles to MiGs up to twelve miles away. The Soviets didn't have anything comparable.

The F-4s carried up to four heat-seeking missiles: either the AIM-9 Sidewinder or its bastard stepchild, the AIM-4 Falcon. These missiles homed in on the hot exhaust of MiGs up to a mile away, thus theoretically eliminating the necessity of having to close within 2,000 feet of a MiG to get a gunshot. Unfortunately for the pilots, the designers of the F-4 failed to realize until too late that most kills had to be made at close range: with friendly aircraft occupying much of North Vietnam's airspace, it was simply too dangerous to fire a missile at a target beyond visual range, because to a radar or infrared seeker an American bomber could look just the same as an enemy fighter. One needed to get very close to an enemy plane to make sure that it was indeed an enemy.

Ted Sienicki almost shot down an EB-66 one day, mistaking it for a MiG-19. "My fangs were hanging out, and I'm thinking, 'We're going to shoot this son of a bitch down in one fucking turn and be out of here. It almost won't cost us any gas. This is great.' And when we got close enough my pilot said, 'It's a goddamn EB-66.' But we had to get close enough to see it, we couldn't tell it was one of our own guys."[55]

In an attempt to rectify this situation, the Air Force early in 1972 sent over a handful of advanced F-4Ds, equipped with Combat Tree sets. Combat Tree enabled the backseat pilot or navigator to interpret North Vietnamese Identification Friend or Foe (IFF) transponders on his radar. The IFF was an electronic device carried by MiGs (as well as by Phantoms) that, when interrogated correctly by a radar, sent back a unique and clearly identifiable return signal. The Tree, in essence, tricked a MiG's IFF into giving out a positive return, which, in turn, the F-4's radar could use to create a fire solution for the long-range Sparrow air-to-air missiles. This was a remarkable coup for the Air Force, but it did not completely solve the technological problems inherent in the F-4.[56]

For all its speed, sexy gadgetry, and awesome power, the design of the F-4 had several major drawbacks. Early models did not carry an internal gun. This meant that targets at 2,000 yards or closer simply could not be engaged. Beginning in 1967, some units began experimenting with the 20-millimeter SUU-16 gun pod, which was carried on the centerline station on the plane's belly. The problem with this configuration is that the gun rested on a station that otherwise could carry 600 gallons of extra fuel—fuel that was often needed on long-range missions to the Hanoi and Haiphong areas. Additionally, the F-4 did not possess a lead computing gunsight; it relied instead on a simple iron sight. For planes flying over 690 miles per hour in a turning, whizzing three-dimensional gun battle, getting an accurate shot was virtually impossible. Eventually the gun troubles would be eliminated with the introduction of the internal gun in the F-4E in 1972, but early-model F-4s continued to be used for air-to-air missions until the end of that year.

Far more serious than the gun situation were the shortcomings of the Phantom's missiles. Many of the 432nd Tactical Reconnaissance Wing's F-4Ds carried AIM-4 Falcon missiles, which had been adopted in 1967 as the Air Force's primary heat-seeking missile. In theory, this missile's internally cooled seeker head could pick up a heat signature from a MiG more efficiently than its predecessor, the AIM-9. In practice the missile was, as Olds succinctly put it, "a piece of shit." Olds had reason to be angry. On 5 June 1967 he would fire six missiles under ideal conditions; five missed and one aborted on the launch rail.[57] All told, the 54 AIM-4s fired during Rolling

Thunder generated only five kills, for a miserable 9 percent effectiveness rate.[58] The missile's firing sequence caused most of the problems. A pilot taking a shot with an F-4 had to go through a complicated sequence of switches; moreover, once armed, the missile only had two minutes of cooling available before it went completely dead.[59]

Because of these deficiencies, Air Force fighter pilots eventually adopted the radar-guided AIM-7E-2 Dogfight Sparrow missile in 1972 as their primary air-to-air weapon. The Dogfight Sparrow functioned in two modes, normal and dogfight. As historian Marshall Michel explains it, "If the radar in its normal mode was like a light bulb in a room, when it locked on, the light narrowed to a flashlight beam that stayed on the target. The AIM-7 followed the beam of the radar toward the reflection of the light off the target." In dogfight mode the AIM-7E-2 had a minimum range of 1,500 feet as opposed to the 3,000-foot minimum range of earlier versions.[60] Even with this improved capability, though, the fragile sparrows often malfunctioned. During Linebacker, 281 AIM-7E-2 missiles were fired and 34 kills achieved for a kill rate of only 12 percent.[61]

With all of these shortcomings, it is no wonder that pilots who flew other aircraft often mocked the F-4. One example of this humor can be seen in the song, "F-4 Serenade," sung by rival F-105 pilots:

> *I'd rather be a pimple on a syphilitic whore,*
> *Than a backseat driver on an old F-4.*

> Refrain:
> *Don't put me in an F-4D, 4D*
> *Don't put me in an F-4D.*

> *I'd rather be a hair on a swollen womb,*
> *Than be a pilot in an old Phan-tomb.*

> *I rather be a pimple on a dirty cock,*
> *Than be an F-4 jock.*

> *I'd rather be a bloody scab,*
> *Than to fly with a bent-up slab.*

> *I'd rather be a rotten bum,*
> *Than fly a plane without a gun.*

I'd rather be a piss in a bottle,
Than fly a plane with more than one throttle.

I'd rather be a peckerless man,
Than fly a bent-up garbage can.

I'd rather be most anything,
Than to fly with a folding wing.

I'd rather give up all my cheatin'
Than to fly a plane with a rotten beacon.

How much lower can you stoop
Than want to fly a droop?

We don't know how they stay alive,
Flying something heavier than a 105.

Just remember, you phantom flyer
You have twice the chance for fire.

We got one engine, you got two,
As a word of parting, fuck you![62]

While many of the problems mentioned eventually got fixed, the song does point out some of the Phantom's most glaring defects, namely its lack of a gun, its complicated controls, its folded wing, and its size and weight. The sexual language of the song is not just another crude rant. When pilots talk about "strapping on" a plane with a long pointy nose, a shark's-mouth paint job, and enough missiles to shoot down a small squadron, they are doing something more than flying a combat mission. Firing a missile up another aircraft's tailpipe can mimic the procreative act and can consume a pilot in just the same way.[63] The F-4C even came equipped with its very own penis—a protrusion under the nose called the "donkey's dick," which housed its cameras.[64] This "pecker," however, didn't necessarily make the F-4's gender male.

Most heterosexual pilots viewed their planes as female. Robin Olds, in an essay entitled "She's a Lady," described the plane as a female bird. "Like a brooding hen, she squats half asleep over her clutch of eggs," he writes. "Her tail feathers droop and her beak juts forward belligerently. Her back looks humped and her wing tips splay upward. Sitting there, she is not a thing of beauty. Far from it. But she is my F-4, and her nest is a steel revetment—her eggs MK-82 500-pound bombs."[65] Robert Clinton, one of Olds' F-4 crew chiefs at Ubon, portrayed the aircraft in more romantic terms in his poem, "Ode to the Phantom":

> *I met you many years ago,*
> *You were quite young then . . . I too.*
> *Known around the world,*
> *Your name instilled fear, respect*
> *To all those who knew.*
> *Together we've fought many battles,*
> *Many places, many times.*
> *We showed them what we can do.*
> *I touched your skin, your soul, felt your heart pound,*
> *I saw you ease, fearless, into the beckoning blue.*
> *I watched when you returned, sometimes I cried.*
> *Each time one of you was lost,*
> *Part of me also died.*
> *Grey, I am now, you too.*
> *Our prime has past, many young anew.*
> *I've known all your kids,*
> *From B to G, the RF too.*
> *I've shined your guns, and armed your tanks,*
> *Loaded your TERS [triple-ejection bomb rack] and MERS [multiple*
> *   ejection bomb rack]*
> *AIM 9s and 88s adorned your wings,*
> *I remember those times we flew.*
> *Thirty years now. We won't quit,*
> *Tomorrow brings something new,*
> *Always another mission, a unique task,*
> *For us old farts to do!*[66]

To Clinton, the F-4 was more like an old girlfriend than a farm hen. It was something he could caress and enjoy in human terms. Ernest Hemingway had earlier put it this way: "You love a lot of things if you live around them, but there isn't any woman and there isn't any home, not any before, nor any after, that is as lovely as a great airplane." The ultimate thrill, Hemingway continues, is to lose your fighter plane "virginity" to a magnificent aircraft because if you do, "there your heart will be forever."

Cultural critic Barbara Ehrenreich defined the late 1960s and early 1970s male culture as the era of the "*Playboy* rebel." A *Playboy* rebel is your typical white middle-class guy who works for a Fortune 500 company. During the week he functions as a button-down, strait-laced professional, but on weekends he breaks out of this mold and indulges in big stereos, flashy clothes, cologne, and most important, fast cars. Assignment to Thailand to fly the F-4 represented the ultimate long weekend for an American male officer in the 1960s; a time when he could shed his blue uniform, put on a flight suit studded with colorful patches, and fly the meanest, grooviest plane in the world.[67]

McDonnell-Douglas could not have invented a better vehicle for the *Playboy* rebel. One Marine unit went so far as to call themselves the "Playboys" and paint the bunny icon on their aircraft.[68] *Esquire*, the upscale men's magazine, even did a color-pictorial piece on the F-4 appropriately entitled "Hotshot Charlie Rides Again."[69] The lead text for the article boasts of the "impulse of delight" one feels when flying this plane.

If the 58-foot-long F-4, with its 14,000-pound payload of missiles, bombs, and fuel, represents the apogee of late 1960s American male culture, the relatively diminutive MiGs flown by the North Vietnamese can be seen as a reflection of a society with different imperatives. The North Vietnamese aircraft were cheap, rugged, maneuverable, and low-tech; in short, perfectly suited for a guerrilla war against a more advanced foe. Furthermore, when employed correctly these fighters could often defeat state-of-the-art American technology such as the F-4.

The MiG-17, North Vietnam's workhorse fighter during Rolling Thunder, could not fly above the speed of sound, nor did it generally carry air-to-air missiles or an advanced radar system. Instead, it relied on the same armament that the Korean War MiG-15 carried: two 23-mm and one 37-mm cannon. Nevertheless, as a dogfighter, the agile MiG-17 proved to be an impressive adversary for the F-4. An Air Force study of the MiG-17 in 1965 stated that "The light weight of the MiG-17 gave it a significant turn advantage over modern U.S. fighters in a slow, close fight—commonly known as a 'Knife Fight'—and the MiG's cannon armament was much more effective in a close engagement."[70] The basic physics of a turning dogfight made this slow-speed turning advantage very significant. As an aircraft turns, gravitational forces make it heavier and slow it down—the heavier the plane, the more it is slowed. As result, a MiG-17 could gradually gain a maneuverability advantage over the F-4 if it could lure the big American jet into a traditional dogfight encounter as opposed to a long-range missile engagement.

Like its older cousin the more advanced North Vietnamese fighter of the war, the MiG-21, often relied on 30-mm cannon to kill other aircraft. But these newer planes rarely engaged in dogfights like the Mig-17s did. Instead, they preferred conducting hit-and-run "slashing" attacks, relying on their supersonic speed and the skill of their ground-controlled intercept (GCI) operators to direct them quickly to a target and then help them escape from any pursuers.[71] The MiG-21 pilots tended to be conservative, and for good reason: their planes could neither outrun the F-4 at high speeds nor maneuver well in a dogfight. The F-4 could fly as slowly as 130 knots, whereas the MiG-21 essentially lost its maneuverability at under 215 knots. The MiG-21 did not carry radar-guided missiles for long-range attacks. Finally, the heat-seeking Atoll missile, essentially a Soviet copy of the AIM-9B Sidewinder, had many of the same disadvantages: it lacked maneuverability and could only be fired at a target from the rear and at relatively close ranges (3,000 to 10,000 feet).

For all its limitations, the MiG-21 could be a formidable foe. Very small and hard to see, the plane worked wonderfully as an interceptor. North Vietnamese ground controllers could vector the stealthy MiGs to the rear of a flight of U.S. F-4s heavily laden with fuel or bombs. The MiGs could then make a quick gun pass or fire a salvo of missiles before the American pilots had time to react. Even if the U.S. pilots did manage to see these bandits coming or receive warning from air- or sea-based friendly radar, the MiGs generally would be in and out before the F-4s could jettison their loads and pursue them. If the tables did turn and the MiG found itself in a defensive position, an armor-plated cockpit protected the pilot from machine-gun rounds, and a bladder fuel tank provided security against incendiary hits.

The final fighter employed by the North Vietnamese during the war was the MiG-19 "Farmer." Similar to the American F-100 Super Sabre, the MiG-19 was a short-range swept-wing interceptor with three 30-mm guns as its main armament. In many respects a hybrid of the MiG-17 and the MiG-21, this plane proved deadly to the F-4 when well flown. Although its top speed of 620 knots was far below that of the F-4, it could out-accelerate the F-4 to 465 knots, and could easily out-turn the F-4 in a slow- or medium-speed dogfight. Fortunately for the American pilots, the MiG-19 did not begin to challenge American fighter planes until May 1972.

F-4 Transition

For his F-4 training Robin Olds went to Davis-Monthan AFB, outside of Tucson, Arizona. Bill Kirk, chief of standard evaluation at the base and a former member of the 81st, remembered Olds' F-4 transition training well. Bill, now a retired four-star general, met his old boss on the tarmac that evening and the two fighter jocks stayed up all night filling out pilot questionnaires. As the sun rose over the Arizona desert, the two men launched into the air in an F-4C. Olds' first ride in the Phantom would be a Mach 2 run. The F-4 was the first operational USAF fighter capable of flying at twice the speed of sound. Developed prior to the revolution of ergonomic sciences, the F-4 had extremely complicated analog control switches, which most pilots spent weeks learning before entering the cockpit. Not Robin Olds—he had to check out in the F-4 and take over the Eighth Wing before his enemies in the Pentagon had the opportunity to kill his assignment. Fortunately for him, Bill Kirk was on the scene to guide him through the process.

A Southerner from Rayville, Louisiana who entered the Air Force in 1951 as a one-stripe airman, Bill Kirk had served with Robin Olds at Bentwaters and respected the man's talents as a pilot. Olds' first test run on the F-4 would be a harrowing near-death experience, but the old ace would soon master the new plane. Kirk would end up training Olds on every aspect of the F-4 weapons system and would travel to George AFB in California to teach Olds how to fire the AIM-7 Sparrow missiles.[72] Kirk, an utterly selfless officer, never once requested to join Olds and the Eighth in Thailand even though he was chafing at the bit to go. Olds sensed this; when he shook Bill's hand goodbye at George, he said, "If you don't think you're on your way to Thailand, you're crazier than hell." Two weeks later Kirk got orders to Thailand.

Olds always worked to reward his subordinates. Loyalty to him went both ways: up and down.[73]

War at Last

The Vietnam War will always be remembered as the war in which civilians hamstrung the military leadership. Yet the appointment of Robin Olds reveals a more complicated story. Although the Air Force's overall commander in Vietnam, General William Momyer, because of his high-profile

position had to produce the high sortie counts and other magic numbers
that the civilian managers in the Pentagon demanded, his wing commanders could play the game a bit more loosely. Clearly Colonel Joe Wilson, a
consummate bureaucrat, was losing too many aircraft in his attempts to
please the Pentagon but Olds, Momyer knew, would gladly sacrifice his own
career to save aircraft and valuable aircrews. That is not to say that Olds
would not expose his men to danger if a target warranted it, but Momyer
also knew that Olds would not send an F-4 out against a target with a single 500-pound bomb just to generate a high sortie count: he would wait
until enough ordnance was available to send that aircraft out with a full
complement of bombs. Similarly, if MiGs became aggressive, Momyer knew
that Olds would not be afraid to temporarily halt bombing missions (the
most significant missions for the civilian number crunchers) to mount a
concerted attack against the MiGs. So despite Momyer's personal dislike
of Olds, he fired Wilson and brought in the feisty colonel in the hope of
fighting President Johnson's Rolling Thunder campaign at a lower cost to
the U.S. Air Force.

Robin Olds arrived at Ubon on 30 September 1966, completely unre-
ceived. Colonel Wilson, who had left that morning, didn't even stick around
long enough to greet Olds or give him a proper change-of-command ceremony. When Olds finally got to the headquarters building, his shock
turned to dismay. Scanning the mission board, he noticed that Wilson had
only flown twelve missions during his entire one-year tour with the Eighth
Wing. No wonder none of the pilots of the wing respected commanders.
Their leaders knew nothing about flying.

That night, Robin ordered the entire Wing to gather in the wing briefing room for a talk. "The challenge was to earn their respect," recalled Olds,
"and you do that by flying with them, not by getting up in front of them
and pounding you chest like you knew what was going on."[74] The room was
dead quiet when Olds entered.

"My name is Robin Olds and it has been twenty-two years since I last
fought in a war. You guys are going to teach me and you better teach me
good and you better teach me fast because I am going to fly Green 16 until
I think I am qualified to fly Green 8 and then I am going to 4 and then to 2,
and finally I am going to be Green 1. One of these days I'm going to be leading and you don't want some dumb shit out front, do ya? So, as long as you
know more than I do, we'll get along just fine, but when I start thinking I
know more than you do, you're in deep trouble."[75] Olds may have been a

cocky and arrogant fighter jock, but he did understand the meritocracy inherent in a combat environment. By allowing junior officers like Stone and Wetterhahn, who grasped the combat environment in Southeast Asia better than he did, to lead combat missions during the first weeks of his tenure at the Eighth Wing, Olds not only gained the instant respect of these veterans but also placed himself in a position to rapidly acquire the skills he would need to eventually lead missions himself.

During the next weeks, Olds began flying with the 433rd Squadron, "Satan's Angels." He loved this outfit and its sporty motto, "Yea, though we fly through the valley of the shadow of death, we will fear no evil, for we are the toughest son of a bitches in the valley." Olds also spent hours in the intelligence shop going over aerial photographs of North Vietnam. "Hell, I spent a good two hours every day in intelligence," he said, "If nothing else, just looking at the new batch of photographs coming in because you might learn something. As a matter of fact, you can learn a hell of a lot."[76] Robin Olds learned where every 85-millimeter anti-aircraft gun position was in North Vietnam. He also learned the geography of North Vietnam so well that he never needed to refer to a map while flying. Knowledge like this contributed immeasurably to his situational awareness in the air. He could jink, do barrel rolls and air combat maneuvers over the skies of the Red River Valley, and still lead his strike force safely home.

Whereas Joe Wilson had distanced himself from his pilots, Robin Olds got to know them intimately by visiting the Officers' Club on almost every night. These club visits helped him pick his varsity team of pilots. Here's what he looked for in a pilot:

> I'll tell you what—I'll tell you what I try to look for in any guy: Is he outgoing? Is he aggressive? In other words, does he like sports? Is he a good party guy? That's part of being outgoing. Is he gregarious? Is he individualistic in the sense of knowing his own mind? Does he have a good grin on his face? Okay?[77]

Hardly a scientific test, but effective nonetheless. From past experience, Olds knew that a pilot's psychological toughness was often the key ingredient of that pilot's success in combat; the best pilot on the training range could be a miserable failure in Vietnam. Therefore, he tended to be partial towards jocks and other "hard-headed" types who could confront the prospect of physical pain and perhaps death with confidence. Ralph Wetterhahn had

boxed as a cadet at the Air Force Academy and was proud of having graduated in the bottom half of his 1963 class. John Stone claimed his sister
got all the brains in his family; he had enjoyed working as a smoke jumper
with the Forest Service before joining the Air Force in 1959. Bill Kirk,
described by Robin as a "hell of a stick," didn't even attend college until after
the Vietnam War. Everett Raspberry flunked his Georgia Tech ROTC classes
in 1954. To Robin, what mattered more than education or social background was raw courage, and all these men possessed that in ample quantity. What these men lacked in academic skills they more than made up for
in flying smarts. Stone and Wetterhahn became self-taught electronic-warfare specialists. Bill Kirk became a leading tactician for the wing, and went
on to develop a highly classified early-warning MiG detection system called
Teaball later in the war.

Time spent in the bar, though, was not all business. Robin Olds loved to
drink, and drank too much. Both he and his wife Ella were heavy drinkers,
and Olds' attraction to alcohol certainly helped to shorten his postwar Air
Force career—he never made it past the rank of brigadier general. On occasion, it also made him less effective in the F-4 than he could have been. Olds
consumed large amounts of liquor the night before Operation Bolo, the
largest counter-MiG operation before 1972, and one could speculate that
some of the "wild" missile shots that he took during that episode could be
traced to his altered mental state. (His inexperience with the F-4 system
probably also contributed to these combat errors.) We never got "knee-
walking, commode-hugging drunk" that night, remembers Ralph Wetterhahn, "but we partied."

Robin Olds enjoyed locking arms with his fellow pilots and sweeping
across the club, destroying everything in his path. He also loved Dead Bug—
a drinking game that required everyone present to lie on the floor and flail
his legs and arms in the air like a dead bug whenever someone shouted
"Dead bug." The game could get particularly nasty after "MiG sweeps,"
when broken glass and other "shrapnel" cluttered the floor. According to J.
B. Stone, "quite a few injuries were sustained in the bar."

Cheap booze only encouraged such behavior. "You could get a fifth of
vodka," recalled Airman Clinton, "for only ninety cents." Robin loved to
go down to the NCO club and buy all the enlisted men booze. "Imagine
it," said Clinton, "a full colonel and the wing commander, God incarnate,
would come down to our club and take time out of his hectic schedule to
reward us and get our feedback."

The colonel and a bar full of sergeants would then sit around and drink beer. "You'd never see this in today's politically correct Air Force," Clinton exclaimed. However, these informal meetings served a distinct purpose. They created a comfortable environment where maintenance people could discuss important issues directly with the boss. Solutions could be hammered out in a matter of minutes rather than days.

Bolo

The opportunity to "beat the shit" out of North Vietnam came in late 1966. From September through December of that year, five Thailand-based USAF fighters were lost to MiGs.[78] Robin Olds, upset by these losses, approached John Stone, the wing tactics officer, and asked him to help come up with a plan for defeating the MiG threat. This plan would be known as Bolo.

Captain John Stone possessed neither the rank nor the background to become the lead planner for the largest, most complex fighter operation in the Vietnam War to date. A country boy from Coffeeville, Mississippi, Stone graduated from the University of Mississippi in 1959 and nearly joined the Forest Service in Montana. He loved the excitement of fighting fires, but figured that flying fighters with the Air Force was probably even more exciting. After an assignment flying the F-102 at Soesterberg RNAFB in Holland, "eating lots of Indonesian food and drinking Indonesian beer," Stone came back to the United States with four other 102 drivers to train in the F-4 and head to Southeast Asia. Of this original group only Stone would escape being shot down or killed.

One should not conclude, however, that John Stone could be characterized as cautious. Before he headed to Thailand, stone's base commander at George AFB in California asked him and another pilot to ferry some F-4s to Nellis AFB. Stone ended up flying an unauthorized low-level flight to Nellis that knocked down a power cable and destroyed a radome on route. Needless to say, his base commander wrote him up for a formal reprimand known as an Article 15. When Stone returned to base, he walked into the commander's office and refused to sign off on the Article 15. Like Olds, this jock hated the "chickenshit" of the peacetime Air Force and refused to play by the rules. The Air Force, desperate for pilots in Southeast Asia, simply threw up its hands and sent the young Turk to Ubon to join the Eighth Wing.[79]

At Ubon, John Stone thrived. Olds allowed his men to raise hell to their hearts' content as long as they fought the war professionally. For aggressive warriors like Stone, such unorthodox leadership was just what they required to succeed; in the end, Stone would end up spending more time in the Wing Operations area than in the bar. It was here that Stone and Olds began to hit it off. As he began to conceptualize the Bolo plan, Stone confronted several major challenges. First, the American rules of engagement during this period did not allow for airfield attacks. All MiG kills would have to be made in the air—a distinct problem since MiGs rarely came up to challenge flights of F-4s. Instead, they preferred to attack the less maneuverable Air Force F-105 Thunderchief, or "Thud." Heavily laden with bombs, and flying in tight formations with large blind spots in their rear quadrants, the Thuds made perfect bait for the fast, highly maneuverable MiG-17. During December of 1966, 20 percent of all Thud strikes against the Hanoi area had to jettison their bombs before reaching their targets due to MiG attacks.[80]

MiGs could differentiate F-105s from Phantoms from the electronic signature emitted by their QRC-160 jamming pod. The jamming pod, though, was a necessary evil for the 105s because it jammed the Fansong range-finding radar of the SA-2 surface-to-air missile (SAM) battery. According to Stone, the QRC-160 transformed a blip on a SAM operator's radar to a solid line. When a flight of four or more aircraft flew with their pods turned on in a tight formation, these solid lines blurred together and rendered the Fansong technology useless.

Stone believed that if the Eighth Wing installed the QRC-160s on a flight of 28 F-4s, the MiGs could be tricked into thinking that those planes were the more vulnerable F-105s and attack. Along with Major J. D. Covington, Lieutenant Joe Hicks, and Captain Ralph Wetterhahn, Captain John Stone set up shop in a tiny storage room in the rear of the operations shed and worked on the plan for two weeks. He pulled several all-nighters just planning the routes and the timing.

When a coherent plan finally emerged, Olds flew to a commanders' conference in the Philippine mountain resort town of Baguio. The Pacific Air Forces Commander, General Hunter Harris, was conducting a farewell tour of his fiefdom and all Southeast Asia (SEA) commanders were required to appear at Baguio for a series of "stupid briefings by a bunch of staff officers from Hickam AFB, Hawaii." It was just the type of event that under ordinary circumstances Olds would have had little patience for.

During the conference, Olds nervously approached General Momyer, the Seventh Air Force Commander, with his plan, but was in essence told to "get lost." A fighter pilot who had fought in World War II and Korea, Momyer possessed a keen intellect, but had a reputation for being a "terrible people person." Furthermore, his chief of staff, Frank Nichols, despised Robin Olds. "That little bastard bad-mouthed everything we did in the Eighth," Olds complained. Nevertheless, shortly thereafter a call came into Eighth Wing headquarters. "General Momyer wants to talk to you, get your ass down here."

Olds flew down to Saigon with Stone that day and briefed Seventh Air Force on the plan. Major General Donovan F. Smith, Momyer's director of operations, loved it and sold it to the rest of the higher headquarters. "Boy, the whole Air Force jumped through its rear end getting us ready for that," Olds recalled. "It was marvelous. The whole supply system and the whole Air Force turned out to support this Bolo mission."[81]

Bolo, named after a Filipino traditional knife, called for three separate strike forces to attack North Vietnam. An "Iron Hand" force of F-105s from Takhli would go in first and attack the SAM sites near Kep, Cat Bi, and Phuc Yen airfields in North Vietnam. An East Force of F-4s from Da Nang would cover the Kep and Cat Bi airfields east of Hanoi and block any MiGs that attempted to retreat to China. The heart of the ruse, though, would be the pod-equipped F-4Cs of the Eighth Wing. These aircraft, known as the West Force, were to attack MiGs coming from the Phuc Yen and Gia Lam air bases just west of Hanoi. The West Force emulated an F-105 Thud strike in every way imaginable. It followed similar approach routes, flew at F-105 airspeeds, and used F-105 tankers to refuel. Overall the Bolo task force consisted of 56 F-4Cs, 24 F-105s, 16 F-104s, plus numerous supporting aircraft: EB-66s for jamming, KC-135s for refueling, helicopters for rescue.[82]

Like the conductor of a symphony orchestra, Stone was mainly concerned about timing. Each instrument in his elaborate symphony needed to play its part at just the right moment. To prevent the MiGs from landing, Stone wanted a flight of F-4Cs flying over each airfield every five minutes for the entire duration of the operation. The MiGs would either be shot down or run out of fuel; escape was out of the question. For three days prior to the mission, aircrews received special briefings for Bolo, originally scheduled for 1 January 1967.

Airman Clinton and the maintenance crews worked nearly 27 hours straight before the mission. "They made us clean every aircraft, take everything off, every rack, bomb, missile, everything!" Olds and Stone told the crews nothing about the mission, and expected the crews to load the ECM pods on the aircraft with little prior training. "In that period of time," according to Clinton, "the only time you flew ECM on an F-4 was if you were flying with nuclear weapons." Because the pods ran on the F-4s' nuclear circuitry, Olds ordered the crew to do a "GWM-4" test of those circuits—a test run only in the event of nuclear war. "'What the hell's going on?'" thought Clinton. "Rumors kind of rolled around."[83]

On 1 January, Robin Olds delayed the mission for 24 hours due to poor weather over Hanoi. Annoyed at having stayed sober for New Year's Eve, many of the Eighth's pilots (including Olds, briefly) went directly to the bar and began to party. At "Oh dark thirty" on the night of the first, Stone and Olds decided that the mission was a go. Usually the coolest hand in the outfit, John Stone disgorged his dinner of liver and onions outside the briefing room that evening. With no sleep that night and no food in his stomach, Stone would go up the next day and shoot down a MiG.

The Eighth Wing's flights that day were all named after automobiles such as Ford, Plymouth, Tempest, and Rambler. Robin Olds, naturally flying in "Olds Flight," led the entire stream of fighters that day. The weather remained "shitty," with heavy cloud cover over Hanoi. Olds, knowing he might only get one shot at executing this plan, pressed on. He led the flight to a point twenty miles from Hanoi, and called "Green Up!"—F-105 jargon for "Arm bombs." Much to Olds' surprise, no MiGs showed up to meet the decoy flight. Olds 3 then picked up a fast radar return about seventeen miles from his 12 o'clock. The MiG was closing at a very high rate, indicating a head-on situation. The MiG zoomed under the flight and ducked into a cloud layer. Olds, continuing to lead the flight toward Thud Ridge, spotted several MiG-21s coming up through the cloud layer. He immediately initiated a hard left turn to gain a firing position. The fight was on. For Olds, this would be his first engagement with an enemy jet; in his excitement he almost "went Winchester" (shot all his missiles) trying to get his first MiG.

First, he salvoed two radar-homing AIM-7Es at minimum range. The missiles failed to guide. Next, he launched two heat-seeking AIM-9 Sidewinders at the MiG-21, now a mile and a half away, but these missiles guided on the clouds instead of the MiG. Meanwhile, another MiG-21 started closing on the flight from the rear quarter and started firing its cannon at Olds 3. Wetterhahn, flying as Olds' wingman in Olds 2, remembered that moment distinctly. "I'm watching this MiG about to kill us,"

Wetterhahn recalled, "and my backseater's [First Lieutenant Jerry Sharp] getting a little bananas." But he stuck with his leaders.

After Olds' Sidewinders failed to guide, Wetterhahn immediately salvoed two AIM-7Es at the MiG in front. The first missile simply fell off the rail, but the second missile did guide and exploded just behind the MiG. "I saw this fireball behind his tail," Wetterhahn explained, "and I thought, 'God damn, I missed him!'" The MiG continued flying for a few precious seconds, and then went end over end, "shedding large portions of the aft section. The aircraft, now emitting black smoke, went into a flat spin, falling through the clouds like a leaf."[84] The Sparrow's warhead, which consisted of expanding rods, had unfolded like a carpenter's ruler and, in the words of Wetterhahn, "basically cut the ass end off this MiG-21."[85]

"Break left, we've got one at six!" Wetterhahn shouted to Olds as soon as Wetterhahn's missiles launched. All three planes then broke left and the MiG overshot. Olds 4, flown by Captain Walter Raedeker, then blasted this MiG-21 out of the sky with a Sidewinder.

As if this fight were not complex enough, another MiG popped up through clouds at Olds' ten-o'clock position and he again took a shot, this time with AIM-9 Sidewinders. "When the first MiG I fired at disappeared," he explained, "I slammed full afterburner and pulled in hard to gain position on this second MiG. I pulled the nose up high, about 45 degrees, inside his circle. Mind you, he was turning around to the left so I pulled the nose up high and rolled to the right. I got up on top of him and half upside down, hung there, and waited for him to complete more of his turn and timed it so that as I continued to roll down behind him, I'd be about 20 degrees angle off and about 4,500 to 5,000 feet behind him."[86] As Olds pulled up low and behind the shiny MiG-21, he let it have his last two Sidewinders, one of which hit and took the delta-shaped wing off the airplane. What was once an aircraft outlined against a brilliant blue January sky became a twisting, corkscrewing, tumbling hunk of metal. No pilot ejected.

Four other pilots from the Eighth Wing would end up with MiG kills— Everett Raspberry, Phil Combies, Lawrence Glynn, Jr., and of course John Stone—for a wing record of seven kills in one day. Stone, flying in the number one slot of the third wave of West Force fighters (Rambler Flight), got his MiG from behind with an AIM-7E. So exhausted was John Stone that he didn't even bother with a victory roll that day. Why push his luck?

In all, Stone's Bolo plan helped raise the Air Force kill ratio from 2.6 to 1 when Olds came on board to 15 to 1 by the end of January 1967.[87] It also whetted Robin Olds' appetite for more MiGs. Perhaps he would emerge as the only two-war ace of the Vietnam War. Robin began to "read every damn combat report written by any outfit that went to Route Pack 6." He even plotted MiG positions at his own desk so he would know "what the hell was happening up there."[88] His hard work would pay off.

Hanging It Out!

Although poor weather prevented Robin Olds from engaging any MiGs until May of 1967, during that month he would shoot down three more MiGs, making him the Air Force's top MiG killer until the summer of 1972, when Richard S. "Steve" Ritchie emerged as an ace with five kills. When asked after the war how killing feels, Olds' answer was remarkably candid: "It feels *great,* compared to the alternative! Remember, for those truly involved in war, civilians and soldiers alike, emotions run deep. You hurt and you hate."[89] By 20 May the war had indeed consumed him. Many combatants in the Vietnam War dreamed of the day they would return home, but Robin dreaded it. He had lived in peacetime long enough to understand that it offered nothing for him. In the Air Force, there were no flying assignments after wing command, only executive leadership positions—and Olds knew that his interest and skills centered on flying and fighting, not paperwork and bureaucracy. In early June, he heard a rumor that the Air Force would end his tour as soon as he got a fifth kill. To get to the bottom of it, he flew to Seventh Air Force headquarters in Saigon and ended up talking to the Seventh AF information officer, Major Lou Churchill, who confirmed the rumor.

For the remainder of his tour, Olds deliberately held back, refusing to allow himself to become a mere public-relations tool. In one instance, a MiG-17 came right between him and some F-105s he was escorting. "I would not have even had to move the airplane," to get the kill, he said. "I could have closed my eyes and hosed off a sidewinder. I just sat there and looked at him. If I had squeezed my finger, I would have lost my job." He claims that he had about nine other opportunities to kill, but he didn't because of that standing threat to his job.

While some former pilots in the Eighth Wing question the validity of this story, most stated that Robin Olds started to "hang it out" a little too much after Bolo. As one pilot said, on a few occasions he became dangerous to fly with, especially for his backseater.[90] For example, Olds once led a gaggle of F-4s over the same target near Hanoi for the second time with no bombs—just to experience the adrenaline rush of being fired at by flak and SAMs for a *second time*. Perhaps Olds himself realized he had a problem after 20 May and used the job threat as a means of reining himself in. Whatever the case, Olds always emphasized that dropping bombs was his major concern, not downing MiGs. Although he will always be remembered in airpower history as a MiG killer as opposed to a fighter-bomber, he constantly emphasized that, "You're not going to win a war by shooting down a damn MiG, you're going to win a war by bombing the bejesus out of whatever you were sent to bomb. Of course we weren't there to win it anyway, so it was all a waste of time."

Old Lionheart Comes Home

The Air Force finally ended Robin Olds' tour with the Eighth Wing in September 1967. Before leaving, he offered some interesting words of advice to his wing. Standing up in the briefing room wearing the jet-black flight suit of the 497th Night Owls squadron, Robin, looking a bit like Clark Gable, offered these words to his boys:

> Now, I won't say good-bye to you. You know we have had some time over here together and I am not going to say good-bye because I know I will see you again. But I just want you to think of something. You have changed! You are not the same young guy that walked onto this base. Things have happened to you inside and you will never be the same for the rest of your life. It's going to take you a while to realize this and it's going to be awfully tough on you when you get home because that little wife that waved good-bye to you is not going to recognize you when you walk back through that front door. She is going to sense immediately that you have changed. And she is going to want to know how you have changed because she wants to know where she stands with this stranger that just walked into the house. So I guarantee you, within the first ten days home, you are going to have a fight. Then you are probably going to go to a party or two in your home town, where they are going to sort of half-ass welcome you back and your best friend from high school or college is going to walk up and tell you what a

dumb shit you are for having been there fighting that stupid war. Then you are going to fly off the handle at him. Or you are going to want to tell him or someone what it was all about, and you are going to realize that nobody gives a goddamn.

True to his own words, Robin Olds went home, fought with his wife the first night, and walked out of a party in Georgetown the second night. Not knowing what to do with Olds, the Air Force gave him an Air Force Cross (its highest award next to the Medal of Honor), promoted him to brigadier general, and sent him to the Air Force Academy to be commandant of cadets. On his first day at the academy, he threw a bouquet of red roses to the wing of cadets from a balcony overlooking the dining hall. "Each one of these roses represents a MiG kill made by *my wing,* the Wolf Pack!" he explained. He then flipped the wing the bird and stormed off. Despite his great love for the Air Force Academy and the United States Air Force, Olds found it difficult to shut his aggression off and transform himself from a MiG hunter to an administrator. Robin Olds would become one of the most popular cadet commandants in the history of the Academy and would influence an entire generation of academy graduates, but his warrior humor and spirit were not appreciated by the academic administration. At a dinner the first night, he got into an argument with the chaplain's wife. After he stormed out of the room Ella Raines, who thought the world of him, offered this as an explanation: "My old lionheart has come home from war."[91]

Fading Away

The old lionheart made several more attempts to roar before his Air Force career finally ended. In 1972, Robin Olds went on an inspection trip to Southeast Asia for the Air Force inspector-general and flew a handful of unauthorized combat missions. When he returned to Washington, Olds not only let General John Ryan, the Air Force Chief of Staff, know that he had flown these missions, but told him that "the fighter forces in Southeast Asia today could not fight their way out of a wet paper bag." Much to Olds' surprise, Ryan agreed with him. "The Navy is shooting down MiGs and the Navy is doing good work," Ryan lamented, "but what's the matter with our goddamn fighter people?" Olds, much to everyone's surprise in the room that day, kept his job.

His luck finally ran out in the spring of 1972. After hearing about the loss of the Air Force's leading air-to-air tactician, Major Bob Lodge, to a MiG on 10 May, Olds immediately flew to Washington and met with his boss the inspector-general, General Lou Wilson.

"Sir, I volunteer to go back. You can bust me to colonel. I want to take about twelve good guys with me. I am going to put them in Korat and Ubon and Da Nang, and we are going to get the show on the road. Then I promise to come home again. But, God, let me do this right now because it's a shambles."

It took Wilson a week to get back to Olds. Wilson's compromise solution was to allow him to travel to Southeast Asia as the head of a missile inspection team. Olds' reply to this offer typified his attitude: "General Wilson, what you are telling me is that you want me to go over there and try to fight that knothead who is the Seventh Air Force Commander [General Vought], all by myself. With no help from the Chief, no support from here, I am supposed to go over and do that all myself, sneak around and do that. You know I am going to fly. You want me to go over and get killed and you guys won't even support me? Nuts!"[92]

Robin turned in his retirement papers that day and left the United States Air Force. Old Lionheart would never again go to war.

Arguably, Robin Olds was the finest Air Force wing commander in the Vietnam War. His wing received two presidential unit citations, and he himself won the Air Force Cross. Overall, he flew 152 missions as wing commander and emerged from the war as the Air Force's fourth leading MiG killer with four MiGs to his credit. The Wing as a whole flew 13,249 sorties over North Vietnam and 1,983 sorties into Laos between 1 October 1966 and 31 August 1967. With all this activity, it only lost 29 aircraft during Olds' tenure. More significant than the numbers, awards, and accolades is what other pilots say about Olds. Ask any Air Force fighter pilot from the Vietnam era who America's greatest air commander was, and inevitably the name Robin Olds will emerge at the top of the list. An informal poll of the 300 pilots interviewed for this book confirms Robin's place in the fraternity of fighter pilots. What was the source of this man's popularity?

Unlike many other leaders during the war, Robin Olds' loyalty extended down to the lowest-ranking man in his outfit. Even if one were only a slick-wing captain, if one had a hot idea Olds would listen, and if one could sell him on that idea, Robin Olds would put his career on the line to see it implemented. Moreover, Olds did not come into the outfit thinking he knew everything. He was willing to learn from others. More significantly, he was willing to share danger with others. That he occasionally made mistakes is evident in this narrative. That his men forgave him when he did had everything to do with his willingness to share risk. Not once in his entire career did Robin Olds ever ask a pilot to do something that he would not do himself.

The most complex element of Olds' character was his warrior ethos. He hated the enemy as much as the youngest lieutenant and allowed the war to consume him in a similar way. He understood how personal and emotional war is: how it often boils down to pure rage and hatred against that person in the other plane who dearly wants to kill you and your best friends. He understood this ethos and believed that a combat leader needed to share it with his men not only in the air but in spirited conversation in the bar. This is what some refer to as the brotherhood of war and it can exact a horrible psychological toll on an individual. Robin Olds lived every day of his life to kill for his country. The rage and anger this attitude created constantly simmered inside him and occasionally came out at the least opportune moments. To unwind, he often needed to drink to excess, even to tear up the bar by leading his men on a "MiG sweep." Certainly Olds' rage, as well as his drinking, often made his marriage with Ella Raines a turbulent one. It also prevented him from rising beyond the rank of brigadier general after the war. That it did not end his career earlier on is a testament to the foresight of a few forward-thinking officers who understood that the Air Force needed leaders who recognized that in an unpopular war like the one in Vietnam, the Air Force needed warriors to take charge and win some victories for the service. The welcome sign over the gate at Ubon read, "The motto of the Air Force is 'to fly and fight' and don't you forget it.'" In war, those skills become of paramount importance, but in peace, they are often more a liability than an asset.

In the end, what made Robin Olds such a fine combat leader was not so much his raw intelligence, his tolerance of drinking and debauchery in the unit, his loyalty to the troops, or his meritocratic approach to combat leadership, although these characteristics certainly helped; rather, it had more to do with his willingness to fight right alongside his men, combined with his extraordinary skills as a pilot. Olds never accompanied a combat flight simply "for the ride," but fought with his men with fierce courage. Despite his initial inexperience with the F-4 system, Olds ultimately mastered the aircraft well enough to become a leading MiG killer in the War. No other wing commander came close to achieving this potent combination of skill and aggression, and that is why Robin Olds is remembered as the finest Wing commander of the Vietnam War.

CHAPTER 2

100 MISSIONS NORTH

Ed Rasimus and the F-105 Experience

As glamorous as it was, Robin Olds' war against the MiGs represented only a small part of Operation Rolling Thunder. Approximately 25 percent of the 304,000 tactical sorties of the campaign were flown by F-105 Thunderchief pilots, and those men paid dearly for their efforts. Over 333 Thunderchiefs were lost between 1965 and 1968.[1] What is more, F-105 pilots stood only a 50 percent chance of surviving a one-year tour without being shot down. For all these losses, the bombing campaign failed miserably. It neither stemmed the flow of supplies from North to South nor convinced the North Vietnamese leadership to end the war on terms acceptable to the United States and the Republic of Vietnam.

Operation Rolling Thunder began in March 1965 and ended in October 1968. During Phase I (March–May 1965), a variety of targets were hit, including ammunition dumps and barracks, in an effort to destroy North Vietnamese Army and Vietcong sanctuaries near the border with South Vietnam. Phase II (July 1965–June 1966) shifted the focus of the campaign to transportation-infrastructure targets: bridges, roads, and rail systems. These targets were not only well defended but also easy for the North Vietnamese to repair with their ample supplies of cheap peasant labor. Theorizing that damaged energy-related (thus more sophisticated) targets would be harder to replace, air-war planners began to target fuel-storage sites during Phase III (June–October 1966) of Rolling Thunder. The Tet Offensive prompted the final phase of Rolling Thunder—a concerted attack against supply depots south of the Nineteenth Parallel.[2]

Over 643,000 tons of bombs rained down on the North during Rolling Thunder; they destroyed over 10,000 trucks, 2,000 railroad cars, 50 percent of the North's bridges, and 65 percent of its fuel storage capacity. However by 1967, the campaign was costing the United States $9.60 for every $1.00 of damage it was causing. Furthermore, by 1968 over 919 fixed-wing aircraft had been destroyed, with 917 airmen missing in action and 356 taken prisoner.[3]

In this chapter, the plight of the F-105 pilot will be examined. Ed Rasimus in may ways typifies the Rolling Thunder pilot. A young ROTC graduate who joined the Air Force to fly fast movers, Rasimus never imagined that he would end up fighting a campaign nearly as dangerous as the daylight B-17 campaign against Germany in World War II. How he came to terms with his fears and transformed himself from a scared recruit into a valued member of his wing will be the focus of this chapter.

Travis AFB Officers' Club, California, May 1966

First Lieutenant Ed Rasimus sat on a barstool alone. Wearing an Air Force blue uniform with shiny new silver wings, he held his bottle of cold Budweiser beer as if it were the stick of an F-105 and struggled to get the bubbly, slightly bitter liquid past the large lump in his throat. Six months ago this proud graduate of the Williams AFB Pilot Training Program proclaimed himself to be "the world's greatest stick and rudder guy"; today, he sat contemplating the prospect of his own demise over the skies of North Vietnam.

"To say I felt sick was an understatement. Did you ever spend much time thinking about death? Not the abstract, philosophical concept. Your death. The end, nothing, darkness, eternity. The sleep from which you don't wake. And you're only twenty-four years old."[4]

The idea of flying fighters had been great fun for Rasimus up to now. As a kid growing up in Chicago in the 1950s, he used to enjoy taking flying lessons for ten bucks a ride, and dreamed one day of flying fast movers with the Air Force. Poor grades in high school, though, kept him out of the Air Force Academy, and he settled instead for an ROTC billet at the Illinois Institute of Technology. At IIT, Rasimus focused most of his energy on his unit and quickly rose up the cadet ranks, ending up as vice commander of the Cadet Corps during his senior year in 1964.

Fortune favored Ed Rasimus in 1964. He applied and was accepted to
the Williams AFB Undergraduate Pilot Training School near Phoenix, AZ,
one of the Air Force's premier undergraduate training program at the
time. "I had about 50 hours of private time in J-3 Cubs and PA-18 Super
Cubs so I knew I was not going to be airsick or be afraid of flying," he
recalled. "Being an egotistical guy, I just said I can do this and I figured
the best thing to do was bluster. So if anyone asked, I told them I was
the world's greatest stick and rudder man. No one had ever been better
than me, no one could beat me. I was good. Which I wasn't obviously, but
the instructors thought this attitude was good and it got me a few extra
points in check rides, etc."[5] Rasimus graduated number three in his class
and won selection to the coveted F-105 Thunderchief program at Nellis
AFB, Nevada.[6]

For him, Nellis was the "cat's pajamas." After three rides with an instructor pilot in a two-seat F-105, Ed soloed in a single-seat B model. He then
went on to practice dropping napalm, firing AIM-9B anti-air missiles, and
even launching large ground-attack missiles known as AGM-12B Bullpups.
"Man, it was fun," recalled Ed. "The napalm made a great big smear. We
were the first class that got to put on our own fireworks display."

When he got his orders for Thailand in February of 1966, however,
Rasimus's world view changed dramatically. "Up to that point I thought the
Air Force was all about fast planes and exotic travel, but I had never read the
small print on the contract that said oh, by the way, you might be killed,
captured, beat up, tortured, permanently maimed, or injured." In 1966
alone, over 111 of these planes went down.[7] For Rasimus, getting assigned
to Thailand to fly combat in the F-105 was "kind of like getting diagnosed
with terminal cancer: everyone is hoping the cure will come before you die.
Maybe the war will end. Maybe they will change my assignment." But in a
few short weeks he found himself being shipped off to Korat Royal Thai Air
Force Base to fly one of the most dangerous missions of the air war: Rolling
Thunder strikes in the F-105 Thunderchief.

From the rumor mill at Nellis, Ed Rasimus knew his odds of surviving his tour were bleak. A few weeks before his scheduled departure he sold
his 1963 Chevy Impala, sent his new wife to Chicago to stay with her parents, and liquidated any other assets of significance. All of his life's pos-
sessions could now fit in his Air Force issue suitcase. Once the cockiest pilot
in his class, Rasimus now sat alone at a strange base, sucking his emotional
thumb.

Absorbed by his travails, Ed failed to notice that a pilot had entered the bar until the officer plopped on the stool next to his. That's when Ed saw something extraordinary. On the pilot's flight suit was one of the most prized badges in the Air Force: not a medal or an insignia, but a simple blue-and-red patch that resembled the Interstate highway emblem. In the red section in white letters was "North Vietnam." In the main section of the shield in blue lettering were the words "100 Missions—F-105." That said it all. Here in front of Ed was a survivor, "someone who had fulfilled the contract, done the job, faced the threat." Only a handful of these patches existed in 1966, and this was the first one Ed Rasimus had ever seen.

The veteran, sensing Rasimus's fear, had some words of encouragement. "Just remember this. Did you ever see one of those Hell's Angels decals that says, 'Death Before Dishonor'?"

"Yeah, what about it?"

"Well, kid, just remember that there are a lot worse things than dying. Living with dishonor is one of them. Think about it. See ya. Good luck." And he was gone out the door with a blonde in a bright red dress.[8] Rasimus never even got his name.

Unlike in the Wolfpack, where MiG kills were the ultimate status symbols, F-105 pilots defined status in terms of numbers of missions flown against North Vietnam and bombs delivered accurately on targets. When a new pilot arrived at Takhli or Korat, he immediately purchased a "Go to Hell" Australian bush hat at the Post Exchange. For each mission flown against North Vietnam, he etched a black hash mark on the front of the hat; for missions into the Hanoi area (Route Package 6), he penned a red mark on the hat. Status in an F-105 squadron often boiled down to how many red and black hash marks a pilot wore, with the ultimate status symbol being the 100-Missions patch he received at the end of a tour. As pilot Jim Gormley put it, "You knew where everyone stood simply by looking at their hats. You couldn't distinguish one day from another—whether it was Monday or Sunday or Saturday. All days were the same—the missions just ground on."[9]

As much as survival mattered to the F-105 community, it was not enough simply to fly a hundred missions and go home. A pilot also needed to put the bombs on target. To earn the respect of his fellow aviators, a 105 pilot needed to do more than simply rack up counters, he needed to "hang it out" occasionally. Hanging it out involved exposing oneself to anti-air-craft fire a bit longer than necessary to put the bombs squarely on the tar-get, or flying multiple passes over a heavily defended area to support a rescue mission. To declare that a fellow pilot had "really hung it out" was the ultimate accolade in an F-105 squadron during the Vietnam War period. It meant more than Air Medals and Distinguished Flying Crosses, it meant that a pilot had upheld his professional commitment to the Air Force to fly and fight. The sense of fellowship created by shared risk-taking also sus-tained these men through periods of great loss.

During the darkest period of 1966, for instance, when most of the 105 pilots were absolutely convinced that survival was impossible, one young pilot named Ronald Bliss approached his commander, Major Roger J. Mathiasen, at the Takhli stag bar and asked him for guidance.

"Major Mathiasen, what are we going to do?" the scared lieutenant asked.

With eyes red from too much liquor, not enough sleep, and twenty straight days of flying, Mathiasen looked up from his drink and said, "We're going to go up there tomorrow, and we're going to put the bombs on target."

"Why?"

Mathiasen put his head down for thirty or forty seconds, looked up, and with tears slowly dripping down his face declared, "Pride. We told them we could do it, and we're going to do it."[10]

For warriors like Mathiasen, the thought of not giving the Air Force a one-hundred-percent effort on every bomb run was worse than dying. The Air Force in the 1960s was full of pilots like Mathiasen. These men knew that their chances of death, capture, and torture were great, but pressed on nev-ertheless. Unlike your typical conscript, these men had worked extremely hard to become jet fighter pilots and were loath to give up this professional status simply because of a combat assignment. Many pilots, like Robin Olds, even welcomed war and the prospect of air-to-air combat as the ultimate test of their pilot skills. But for those who mainly dropped bombs for a living, maintaining their proud membership in the elite fighter-pilot fraternity was usually a strong enough motivational element to allow them to overcome their fears and fly and fight for the Air Force. For Vietnam-War-era F-105 pilots, the ultimate proof that they had paid their dues to the fraternity was the 100 Missions, North Vietnam patch. No medal, rank, or citation means more to this very special group of individuals.

Clark AFB, Philippines

While the 100-mission veteran enjoyed an evening in San Francisco with an attractive date, Ed Rasimus boarded a charter flight to the Philippines to undergo jungle-warfare training—a necessary prerequisite for pilots bound for combat duty. The flight, staffed by the "ugliest stewardesses ever assembled in one place," carried 300 soldiers, sailors, and dependents all seated six abreast on a narrow DC-8 aircraft.

Rasimus's transformation from a scared first lieutenant to a valued member of the Korat team began as soon as his C-130 flight from Clark touched down at Korat. The 388th Wing received a cable from Clark that Rasimus would be on the inbound supply flight and sent two lieutenants, Ken Kerkering and John Russell, to meet him and get him checked in. There would be no "new-guy treatment"—the practice of giving a new pilot the silent treatment until he proved himself in the outfit. Ed soon found out why. In the previous seven days, the wing had lost eight out of its complement of 40 aircraft. These guys, in their Australian go-to-hell hats and sage-green flight suits, were genuinely happy to see fresh cannon fodder for the flight schedule.

Rasimus's first stop was the personal-equipment area. He started with his helmet, which he had brought with him from the States. The life-support sergeant told him to put it on, then adjusted an oxygen mask to his face. The mask had to be snug enough to prevent oxygen from leaking out but not so tight that it would crush his nose or blur his vision. Next he got fitted for a G-Suit, which consisted of chaps that fit around the legs and a stomach bladder. When a pilot pulled Gs, the suit filled with air and prevented blood from pooling in the lower extremities of his body.

Rasimus then requested 18 rounds of ammunition for his Air Force-issue Smith & Wesson 38-caliber Combat Masterpiece revolver. In addition to this weapon, he intended to carry a small semiautomatic Beretta .38 pistol in a James Bond-style thigh holster. This would be his last-ditch weapon. He also requested a second UHF radio, a 200-foot nylon letdown rope for rappelling out of trees, a cut-down machete, a Marine hunting knife, two 16-ounce plastic containers, two 12-ounce cans of water, and a medical kit. The medical kit, incidentally, carried a virtual smorgasbord of drugs: morphine, Dexedrine, quinine, and Darvon. Few pilots would have enough time on the ground after a shootdown to utilize these drugs, but it was very comforting for them to know they had such medications should they need them.

Rasimus opted to carry all this gear in a survival vest. Until a pilot has worn his gear for a week or two, it is uncomfortable: it develops little hot spots and pressure points that bore into the skin, forcing the pilot to adjust his equipment constantly until things feel right. Sometimes the awkward placement of survival equipment could even prevent a pilot from reaching the switches on his rear consoles. To free up the use of his upper body, Carl Richter, one of Ed's close friends, chose to wear his equipment in chaps that were suspended by a webbed pistol belt over the outside of his G-Suit. Richter later suffered severe compound fractures on his legs after bailout in Pack 1, and died from shock during his rescue. Many pilots believed that the weight of the equipment that Richter carried in his chaps caused his legs to flail during bailout, creating the compound fractures that put him into shock. Regardless of how Richter died, a poorly-packed survival kit could cause injuries in a bailout—and could also diminish a pilot's performance in the cockpit. On the other hand, a well-managed kit bolstered a pilot's confidence and even enhanced his chances of survival in the event of a shootdown.

Rasimus's tour of Korat ended with a stop at the flight surgeon's office. If Rasimus decided to quit, Dr. Ron Goldman would be the person he would have to see: the Air Force sent all pilots who refused to fly to the flight surgeon for a psychological evaluation. "Things were happening very quickly at this point," recalled Rasimus. "There wasn't time to quit and there didn't seem to be anyone who would have the time to listen even if I wanted to quit." He simply told Goldman that he felt fine; Goldman signed his papers and dismissed him from the office.

After getting him cleared for combat, the lieutenants led him to his quarters. At Korat, the Air Force treated its pilots well. In contrast to the miserable Clark BOQ, Rasimus's quarters at Korat consisted of a teakwood hootch with four air-conditioned bedrooms, a bathroom, and a central sitting area. A local Thai woman would clean the hootch, make the beds, and do everyone's laundry. She literally pressed Rasimus's flight suit, socks, and underwear every single day. The cool blast of an air conditioner welcomed him, and after a quick shower, he crawled between two freshly laundered sheets and was asleep in seconds.

The Orientation Ride

The next day, the 421st Squadron Operations Officer grabbed Ed Rasimus and told him to suit up for an instructional ride that afternoon. The F-105 was originally designed by Republic Aviation to be a high-speed, low-level nuclear-attack fighter. In the event of a nuclear war, its mission was to fly ahead of the B-52s and bomb Soviet airfields and SAM sites with nuclear weapons. During the Vietnam War, the Thunderchief became the work-horse fighter-bomber for the Air Force, delivering 70 percent of the bombs dropped on North Vietnam during the period 1965–1968. In all, Republic manufactured 833 of these aircraft; 383 were lost in combat.[11]

The Thunderchief weighed 52,000 pounds and had a maximum speed of 730 knots at sea level. It could carry a payload of up to sixteen 750-pound bombs, plus AIM-9 Sidewinder missiles and a 20-millimeter Vulcan cannon for air defense.[12] The short 35-foot wingspan of the F-105 gave it poor turn-ing capability and maneuverability, but its Vulcan cannon and high speeds at low altitudes meant that it could generally hold its own against MiGs once its bombs were dropped.[13] The ultimate curse of the 105, however, was its hydraulic system—the system that powered the control surfaces of the aircraft and allowed a pilot to steer this large, heavy plane. "She was prone to lose control when the hydraulic system took even the smallest of hits," recalled pilot Jack Broughton. "There is just no way to steer her once the fluid goes out. . . . You can lose two of the three hydraulics systems that run your flight controls by the time you realize you are hit."[14]

For Ed Rasimums and other pilots fresh out of pilot training, another daunting aspect of the F-105 was its complex cockpit. With all of his sur-vival gear on, Rasimus could barely see his legs or his control stick. At the center of the cluster of flight instruments in front of him was a flight-director system: a collection of moving tapes, controlled by a computer, that told Ed his altitude, compass heading, airspeed, vertical velocity, Mach, and Gs. The director-system tapes swiveled up and down under a horizontal index line to inform Ed of his flight-performance characteristics. The rest of the cockpit controls consisted of a maze of weapons switches, engine-monitoring instruments, autopilot controls, navigation-system controls, drag-chute handles, refueling-probe controls, external fuel-management cir-cuits, and so forth. A radarscope sat beneath the flight-director system. Above it was a radar-controlled gunsight that could be used for strafing, bombing, and air-intercept attacks. The 105 had so many switches and gad-gets that the aircraft designers could not fit them all onto the front control panel. Along each of Rasimus's legs were additional fold-out panels with more weapons-control switches.

As if the crowded conditions of the cockpit were not daunting enough, Rasimus discovered that the heat and humidity of Thailand had sapped much of his energy before he even got strapped into the cockpit. Fortunately, his crew chief had just filled a two-quart water bottle with ice water. He immediately reached behind his right shoulder, shoved the feeder tube of the bottle in his mouth, and squeezed the release valve to allow a pull of cold water to cascade down his parched throat.

"Sir, can you read me on ground intercom, over?" Rasimus's crew chief chimed in over the ground intercom. Rasimus heard the call over his headset and responded, "You're five-by, Chief, stand by for the prestart checklist."

Suddenly, all his training took over; he could no longer worry about his anxieties. Now attached by tubes, wires, and harnesses to his aircraft, Ed Rasimus began to become one with his machine. He carefully went through the system checks, and then ordered the crew chief to fire the start cartridge. In the States, F-105s were started with external electrical power, but here in Thailand a black-powder cartridge was used. These cartridges were loud and expensive but provided a simple way of starting numerous engines at once in areas lacking adequate electrical power or power generators. A canister of black powder was placed in a compartment under the fuselage of the aircraft and ignited. The combustion of the black powder in a small compartment produced enough gas to get the starter turbine moving. The crew chief gave Rasimus the two-thumbs-up sign, signaling him that all was okay and he could begin to taxi to the runway.

Ed Rasimus's heart began to pound a bit harder as he eased forward the throttle of his Pratt & Whitney J-75P-19W turbojet engine. The smell of jet fuel, exhaust, and cordite from the cartridge burned his nose.

"Oak 2, let's taxi," the flight leader radioed.

"Roger, flight lead," Rasimus responded as he eased off the brake pedals. The 26,500 pounds of thrust of the J-75 caused the plane to literally lurch out of its revetment. He had to tap the brakes constantly to keep his 52,000-pound aircraft under control. Since no weapons were carried on this orientation flight, Ed cruised past the arming area and was cleared as number one for takeoff. Ed clamped down the brake pedals, pushed the throttle to full power, and waited for the engine to reach full power. When his meter read full power and his ears heard the strain of the engine against the brakes, he released the brakes, threw the throttle outboard to light his afterburner and felt the acceleration smash him back into his seat. At the 2,000-foot marker he checked to make sure his speed exceeded 100 knots—the minimum speed needed for takeoff. With that threshold crossed, Ed switched on his water injection system and gently eased back on the stick.

(The injection of water into the combustible fuel mixture of an engine improves combustion within the engine and provides additional cooling). Within seconds he was airborne. Ed flew his F-105 over each of the major air bases in Thailand (Takhli, Udorn, Nakhon Phanom, Ubon, Don Muang, and U-Tapao), tapped a tanker (that is, refueled in the air), and came back and landed. "No sweat," he thought. "My plane works, I can still fly, and perhaps I am even ready for a mission in Pack 1 [a relatively low-threat area where new pilots generally flew their first combat mission]." Rasimus reasoned that it would be less cowardly to quit after an easy "counter" than to drop out before even experiencing a combat ride.

The First Counter

True to his predictions, Ed Rasimus's first combat mission was remarkably uneventful. It occurred on his fifth day at Korat. The target was a little storage area near the old airfield at Dong Hoi, about 75 miles north of the 17th parallel, right on the coast. The airfield was badly cratered and totally unusable. Rasimus simply dropped his bombs near the smoke from his lead's bombs, even though he could not make out a target. "Hell," he reasoned after the flight, "that wasn't bad, maybe I can do another."[15]

When Rasimus landed at 1100, he immediately went to his air-conditioned quarters to get five hours of sleep before the next day's schedule was posted at 1800. Young lieutenants with no command responsibilities *could* sleep—a factor that greatly reduced their stress and improved combat performance. "Once the schedule was posted," recalled Rasimus, "the tension started to set in and you simply tossed and turned until you had to wake up at 0300 for breakfast and the morning briefing: I could only sleep well during that golden period between 1100 and 1800 when I had no idea what tomorrow would bring."[16] If he was not on the schedule, a pilot usually went to the Officers' Club, got drunk, and celebrated his precarious survival up to that moment.

Typically, a combat mission lasted three hours from start to finish; briefings and debriefings generally added another four and a half hours to the equation. Launch times were based upon a strike force's ability to achieve a time over target of 0700. That meant that pilots needed to wake up at 0300 to have enough time to grab a quick shave and eat a glob of eggs, a couple of pieces of toast, and a cup of coffee. Some pilots couldn't dine before combat; others needed to throw up their meal before getting into the cockpit. For those who could eat, though, breakfast was important—in the event of a shootdown, it would be the last hot meal a pilot would receive for quite a while.

Following breakfast, pilots would attend a force briefing in the main auditorium of the command center. That would be the mass briefing, lasting about 45 minutes. In it, the force commanders would take the stage and discuss the target of the day and its defenses. Maps and target photos would then be issued, followed by discussions of weather, tanker procedures, and other combat-support issues. Next, pilots would break up into squadrons and eventually into flights to discuss the more specific elements of the mission. An F-105 strike package during 1966 generally consisted of four flights of four F-105s plus one or two F-105F Wild Weasel flights. Wild Weasels were two-man aircraft, equipped with special electronic gear and antiradar missiles, designed to destroy the radars of surface-to-air missile sites.[17]

A force generally launched at 0500, and rendezvoused with the refueling tankers before striking the target. Before their duty in Thailand, many 105 pilots had never refueled air-to-air before. Here they discovered that F-105s often needed to tank twice during the course of a mission. To refuel, the F-105 pilot needed to carefully maneuver his aircraft behind a KC-135 and allow the tanker's boom operator to plug a fuel probe into a receptacle in the fighter-bomber's nose. Unlike the Navy, which equipped its fighters with a probe and its tankers with a basket-receptacle that trailed the tanker from a hose, Air Force planners decided early on that the most challenging aspect of refueling is jamming the probe into a receptacle. Pilots, these planners reasoned, would be better served by a rigid boom and an enlisted boom operator who could devote himself full time to the art of manipulating a probe. As pilot Jack Broughton put it, fighter pilots could depend "on a stable refueling boom hanging there in space, as well as the skill of the refueling boom operator, or boomer, in the back end of the tanker. Those boomers saved lots of fighter pilot asses."[18]

The image of sex that aerial refueling conjures is difficult to deny: a phallic fuel probe plunging into a receptacle, the object being the transfer of vital fluid. Stanley Kubrick opened the movie *Dr. Strangelove* with a suggestive clip of refueling, but one can also see sex in the language pilots use. Pilot Ken Bell wrote in his memoir that he "almost went limp" during one refueling when the "nozzle moved into the receptacle, and the locking latches closed with a sharp clunk." As the fuel began to flow, he shouted orgasmically: "Hallelujah, praise the Lord and that beautiful boomer!"[19] The sexual nature of the refueling act is equally pronounced in Bell's description of his first tanking. Like a young man recounting his first coitus, he writes:

> I took a nervous drag on my cigarette, switched to 100 percent oxygen, and secured the cockpit for refueling. I was very tense as I slid in behind the tanker. I tried to stabilize in position but I could feel myself starting to overcontrol the airplane. Before I could settle down, the boomer took a chance and stabbed my receptacle. Away she went! In seconds, my airplane rolled to the outer limits of the refueling envelope, triggering an automatic disconnect. I backed off and tried to settle down. "If only I could calm down enough to get a full load, just two measly minutes. Then I could relax and regroup," I chided myself. The boomer extended the nozzle and stabbed again. The harder I tried the worse it got.[20]

Eventually, the over-eager Bell managed to get the nozzle into the receptacle, but then he could not disconnect it. "The situation came unglued," he explained. "I heard a loud snap, the nozzle tore out of the receptacle, and the tanker and I parted company."[21]

Bell's first experience proved rather unnerving, but with time most pilots became very comfortable and proficient with the process. Jim Gormley had never refueled in the air before transferring to 105s, but did not have any difficulty with it. "You just put your receptacle near the boom and the boomer would plug in," he said, "Everyone would cycle through the tankers twice—once to get filled up and then a second time to top off the tanks."[22]

"Holy Shit, They're Shooting at Me!": Ed's Third Counter

After his first counter, Ed Rasimus flew another milk run into lightly defended Pack 1 before flying a truly challenging mission on his seventh day at Korat. Both he and Carl Richter were assigned to fly as spares for a strike against a SAM site in Route Package 2. As often happened in a combat environment, two pilots in the original strike package had aborted due to mechanical problems. Rasimus, with only two missions under his belt, ended up flying a varsity mission as a freshman. Fortunately for him, he was so busy when the aborts were called in that he didn't have time to worry about his predicament: "The workload is so heavy that you can hardly think about consequences; you are thinking about the mission, about formation flying, and navigation." On this mission in particular, navigation proved challenging. A wall of thunderclouds was starting to build over the target area as the first flight went in to deliver their bombs.

Suddenly, Rasimus heard yelling and shouting over the strike frequency: "Flak, look out, move it around!"[23] For someone on his third mission, this chatter was "petrifyingly scary." But Rasimus's flight pressed on. They entered the valley from the south, and immediately began taking hits from radar-controlled artillery. Arranged in a circle around a "Firecan" radar, these 85-millimeter guns spat shells at Rasimus one gun at a time in a circular pattern. "They looked like spots around a ring," he recalled. "But to tell you the truth, I was too busy to say, 'Hey, I'm about to get shot.'" He followed his leader towards the target and dropped his two 3,000-pound bombs as soon as he saw his leader's bomb begin to impact on one of the 85-millimeter gun rings. "I remember pulling off the target and seeing all the flashes on the ground. Holy shit, they're shooting at me, and I ducked in a cloud and felt safer, and then 85-mm bursts started popping in the clouds because they were radar-guided guns. This was my first encounter with guns."

In the confusion of the moment, Rasimus punched not only his bombs off, but everything else on the airplane as well: bomb racks, fuel tanks, and Sidewinder missiles. At least he learned something. More importantly, the mission helped him begin to turn the tables on his fear. "Hell, after that one, I realized that this thing is survivable, and I even began to get a little pompous: I thought to myself, 'I do something other people can't do.'" He was in many respects correct in this observation.

In 1966, F-105 pilots were a rare commodity in the Air Force. During the Vietnam War, the Air Force simply could not keep up with F-105 pilot attrition in Southeast Asia. Ideally, the service wanted to station 1.5 pilots per aircraft in Thailand, but limited resources meant that the ratio generally stood at 1.25. To keep up with pilot demand, the Air Force literally commandeered pilots from around the world and sent them to Thailand on temporary-duty (TDY) assignments ranging from a couple of weeks to a couple of months.[24] Dick Guild served an entire 100-mission tour through a series of TDY assignments. During one TDY, he could see the attrition rate in his own hootch at Takhli. "When I went down in early spring of 1967," Guild said, "I entered a hootch and said, 'How come all these spaces are empty?' 'They all got shot down,' one of the guys responded. I picked one of the empty beds. My logic: you can't clean out the whole side of a hootch twice."[25]

Another method that the Air Force employed to remedy the pilot shortage was to take pilots from the Strategic Air Command, Air Defense Command, and Air Transport Command and put these men through short—70–80 hour—combat-crew-training courses for the F-105. This meant that a guy who graduated last in his Undergraduate Pilot training class and ended up in tankers could find himself flying one of the most sophisticated tactical fighters in the Air Force after only a very short refresher course in the 105. Needless to say, this created many problems at the operational level.

Ed Rasimus remembered that many of these guys became dead weights in the squadron. A pilot who flew F-86Ds with the Air Defense Command, for example, claimed he could not fly the 105 because his back could not take an ejection. "That was very clearly an excuse to avoid combat," Rasimus explained. "He couldn't fly an ejection seat but he could still fly and stay in the Air Force as a pilot. Guys at the bar would say, how the hell did this guy draw a paycheck for eighteen years? When it comes to people shooting at him, now he can't do it." For Rasimus, seeing guys quit actually inspired him to press on. "On the one side," he explained, "you see people quitting and refusing to fly so you don't want to be put in that category: and on the other side, as you take each step in the process, you are surrounded by the assumption that you are going to continue to do it and that you are okay, and that you are not scared, and it just kind of sucks you along."

What did eventually anger Ed Rasimus and other young pilots who put their fears aside and flew the missions was that the leadership often allowed inexperienced majors and lieutenant colonels from outside the tactical-aviation community to lead missions. Cal Tax from Long Beach, New York, a young lieutenant in 1967, kept a diary during the war. On 6 October he complained:

> At this point of my combat tour I am getting very disgusted with the people running my squadron, to name names, I particularly dislike Major Jim Gormley, my operations officer, whom I consider a liar at times and a poor politician at others. Although I am one of the highest time pilots in the F-105 and have more route package 6 mis-

sions than 90% of the pilots, he refuses me the right to lead a flight. The only reason being, which he would not say, is that I am a lieutenant. This unwarranted shortsightedness on his part makes me very bitter. This was the old rule around here "Lieutenants—NO!" That was all, but it was wrong and they know it. I'm better qualified than any of these retread Majors and Captains he has with their 4,000 hours of B-47 [SAC Bomber] time, etc., and he knows it. He just can't stomach the fact that a lowly lieutenant can fly better than one of his crony friends.[26]

Jim Gormley, a retread from the Air Defense Command who had originally flown F-86s and F-106s before going through a short 105 course at Nellis in 1966, probably saw no problem in assigning other retreads to command roles in the unit.[27]

Retreads, however, often lacked a tiger attitude towards combat flying. Cal Tax, known throughout Takhli as "Super Jew," describes what can happen in the absence of tigers leading the pack in a 7 October 1967 journal entry:

> We had the same old "hit and run scared" guys on our target. The rule is, see, to drop your bombs as fast as you can, no matter where they hit, and then go full throttle till you get to the border! Don't wait for anybody! First guy there wins! That's the name of the game with the gutless wonders around here. Every plane they see, it's a "MiG!!! MiG!!!" and wham! Afterburner and run. Sort of makes you real proud to be a member of the team![28]

In another instance, Tax described a mission where his force commander, Dale Leatham, got off course and put the whole force over Kep airfield, one of the most heavily defended areas in North Vietnam. Since Kep was off limits as a target that day Leatham aborted the mission, but only after the North Vietnamese peppered the force with SAMs and AAA. One SAM came so close to Tax that he could see the little canards on the nose of the missile. According to Tax, the force had to dump its bombs in the Gulf of Tonkin because the Route Package system was not flexible enough to permit Air Force planes to bomb Navy targets at this point in the war. "Air Force cannot bomb Navy areas," Tax bitterly complained. "You'd never know we were fighting the same enemy. The bosses would rather have us waste all our bombs in the Gulf of Tonkin, before making a road cut in a "Navy" area. It just makes me so mad, I'd like to go and bomb Saigon!"[29]

The Hubcap Thief: Ed Rasimus Hits His Stride

By the end of May, Ed Rasimus had 18 counters, and by the end of June 40. "On the front side," he explained, "a hundred missions sounds like an incredibly long time but when they're done they always turn out to be much shorter. You've been there sixty days and you're approaching the halfway mark." Ed began to view the mission in the same way he viewed stealing hubcaps as a high-school kid in Chicago. First, the mission needed to be planned. "Would we steal '58 Plymouth cones or Lincoln Continental spinners?" Once a target was selected, the gang would scout out a car in the neighborhood, plan an ingress and egress, and decided who would work on which wheel. Like a flight of F-105s, a hubcap theft mission consisted of four guys. After dark, the gang would carefully make their way to the target, begin to pry the caps off the wheels, and then all of a sudden someone would drop a hubcap and it would go *bang!* A porch light would come on, and some big guy in a spaghetti-strap undershirt would come out and sound angry. A chase would then ensue.

Always the philosopher, Ed Rasimus theorized later that he and his band of thieves were not in the game for the hubcaps, they were in it for the chase. Inevitably, someone would make noise and tip off the opposition. "For most guys who really like flying fighters, going to the range, going to war, the pilot is not a patriot, he's a hubcap thief. He's out there doing it for the rush. To go downtown was to go in there and drop a hubcap and get a chase."

Rasimus began to see the old hubcap thief in himself on the day he earned a Silver Star. The target was an oil-storage area five miles from downtown Hanoi, and that day he was placed on the flight list as a spare. When he started his airplane, he immediately noticed that his gunsight was down, but since the flight was short an aircraft, he pressed on. Now Rasimus could easily have aborted with no hard feelings at this point. Not only was he a spare but if the flight got jumped by MiGs he would be nearly defenseless without a gunsight. Why did he press on? He needed the rush. As he later described it, "I got carried away with the moment, went in extremely low, and ended up putting the bombs on the target with no sight." Rasimus's bomb run got captured by a photo-reconnaissance aircraft, and he ended up receiving a Silver Star for his heroism. On that day, Korat lost two out of twenty aircraft.

Evidence of hubcap thievery could also be seen in the actions of other F-105 pilots. Cal Tax, for instance, expressed disappointment about flying "easy" missions in the lower route packages in several of his diary entries. On 16 September 1967, he wrote:

> I was number two on Ted Tolman's wing as we went back up to the same exact place we hit yesterday. A typical stupid move from those jerks at 7th [AF Headquarters in Saigon]. This time however, the weatherman really flubbed and the target was overcast so we turned around and dropped on the northwest railroad, near Yen Bay. No SAM's, flak or MiGs and it was kind of boring.[30]

Similarly, in an earlier entry on 7 August 1967, he wrote:

> Poor weather in the primary target area forced us to go to our second alternate in RP I. Here we were under control of a FAC [forward air controller], in one of the new Cessna O-2's. (Pusher-puller). We bombed and strafed an area he said was suspect of ground fire, but drew none ourselves. A very boring and routine mission. I can see why we lose so many planes in this area. Guys just think they are on a gunnery range and press in for a close look. They've got plenty of guns in these places and they usually don't open up unless a good target presents itself. I even found myself down to 3,500 feet once.

Pilots like Tax would increase their exposure on an "easy" mission to increase their excitement. Some pilots enjoyed the rush of combat so much that they actually volunteered to fly the toughest missions. Dick Guild, for example, went against the trend of flying easy Route Pack 1 missions toward the end of a tour by volunteering to fly his last ten missions into Route Pack 6. On his hundredth mission, his flight got strung out in their approach to a bridge target, and as he began to roll in he spotted two MiGs in front of him. Knowing full well that his number three guy was too far behind him to cover his six o'clock and also knowing it was his last mission, Dick could have aborted his run at that point. Instead, he chose to hang it out and press on:

So I roll in and this MiG turns on me and he's pulling like a son of a bitch and goes right in front of me and I'm lining up to the target and I look out and see he can't get his nose on me, he ain't going to be able to gun me—I'll take the bridge. I hit the bridge and the MiG departs, goes uncontrollable and crashes. Meanwhile, Robin Olds [flying MIGCAP for the strike that day] is lining up on that MiG—it would have been his fifth. No one got credit for that MiG. If I had pulled the trigger, I would have gotten credit for it. I've never talked to him about that.[31]

A fighter pilot assigned to the Pentagon shortly after serving in combat in Vietnam mentioned that he was once approached by antiwar protesters and asked, "How can you work for an organization devoted to bombing a poor, underdeveloped country into submission?" To which the pilot responded, "Hell, that's the only fun part of my job!" Though no doubt apocryphal, the underlying message of this story dovetails with how many F-105 pilots viewed the war. Pilot Jerry Hoblit put it this way: "This was our war and we wanted to make the very best of it."[32] Despite all the danger and fear associated with combat, combat flying could be enjoyable in a perverse way: the adrenaline rush associated with hanging it out mitigated even the worst horrors of war. "You enjoyed the fact that you were getting out there and getting a combat mission," explained pilot Dave Groark.[33]

Wild Weasels: The Guys who Went After the Cadillacs

In the F-105 community, ultimately, the very best pilots gravitated to the Wild Weasel program. The F-105G Wild Weasel was essentially a two-person version of the standard F-105 with additional electronic equipment designed to pick up the radar signal emitted by a SAM's radar controllers. These aircraft killed the SAM-controlling stations by forcing the controllers to launch a missile at them, which they would evade, and then bombing the pad from which the missile originated. Weasels also sought to suppress SAM fire in a strike zone by intimidating the operators with their antiradiation missiles. These missiles homed in on the electronic emissions of the SAM radars. When Weasels operated effectively, a SAM operator could not turn on his radar or fire a missile without provoking a counterattack. Due to the nature of their mission, Weasels were the first aircraft to arrive in the strike zone and the last to leave. During the war in Southeast Asia, very few missions proved more dangerous than those of the Wild Weasel.

Clearly, it took a special type of pilot and backseater to endure the extreme danger of the F-105 mission. One of the best crews in the business in 1966 was Jerry "Hob Nose" Hoblit and his EWO [electronic warfare operator], Tom Wilson. Hoblit, the son of an Air Force dentist, grew up on Air Force bases around the world, attended West Point, and eventually entered the Air Force upon graduation in 1958. After a series of Stateside assignments in the F-100 and later the F-105, Hob Nose did two TDY tours at Takhli in 1964 and 1965. He then attended the Fighter Weapons School at Nellis and volunteered for a third tour in 1966 as a Wild Weasel pilot. When asked why he volunteered for so many tours, he replied, "You have to march to the sound of cannon. I was a professional military guy, the cannon was going off and I had to get there. That's what was driving me."[34] Hoblit arrived at Takhli with over 2,000 flying hours, plus experience as a 105 instructor at both Yokota AFB, Japan, and Nellis AFB, Nevada. Very few Thunderchief pilots could match him in terms of flying knowledge and ability nor could they match his professional officer's credentials: he had over eight years of experience in the USAF as well as a West Point diploma.

Tom Wilson, Hoblit's backseater, came from a very different background. The son of a construction worker, Wilson enlisted in the Air Force soon after graduating from high school in the small Northern California town of Ukiah in 1956. Wilson went through basic training at Parks AFB outside of San Francisco, scored extremely well on various aptitude tests taken there, and was tapped to attend a highly selective nucleonics school at Tracer Labs near Livermore, California. For the next four years, Wilson worked in nuclear-weapons development at Tracer Labs and took college courses at UC Berkeley. When he finished two years of college in 1960, Wilson applied for and was accepted to Officer Candidate School at Lackland AFB, Texas. Wilson tried to win selection to pilot training, but poor eyesight kept him out; he instead ended up in navigator school at Mather AFB in California.

From Mather, Wilson went to Castle AFB, California, and later Columbus AFB, Mississippi, as a B-52 electronics warfare officer for the Strategic Air Command (SAC). Wilson hated SAC because of the boring and repetitive nature of the B-52 mission. During the long 24-hour flights along the periphery of Russia, he thought of nothing but getting out of the Air Force.

Wilson wanted to move up to a wilderness fishing and hunting area in Canada as soon as he could get out, but the Vietnam War foiled his plans. Just as he submitted his paperwork to separate from the service, his B-52 unit got transferred to Guam to fly missions into South Vietnam. The eight-engine B-52 jets could carry 20 tons of bombs and could take out every living and breathing thing within a box approximately five-eights of a mile wide by about two miles long. These strikes, appropriately labeled "Arc Lights," initially promised a break from peacetime B-52 missions, but they actually confirmed Wilson's worst view of both the B-52 and its mission. "It was abysmal. We flew the airline routes. I was beside myself with boredom."[35] To make matters worse, Wilson soon learned that policymakers in Washington were contemplating the use of these slow-flying aircraft in high-threat areas in North Vietnam—a mission that he considered suicidal. Therefore, after 47 missions, he took some leave in the United States and put in for a transfer to the Wild Weasels.

Both Jerry Hoblit and Tom Wilson were rushed through training at Nellis because all five of the original Wild Weasel aircraft based at Takhli had been shot down. The night Wilson showed up at the bar in Takhli, a guy there informed him that his chances of living through his tour were less than 37 percent. A few days later, Jerry Hoblit picked Tom Wilson to fly a mission with him. Being an arrogant single-seat fighter pilot, Hoblit was not pleased with the idea of fighting in a two-seat plane, but chose Wilson because he appeared to be the most knowledgeable and aggressive EWO of the bunch. As an aircraft commander, Hoblit also looked forward to delegating much of the paperwork associated with combat flying to his new crewman. After their first mission, Hoblit got out of the aircraft, handed Wilson a stack of forms, and said, "Here, go fill these out!" Hoblit then turned around and started walking away. Seconds later he distinctly felt the palm of a hand smacking the back of his head: "Go fill out your own fucking forms!"

That night, Hoblit and Wilson met over beers at the Officers' Club and tried to arrive at a new plan for knocking out SAM sites. At this point in the war, many of the Weasel pilots were so terrified by their mission that they spent most of their time hiding from enemy radars behind a line of mountains northwest of Hanoi known as Thud Ridge.[36] Occasionally, these planes would pop up and fire an antirado-Shrike missile at a SAM-site radar. These missiles, however, rarely caused much damage because a SAM operator could simply turn his radar off to foil the weapon, making it go ballistic. Even if the missile did manage to find its way to a Fansong radar van, its small warhead rarely destroyed more than a SAM's radar—launchers and missiles generally remained unscathed.

Hoblit and Wilson understood implicitly the limitations of the Shrike. Killing a site, reasoned these men, required a much bolder plan. After flying a number of missions, they figured out that the best weapons for killing sites were not missiles but cluster bombs. They also learned that the easiest way to find a site was to lure it into firing a missile. After a well-camouflaged site was identified by the flame and smoke of a missile firing, a Weasel could go right in and kill the missile operators with one of the six CBU-24 cluster bombs carried by his aircraft. Each cluster bomb consisted of 500 baseball-sized bomblets, each capable of penetrating the armor of a light tank as well as saturating the impact area with fragments. Another single-seat 105 would follow and "scoop out" the control vans in the center of the site with MK-82 500-pound bombs.

Using this hunter/killer tactic, Tom Wilson and Jerry Hoblit killed seven SAM sites and ended up having to dodge over sixty SAMS in the process. On one occasion, a SAM exploded so close to their aircraft that it flipped the plane completely over on its back. From the back of the cockpit Wilson radioed, "Aren't you going to get him?" That was all the pep talk Hoblit needed. He quickly righted the aircraft, rolled into the site, and bombed it.[37]

Jerry Hoblit recalled,

> The intensity of the radio noise, the vital nature of the decisions that have to be made—*right now*—the requirement for accelerated brain traffic; they were often more than a guy could effectively handle. Tom had one mission in life; he lived to be ultimately involved in the super-specialized thing that he was doing with his head locked in his electronic gear and his mind sorting out things that cascaded on him like an overpowering waterfall. He knew what he told me had to be right or else we, the other Weasels, and the strike force could go down the tube right now. He had to sort out what none of the rest of us could sort out and he had to assign the correct priorities to the realities that meant life or death over the North.[38]

So respected were Weasel crews that when this team diverted to Udorn one day after receiving battle damage, the F-104 pilot who picked them up at the flight line felt obliged to apologize for not bringing a wheelbarrow. "Wheelbarrow?" asked Wilson. "Yeah," the pilot explained, "to carry your balls."[39] For Tom Wilson peer recognition, however juvenile, meant more than the four silver stars he earned for his tour. But Wilson never believed he was brave. Unlike Ed Rasimus, he felt no fear. "I feel I am not brave because I just don't know fear," he explained. "I am just not too good with fear. You really get cold at heart. I didn't give a damn that my closest friend had been shot down. It comes back to haunt you."[40]

The Last Walk

One of the most famous examples of aviation art to emerge from the Vietnam War is a painting entitled "The Last Walk," by artist Maxine McCaffrey. The painting depicts Jerry Hoblit and Tom Wilson walking away from their 105 after their hundredth mission North. Hoblit carries a bottle of Champagne and both men sport long "bullet-proof" mustaches. As this painting implies, the hundredth mission was a bittersweet affair for the pilots who hung it out in the air war in the F-105. On the one hand, it meant surviving one of the most difficult flying assignments of the air war and a job well done. On the other hand, for most pilots, it would be the last ride they would ever take in the 105. Because of its high losses relative to the F-4, the Air Force slowly phased the F-105 out during the course of the war, so that by 1972 only the two-seat Weasel variants flew. Pilots who chose to continue in tactical aviation would inevitably transition to other aircraft, such as the F-4 or the F-111. More significantly, for some pilots the hundredth mission would be their last combat mission.

Pilot Ken Bell described how he felt after his hundredth mission party in the O Club:

> As I walked back to my trailer, reality began to sink in. I realized more completely that I had flown my last combat mission and my part in the war was over. Without thinking, I passed my trailer and continued across the airfield along a familiar path to the flight line. I wanted another look at the airplane I had flown on my last mission. The ground crews were going about their normal duties and it was business as usual. No one noticed as I stood there quietly reflecting. I felt alone and terribly sentimental. In one short day, the celebrity was gone and I suddenly felt like a has-been. It was a poignant moment indeed and it ended my combat story—a story I would remember proudly.[41]

Ed Rasimus, similarly, felt a sense of profound loss after his final mission: "When you graduate and go to an aircraft like the 105, that's the high end, that's as good as it gets. And you come back and you think you have done something worthwhile and the reward is to fly T-37s at a pilot-training base."[42]

Interestingly enough, Ed Rasimus's last mission turned out to be one of the toughest of his career. Although the command tried to give him an easy mission for his hundredth, he ended up flying as a single-seat escort on a Wild Weasel mission fifteen miles northwest of Hanoi. On that day, a pilot in another flight was shot down and Rasimus volunteered to fly fighter cover for the rescue. As his flight of four 105s was refueling, the rescue forces radioed that the pilot had been picked up. The tanker then departed without filling up Rasimus's tank. Ed, fearing he would miss his hundredth-mission party if he diverted to Bangkok, decided to push it to Korat, and ended up landing with about ten pounds of fuel in his tank, enough gas for 30 more seconds of flying. He left Korat the next day. For his service in Thailand, Ed Rasimus earned two Distinguished Flying Crosses in addition to a Silver Star.

When Rasimus returned to the States and began his new job as an instructor pilot at Williams AFB in Arizona, his melancholy turned into resentment. "It's inevitable that you feel that one, this is no thanks for a job well done, and two, that this is a terrible waste of knowledge and experience. It was frustrating. I used to laugh and say I could fly an entire training mission in a T-37 and never reach the take-off speed of a 105."[43] Despite Rasimus's experience and obvious desire to get back into the 105 business, the Air Force wanted every pilot to serve at least one tour Stateside before going back to SEA on a second tour. Ed was stuck: he would have to wait to begin stealing hubcaps again.

With its wonderful gift for matching personality types with jobs, the Air Force then compelled Ed Rasimus to bide his time on the personnel staff of the Air Training Command in San Antonio, Texas. After 20 months in this assignment, he approached his boss, a Korean War fighter pilot named Jack Denton, and asked to be sent back to the war.

Denton not only agreed to his request but allowed him to work with the people in the military-personnel center to negotiate the next available fighter slot. As Rasimus put it, "he basically allowed me to facilitate my own transfer." He was ecstatic when he came home that day to announce his new assignment to his spouse. She was less pleased, and by the time Ed shipped out, she had presented him with the paperwork for a separation. She sim-

ply could not handle the stress of another combat tour, and the life of constant separations, that an Air Force career promised.

Ed Rasimus ended up flying 150 more combat missions (including 50
in North Vietnam during Linebacker I and II) with the 469th Squadron in
Korat as an F-4 Hunter/Killer for the Wild Weasels. Admittedly, Ed found
this mission a bit grueling, but he preferred it to serving in the Stateside Air
Force. "I did not like the idea of flying Pack 6 every day, but by working with
the same crew every day, everybody knew each other and the tactics, and
there were no weak sisters that you had to take care of. It was a case where
everyone was qualified to do the job, and everybody could depend on everybody else. 'First in, last out' was our motto."[44]

Ed Rasimus had come of age. Once a scared freshman pilot contemplating his own death at a Stateside bar, he now flew the toughest Weasel missions over North Vietnam with few complaints. Ed and many others willingly
volunteered for second or even third tours, flew more tough missions than
were expected, and hung it out on a daily basis. Why? They clearly enjoyed
the stimulation and rush of combat flying, but more importantly, they also
prided themselves on being part of a unique brotherhood of warriors committed to fighting the war and hurting the enemy. "They reveled in being the
elite knights of the airborne round table of Downtown Hanoi . . . and squab-
bled amongst themselves for a spot on the toughest missions" wrote pilot
Jack Broughton.[45] Surprisingly, this attitude not only existed among the fast
movers at the beginning of the conflict but, with only a few notable exceptions, remained in effect throughout the war. The desire to fly, fight, and
kill had little to do with the political undercurrents of the time. Instead it
stemmed directly from the personalities and patriotism of America's professional aviators. These aviators could be relied upon by policymakers to
rapidly transition from a tranquil domestic life in the States to an extremely
dangerous combat environment overseas. F-105 pilots endured the danger
and hardship of their job because their status within the pilot brotherhood
demanded such sacrifice. As Ed Rasimus emphasized after his first engagement with radar-controlled 85-mm flak guns, to "quit" meant falling into a
dishonorable category where you never wanted to find yourself. However
sophomoric this may sound to the uninitiated, Rasimus and others cherished
their membership in the elite brotherhood of fighter pilots more than even
their marriages. As Tom Wolfe succinctly put it, they reveled in the hyper-
masculine notion that they had the "right stuff," and they would sacrifice just
about everything, including their lives, to retain this status.

CHAPTER 3

VULTURE FLIGHT

The Odyssey of Marine Squadron VMA (AW)-224

In sharp contrast to Rolling Thunder, Linebacker I was arguably the most effective application of U.S. airpower in the Vietnam War. Its objective was straightforward: to prevent North Vietnam from using conventional military troops to win the war. During the spring of 1972, North Vietnam invaded the South with fourteen divisions of regular troops. U.S. airpower not only provided close air support for the Army of the Republic of South Vietnam (ARVN) during the invasion, but simultaneously attacked the North Vietnamese transportation system and military bases.

Although similar targets had been struck during Rolling Thunder, Linebacker proved much more successful for several reasons. First, wing commanders were given much more latitude in choosing targets and devising the best tactics and weapons to employ. Second, technological advances such as precision-guided munitions and improved navigation systems made it possible for the U.S. forces to attack heavily defended targets with fewer aircraft and minimal collateral damage to civilians. With smart bombs and smart planes, the Navy and Air Force, for the first time, could attack warehouses and truck-repair facilities in residential neighborhoods. Finally, the fourteen North Vietnamese divisions involved in the Easter Offensive, being conventional forces, needed 1,000 tons of supplies a day to maintain their offensive. Their trucks and tanks consumed fuel, and their artillery, shells—war materiel that could not easily be transported South without a functional transportation infrastructure. Peace talks resumed between North Vietnam and the United States soon after the first Linebacker attacks, and by October a peace agreement acceptable to President Richard Nixon emerged and bombing north of the Twentieth Parallel was halted.

One of the most significant actions of the Linebacker campaign was the U.S. Navy's mining of Haiphong Harbor on 8 May 1972, executed by three Marine A-6 Intruders and six Navy A-7 Corsairs from the aircraft carrier *Coral Sea*. This was the first time in the war that this logistically critical port was blocked off by mines. And this blockage was a key factor behind North Vietnam's eventual acceptance of a peace settlement to end hostilities. For the aviators of Marine Squadron 224 who participated in the attacks, though, the raid had even greater meaning. It proved beyond doubt that Marine aviators could operate just as effectively from a carrier as their counterparts in the Navy. More important for the sea services overall, it demonstrated that carrier-based air power could achieve tangible results if it were allowed to destroy high-value targets with advanced technology, and if the on-scene wing commander and his staff were given the latitude to plan and execute the mission as they saw fit. Not surprisingly, morale in this unit was much higher than in Ed Rasimus's F-105 wing during the Rolling Thunder period.

Naval Air Station Miramar: 6 April 1972

Commander Roger Sheets looked forward to taking command of Carrier Air Wing Nine on board the aircraft carrier USS *Constellation*. This job would be the crowning assignment in the 42-year-old Navy fighter pilot's career: an opportunity to be a carrier air group commander or CAG. However, as Sheets emerged from a DC-3 that evening at NAS Miramar, an officer greeted him and told him that the commander of Naval Air Forces in the Pacific needed to talk to him as soon as possible. A crisis was unfolding aboard the USS *Coral Sea*, on station in the waters just off the coast of North Vietnam in the Gulf of Tonkin. The *Coral Sea's* CAG, Thomas Dunlop, had just been shot down by a SAM, and a leadership vacuum now existed on a carrier destined to play a central role in President Nixon's upcoming Linebacker campaign.

Roger Sheets was told to get his vaccinations together and prepare to take immediate command of Carrier Air Wing Fifteen on the *Coral Sea*. The next day, a Friday, Sheets got his vaccination shots, and by 0700 on Saturday morning a yeoman was knocking on his door at the BOQ in Miramar with the orders to assume command. Sheets left that evening for Da Nang air base, spent the night there, and took the Carrier Onboard Delivery plane to the *Coral Sea* the next morning.

The trip to the *Coral Sea* was a homecoming for Sheets. During the early 1960s he had flown F-8 Crusaders off the carrier with VF-154, and from December 1967 to April 1969, he had commanded VF-161, and F-4 squadron on the *Coral Sea,* so he knew the ship well.

As he emerged from the plane, an old friend of his, Captain William Harris, the ship's commander, said, "Welcome aboard, CAG! The air wing is yours to run; my job is to provide the support and put the ship where you need it. If any of my people aren't doing what you want, let me know."[1] The two men then met Admiral Jesse Greer, the carrier battle group commander and another close friend of Sheets. Echoing Harris's welcome, Greer said, "Welcome aboard, CAG. Your job is to run the air wing and my job is to keep the people up the line off your back and get you whatever authority you need to do the job."[2]

Sheets couldn't have asked for a better situation. "It was just superb; they really meant it."[3] One of Sheets' initial challenges was to improve the morale and the performance of the carrier's A-6 Intruder squadron, a Marine unit filled with pilots and navigators unfamiliar with carrier operations. During the carrier's initial work-up period, Sheets' predecessor had exacerbated the situation by being overbearing and criticizing the Marines at every opportunity. According to Marine Captain William "Charlie" Carr, Jr., "Tom Dunlop, an A-7 driver and the first CAG, just about wrote us off. He figured the only reason we were on board was to screw him up."[4] The squadron's executive officer and later its commander, Ralph Brubaker, described the situation this way:

> The Marines got hind tit—the worst maintenance shops, quarters, ready room, you name it. We accepted that because we were used to it, but once we started doing our job, it did bother us somewhat to be ridiculed for things that weren't the squadron's fault, and CAG Sheets corrected that.[5]

One of first steps Sheets took to improve the situation was to fly with the squadron as much as possible. Although an F-8 and F-4 fighter pilot by trade, Sheets, during his CAG training, had already made up his mind to devote most of his flying time to the A-6 because he understood that the A-6 bore the brunt of the tough missions in the naval air war in Southeast Asia. The plane had a maximum speed of only 648 mph, but it could carry up to thirty 500-pound bombs. With its Digital Integrated Attack and

Navigation Equipment (DIANE), the A-6 could attack preselected locations or targets of opportunity without the crew ever having to look outside the cockpit from launch to recovery. A bomber/navigator (BN) sat adjacent to the pilot and managed DIANE. Steering instructions from the navigator's systems were displayed to the pilot through a visual display terminal (VDT); all a pilot did in this mode was respond to the steering blip on his VDT.[6]

Since Sheets wanted to lead all major strike missions, he also saw real advantages to having a bomber/navigator in the cockpit to turn pages and answer questions. "I was going to fly a lot and I was going to be very aggressive because I wanted to set the tone for the air wing."[7] Therefore, a competent crewman to take care of navigation and other mission details was a must. That first day aboard the carrier, Sheets sauntered down to Ready Room 5, deep in the bowels of the carrier, took a look at the flight list of bomber/navigators, and immediately saw that a man named Carr was far and away the most experienced BN in the squadron, if not the entire Marine Corps.

"Who's Carr? I'm flying with him!"

Charlie Carr, who had just returned from a hop, remembered coming into the Ready Room and seeing this guy with a hat too big for his head and an eye twitch. "He looked like Don Knotts, but he was wearing a commander's silver leaf on his collar tab."[8] Carr didn't know what to make of this unusual-looking pilot but immediately agreed to fly with him. Sheets, after all, was the CAG—the closest thing to God in carrier aviation. Sheets took a liking to Carr immediately. Before him stood a warrior—a guy who, like him, had served multiple combat tours in Southeast Asia. When the two men strapped themselves into an A-6 the following day, they put a combined total of 12,000 hours of personal flight experience into that aircraft.

"Almost right off the bat," recalled Sheets, "we got each other's attention and I think it was almost an immediate mutual respect."[9] The mission that day was to work with a forward air controller (FAC) to support a South Vietnamese machine-gun position that was being overrun by a North Vietnamese regiment. Heavily overcast skies and thunderstorms made it almost impossible for A-6s to descend into the target area, which was in a punchbowl valley. After the FAC reported that he did not know how to guide the A-6s safely into the valley, CAG Sheets took over the mission. First he asked the FAC how fast he could spiral down through the valley; to which the FAC replied, "A couple hundred knots." He then ordered the flight to form up in formation on the FAC's wing and let the small plane lead them down into the valley. According to reports from the ground, the flight ended

up killing 250 enemy troops with low drag 500-pound bombs[10] and cluster bomblets. The friendly machine-gun position also got rescued by a helicopter. "That was kind of a start to things," explained Sheets.[11]

Shortly after this mission, the Marines repainted one of their aircraft
and designated it 500. On the pilot's side was lettered CMDR/LTC ROGER
E. SHEETS, USN/USMC, CAG. They also had a flight suit made up for him
with A-6 patches and a joint Marine/Navy rank insignia. The Marines of
VMA (AW)-224 now accepted Roger "Blinky" Sheets as one of their own.
"He was super to fly with," remembered Charlie Carr. "He had guts, and
though he did not appear to be meticulous, he was meticulous in planning;
he made decisions when decisions had to be made; he led that air group better than any one could have."[12]

The story of CAG Sheets and VMA (AW)-224, like Robin Olds' story,
reveals the significance of wing-level command in Southeast Asia—in short,
how one skilled leader can turn a situation around and produce tangible
results with even the weakest of units: VMA (AW)-224 emerged from its
adjustment problems to become one of the Navy's lead units in Linebacker
I. Sheets, though, differs from Olds in several significant ways. Unlike Olds,
he commanded not only the confidence of the sailors and Marines under
him but also that of the admirals and captains over him. Sheets knew how
to suppress his fighter-pilot ego and act professionally. As a result, his superiors tended to give him the latitude he needed to make his unit a success.
The differences between Olds and Sheets stem in part from the differences
in their social backgrounds. Robin Olds grew up in relative privilege under
the tutelage of an iconoclastic Army Air Corps general, attended all the right
military schools, including West Point, and was groomed practically from
birth to become a military officer. Roger Sheets, by contrast, was the son
of a humble Navy chaplain and ended up in the Navy more by accident than
by design. Sheets dropped out of college and joined the Naval Aviation
Cadets because his interests lay more in flying than in academics. To him,
flying in the military was always a privilege, not an entitlement. He therefore treated his superiors with more caution and respect than did Olds. Like
Olds, he understood that his fighter-pilot status made him special, but he
tried not to flaunt it too often. Being the son of a chaplain taught him early
how important discretion and subtlety can be in a military environment.
Like his father, Roger Sheets also knew how to inspire men without getting overly familiar with them. Frederick the Great once remarked that a
responsible commander:

. . . should practice kindness and severity, should appear friendly to the soldiers, speak to them on the march, visit them while they are cooking, ask them if they are well cared for, and alleviate their needs if they have any. Officers without experience in war should be treated kindly. Their good actions should be praised. Small requests should be granted, and they should not be treated in an overbearing manner, but severity is maintained about everything regarding duty.[13]

Sheets knew how to achieve this subtle balance; Olds did not. Whereas Olds reveled in his iconoclasm, Sheets took pride in being a professional officer. In simpler terms, Sheets might eat dinner with his officers or even have a drink with them in the Officers' Club, but he never closed the bar with them.

Beyond Sheets and his role in transforming VMA (AW)-224 into a premier fighting unit, the story of the Marine squadron is important for several other reasons. First, it debunks the myth that only naval aviators can fly off of aircraft carriers. The vast majority of the pilots and navigators of the VMA (AW)-224 had spent their entire careers up to their *Coral Sea* deployment flying from airfields, both in the United States and abroad. Some had even been trained by the Air Force and only later received a carrier qualification. The VMA (AW)-224 experience, therefore, stands out as a lesson in interservice cooperation in wartime. This story suggests that given patience, proper equipment, and adequate training, there is no reason why Marine or even Air Force or Army aviation units can not be deployed on a Navy carrier in a future conflict.

Another lesson to be learned from this story is that technology is no substitute for skilled air crews. Unquestionably, the A-6 Intruder was the most sophisticated piece of aviation technology deployed by the armed services during the Vietnam War. It could carry almost as many bombs as a World War II-era Superfortress (about 18,000 pounds worth, versus 20,000 for a B-29), and deliver these bombs accurately against targets even at night or in bad weather. Despite the plane's sophisticated navigational and targeting systems, though, inevitably it was the pilot and navigator who in the end proved instrumental in putting the bombs on target during the most difficult sorties.

Finally, 224 supports historian S. L. A. Marshall's theory that in a combat situation it is always a small number of individuals who put most of the fire on a target. During World War II, Marshall found that out of every hundred men in a combat unit, only fifteen to twenty "would take part with their weapons."[14] In VMA (AW)-224, the eight air crewmen who comprised Vulture flight flew most of the tough missions against Hanoi and Haiphong. The remainder of the squadron (forty officers) bombed targets in lower-threat areas or flew combat-support missions, such as tanker or electronic-warfare runs. One might expect the pilots and navigators of Vulture Flight to be predominantly long-term careerists with ROTC or service academy backgrounds; however, most stumbled into the military almost by accident. Once there, they became addicted to flying and, like Rasimus, began to enjoy the adrenaline rush of combat.

Wings of Gold: The Naval Career of Roger Sheets

The incongruous-looking CAG arrived on the *Coral Sea* not only with a wealth of flying experience behind him but also with a wealth of knowledge on the war in SEA. As the son of a Protestant Navy chaplain, Roger Sheets had grown up on naval bases across the United States. During World War II, the still under-age Roger felt embarrassed walking around post without a uniform. Consequently, as soon as he turned 17 in 1947, he joined the Naval Reserve as a seaman; he did summer cruises in a patrol craft on Lake Michigan and on an auxiliary ocean tug out of Norfolk, Virginia. In the Navy, Sheets "found something he really liked."[15] The same could not be said for academic pursuits. He tried taking courses at Wabash College in Crawfordsville, Indiana, and at Bethany College in Bethany, West Virginia, but found that his interests lay more in music and the Navy than in academic subjects. Consequently, he left college early in 1950 to enter the Naval Aviation Cadet Program.

Roger Sheets did his initial flight training in the propeller-driven SNJ (the Navy version of the T-6 Texan) at Pensacola, Florida, and then got selected along with five other pilots from his group to attend jet training in the T-33 at Kingsville, Texas. Earning his wings in 1952, Sheets barely made it to the Korean War before it ended. He transitioned to the F-9 Panther at Naval Air Station Alameda in Oakland, California, and then joined VF-151 aboard the USS *Boxer* on 30 March 1953. Sheet's initial experiences flying the F-9 off the *Boxer* were trying; she was a straight-deck carrier with catapults barely adequate for launching jets and no storage space for jet fuel. She had fourteen accidents, including two fatalities, in the first week after he arrived, but Sheet' morale remained high. "I loved the combat flying. It didn't take me any time at all to decide that I liked doing that."[16]

In Korea Sheets mainly flew interdiction missions against rail lines and other supply targets. On one mission, he got hit by a 57-millimeter shell and lost his entire rudder as well as a third of each elevator, but still managed to land the aircraft at K-18, an airfield near the DMZ. Before the war ended on 27 July 1953, Roger Sheets had racked up a total of fifty combat missions, earning four Air Medals and a Navy Commendation Medal with a Combat V device. He stayed with the *Boxer* through 28 November 1953, then did another cruise with VF-151, this time aboard the *Wasp*. From there, he became a T-33 instructor at Memphis, Tennessee, and stayed in that assignment until 1958.

Almost from the outset, Roger Sheets' Navy career was hampered by the fact that he had neither attended the Naval Academy nor earned a four-year college degree. "At that time in the Navy," claims Sheets, "the ring knockers kind of ruled and they looked after one another."[17] To teach Sheets basic seamanship and get him educationally on a par with the Academy graduates, the Navy sent him to the Navy Line School at Monterey, California. Upon graduation in 1959, he transitioned to one of the Navy's hottest fighters at the time, the F-8 Crusader, with VF-154. The "'Sader" was the most demanding aircraft Sheets ever flew. It was a huge fighter that allowed almost no margin for error on a carrier approach because some of the control surfaces were dual purpose, serving as both flaps and ailerons. Sheets, though, excelled in the F-8, and eventually became a Landing Signal Officer (LSO) aboard the *Coral Sea*. Usually one of the most skilled pilots in a squadron, the LSO controlled carrier landings by telling each returning pilot how well he was flying approach relative to the optimum flight path for a successful landing. For the brief moments of the landing cycle, often referred to as a "controlled crash," a pilot's life rested firmly in the hands of his LSO. The LSO guided a pilot's every move, telling him when to slow down, add power, add rudder, and so forth. He could even order a pilot to abort a landing by waving him off. The job, in short, required nerves of steel and expert knowledge of the unique flight characteristics of every aircraft in the wing.

In 1963, Roger Sheets returned to shore to train at Naval Air Station Glencoe in Brunswick, Georgia for his next assignment as an assistant air operations officer on the *Constellation*. He then served on the carrier for two and a half years as a lieutenant commander. During this tour, the carrier was on station off North Vietnam during the famous Gulf of Tonkin incidents in 1964. In fact, on the night of the 4 August attack on the destroyers *Maddox* and *Turner Joy,* Sheets served as the carrier control approach (CCA) officer. During this second attack on U.S. forces, both destroyers reported hostile torpedo-boat attacks, but the commander of the *Maddox* later admitted that his contact data might have resulted from the effects of bad weather and nervous radar operators.[18]

Roger's job that stormy evening was to guide the aircraft making reconnaissance runs over the destroyers and back to the carrier. Everett Alvarez, one of the officers who flew that night, attributes his successful landing that night to Sheets' skill as a CCA:

> This time, as the carrier control approach (CCA) directed me down by radio and I approached the ship, I knew they really weren't ready to take me on. I saw a plane taking off and knew they wouldn't have time to clear the deck. When they turned me back out I was concerned because once before, when I had been in a similar pattern, they lost me through the ground clutter on the scope. I didn't want them to keep me going around this time on account of my low fuel.
>
> "Hey, you guys are running me out of fuel!" I radioed in.
>
> "Where are you?" responded the CCA.
>
> In that instant I recognized the voice of Lt. Cmdr. Roger Sheets, the very able CCA officer in charge. I knew if he was in control nothing untoward would happen. Sure enough, within seconds Sheets' voice came over the headset, "We have you." Fortunately, everything went well and I landed without incident.[19]

Unfortunately for Alvarez, his next mission, on 5 August, did not go as smoothly. In a reprisal attack against four North Vietnamese torpedo boats, Alvarez got shot down by anti-aircraft fire, earning the distinction of being the first American pilot shot down over North Vietnam.[20]

In 1965 Roger Sheets attended the Naval War College at Newport, Rhode Island and was later promoted to commander. In 1966, he spent eleven months in Kingsville, Texas, as an F-9 instructor. He then received an opportunity second in prestige only to his eventual CAG assignment—command of an F-4 squadron on Yankee Station in Vietnam. Sheets, however, was "almost a little disappointed at first and had to think about it for a while."[21] The problem with the F-4 was that it was a two-seat fighter, and up to this point, all of his fighter time had been in single-seaters like the F-9 and F-8. "In flying a single-seat aircraft," he explained, "there are certain times when you are really going to hang it out on something that might put you in jeopardy. Since you only have to think of yourself, you are apt to go ahead and do it. I was concerned that with someone else in the plane, I might feel a certain hesitancy to do that. What I discovered was that with only rare exceptions, the guys in back were as gung-ho as anyone else and you almost had to guard against letting them talk you into something that was really hare-brained."[22]

Under ordinary circumstances, the route to squadron command in the U.S. Navy involved a year of service as squadron executive officer (XO), the number two man in the squadron.[23] After a year, the XO then took over the squadron as the skipper. However, because VF-161 had lost its XO a week before Sheets was slated to come aboard, he ended up bypassing the executive officer's job and moving right into the top slot. Sheets also managed to convince the Navy Bureau of Personnel to extend his command from one to two years as compensation for skipping the XO tour.

As the squadron commander of VF-161, Roger Sheets stressed a theme common among Vietnam War fighter pilots: "It isn't much of a war but it's the only one we've got, so let's make the best of it."[24] In other words, this might be the only opportunity these men would have to test their skills in combat and perhaps even earn the ultimate status symbol in the pilot fraternity, a MiG kill. Sheets made the best of the war by "playing everything up to the edge of what he was supposed to do."[25] That meant flying as low as 100 feet above the ground with the F-4, and experimenting a lot with different types of bombs and bomb loads. One bomb that Sheets adapted for use on bridges was the "daisy-cutter"—a 750-pound bomb with a 3-foot-long fuse extender. Prior to Sheets' tenure daisy-cutters were employed primarily as antipersonnel weapons: the fuse extender caused the bomb to explode just before hitting the ground, thereby maximizing the spread of the blast. Sheets reasoned that the same principle could be applied to bridges. In a bridge attack, the fuse extender concentrated the force of the blast at the surface of the bridge rather than in the open air beneath it; this proved extremely effective at breaking up the spans and road surface of a bridge.

One type of target that Sheets did not have much luck destroying was MiGs. During most of the period when Sheets commanded VF-161 (1968–69), various bombing halts against North Vietnam mostly prevented his fighters from encountering MiGs. "On three occasions, I had solid radar locks and good visuals on MiGs. They stayed just over the coastline, kind of tormenting and testing, and we couldn't get approval to fire."[26] During the 1968–1972 bombing halt against the North, American planes generally could fire on MiGs over North Vietnamese territory only if they were fired upon first. Most of Sheets' missions during this period were close-air-support missions in South Vietnam and interdiction missions in southern Laos against the Ho Chi Minh Trail.

"Blinky" Sheets stayed with VF-161 until May of 1969. He then transferred to the Carrier Division Nine staff, and served two more Vietnam tours during the 1969–70 period as a staff officer aboard the *Coral Sea* and the *Kitty Hawk*. In different capacities, Sheets witnessed just about the entire naval air war in Southeast Asia before arriving as CAG on the *Coral Sea* in 1972. Very few aviators in the Navy had served in Southeast Asia longer than he had, yet he still volunteered for a sixth tour. Why? "I always felt we could win the thing if anyone decided they wanted to win it." In 1972 it appeared that Nixon just "might have the guts to start taking steps in that direction."[27] As it turned out, Sheets' predictions about those steps would prove out correct.

Taking the War North: 16 April 1972

During Sheets' tour as squadron commander of VF-161, he participated in one of the last missions into Haiphong before the bombing halt. In an ironic twist of fate, he would fly the first Navy mission into that area nearly four years later as CAG-15. The mission called for Sheets' A-6s to fly ahead of a B-52 raid against the tank farms in Haiphong and "suppress" the SAM sites there with cluster bombs. "What wasn't stated but what I recognized as a reality is that they wanted us to soak up an awful lot of those SAMs that had been stockpiled so they wouldn't be available to shoot at the B-52s."[28] The Marine A-6s, in short, would be SAM bait.

For this mission, Sheets ordered his A-6s to fly the classic Intruder mission: each plane would fly alone, at night, and at low altitude against a single SAM site and then return to the carrier. Bill Angus, one of the A-6 pilots, remembers having "cotton mouth" when he launched: "Our strike was about thirty miles outside of Haiphong and there were already five or six SAMS in the air and we were not even in range. The whole thing was surreal. The threat indicator looked like a sparkler. It was emitting strobes in every conceivable direction in the world and we turned the damn thing off and proceeded. It was distracting. But everybody got home."[29]

During the mission, at least 29 missiles were fired at Sheets' A-6s. "When we started dropping the CBU-24s," Sheets recalled, "they seemed like they would never come off the plane. You can't imagine how long three hundred milliseconds can become when you are waiting for all those bombs to come off the airplane, but it seemed like an eternity. When we finally got back out over the water, both of us took off our masks, shut off the oxygen, and Charlie said, 'Oh, good, I can smoke again. I thought there for a while I would never get a chance.'"[30]

Interestingly enough, after all this effort the B-52 mission nearly got cancelled. The American ground forces commander in Saigon, General Creighton Abrams, objected to the diversion of B-52 assets from targets in the South, and Nixon and Kissinger nearly halted the raid. However, when Admiral Thomas Moorer, the chairman of the Joint Chiefs of Staff, pointed out that the B-52s were already in the air and would have to ditch their bombs in the Gulf of Tonkin if the mission were scrubbed, Nixon chose to press on. The B-52s went on to destroy more than thirty oil tanks in Haiphong with no losses.[31]

With the resumption of the air war against the Haiphong area, Sheets and Carr began to spend much more time in the *Coral Sea*'s Air Intelligence (AI) center planning missions. As military personnel often do, the intelligence officers on the carrier had decorated their shop with numerous posters. The most popular of these was a picture of two vultures in a desert scene with the caption, "Patience my ass! I'm going to kill something." During one briefing, one of the AI guys pointed to Carr and Sheets sitting hunched over and intent in the first row of Ready Room 5 and started to laugh.

"What's the matter, Lieutenant?" Sheets asked.

"Sir, the two of you look like those vultures in the poster."

The entire ready room roared with laughter, and Sheets ordered the poster removed from AI and displayed in Ready Room 5. From then on, the call sign for Sheets' flights would be Vulture, and at the end of every briefing, Sheets would point to the poster and say, "Gentlemen, LET'S GO KILL SOMETHING!" The room would then erupt in classic Marine grunts and groans, led of course by Carr himself, who soon adopted the "Vulture" nick-name as his own. With his big nose and brash attitude, Carr personified his nickname perfectly.

The Vulture

The similarities between Roger Sheets and William "Charlie" Carr, Jr. were as remarkable as their differences. The two men were roughly the same age, both were superior aviators, and both enthusiastically volunteered for mul-tiple tours. That's not all. Both men had rejected college as a means to suc-cess and chose the military instead, initially as enlisted men and later as aviation officers. Naval aviation provided both men with a military com-munity where they could rise based on merit, as opposed to connections or prestigious service-academy degrees.

That was where the similarities ended. Whereas Roger Sheets was extremely aggressive in his flying yet somewhat reserved and cerebral in his personality, Carr's personality tended to be aggressive and iconoclastic. The son of a wealthy lawyer and banker in New York City, Carr had lived a life of privilege during his youth. He attended primary school at prestigious St. Bernard's School on Manhattan's Upper East Side and later transferred to Short Hills Country Day School in Short Hills, New Jersey. For high school, his parents sent him to the Loomis-Chaffee prep school in Windsor, Connecticut. At Loomis, the only thing for Charlie Carr to do on week-ends was go into Windsor occasionally, and maybe see a movie; the remain-der of his time was spent on campus. After this austere experience, Charlie literally went wild at Williams College in Williamstown, Massachusetts: "I had probably the most spectacular freshman career they have seen at Williamstown for a long time."[32]

Carr joined a fraternity, became a football cheerleader, sang in the octet, drank a lot of beer, and generally partied his way through his first semester. The crowning moment of the semester came on the night before Thanksgiving of 1952. That night, he and a friend decided to drive down to New York City to meet a couple of girls they had met at Miss Hall's [prep] School in North Adams, Massachusetts. His friend Tucker, the dri-ver, ended up drinking one too many beers at the fraternity and smashed up the car. Tucker wound up in jail that night and Carr spent the evening in the hospital. "We both hitchhiked back to Williamstown the next day.

Tucker was immediately suspended, and I was put on academic probation. We still made it to New York the following night in the car with no front windscreen."[33]

In January when his grades came out, Charlie Carr was promptly summoned before the dean of freshmen, whom Carr paraphrases thus: "Mr. Carr, we'll see ya."[34] Thus ended the illustrious college career of Charlie Carr. Several days after getting kicked out of Williams, Carr received a draft notice and took a subway trip downtown to Church Street, near New York City's financial district' to explore his recruitment options. "I put my nose in the Marine recruiter's office and they promised to make me a general in a week if I just went down to Parris Island and got a little training. I said, 'Hey, that sounds good to me.'"[35]

The Marine Corps traditionally does not draw very many wealthy kids from the northeast United States. In fact, Charlie Carr never met a single Marine officer in his forty-year career who had attended Williams College. Nevertheless, Carr adapted to Marine Corps life with extraordinary grace. "If I had gone into the Marine Corps after Loomis, did a normal two- or three-year tour, and then gone back to Williams, I would have graduated, no question about it. It gave me a huge dose of discipline that was intense and all-pervasive, something that sticks with you your whole life."[36] One day, for instance, Carr showed up for inspection with an untucked blouse. As punishment, the drill sergeant made him puff a cigarette under a bucket while running in place until he passed out.

When Carr graduated from basic training, he applied for and was accepted to the eight-month Marine navigator school at Cherry Point, North Carolina. Of the twenty enlisted men who entered the program in the fall of 1953, only six graduated. According to Carr, the most demanding part of the course was staying up all night locating stars with a sextant, then having to navigate a blackened transport plane around North Carolina the next morning.

When he graduated in the spring of 1954, the Marine Corps sent Charlie Carr to Itami, Japan as a C-119 "Flying Boxcar" navigator. He immediately fell in love with Marine life in the Far East: "I did a fifteen-month tour, 1954–55. The yen was 360 to a buck, it cost a hundred yen for a huge bottle of Asahi beer, and the women were plentiful and really cheap."[37]

When Carr returned to the States, his father had a banking job lined up for him at the First National City Bank. Naturally, Carr deplored the idea of "hanging on a subway strap every morning and working in a bank," but the banking job fetched a handsome salary and would even allow him to finish his college degree at nights at Columbia University. The night of his discharge, he sang Japanese songs all night in a barracks full of Marines just back from the Far East—and the next morning he reenlisted. As he put it, "It was sort of like prostitution, you gave up six years of your life, and they gave you a thousand bucks."[38] Carr took his bonus, drove out to Tucson, Arizona, traveled around the West Coast with his girlfriend, and wound up hitchhiking back to Los Angeles, very nearly AWOL. He shipped off to Japan the next day without a dime in his pocket.

After another tour in Japan, followed by a tour in Antarctica, Carr applied for a commission as a warrant officer and attended OCS at Quantico, Virginia. It was during this period that he married his first wife, a woman from Yarmouth, Massachusetts whom Charlie had met during a brief vacation to Cape Cod. "Actually, I was dating another girl at the time, but then I met my first wife and thought she was a better deal. Well, I thought so for a while."[39]

Charlie then flew another tour as an electronics countermeasures (ECM) officer in F-3Ds in Japan, and finally transferred back to Cherry Point for a Stateside tour. The year was 1964, and the Marine A-6 program was just starting. Fortunately for Charlie, the naval flight officer coordinator on base was a friend. One night, Charlie plied the coordinator with beer and convinced him to secure orders for Carr to undergo A-6 bomber/navigator (BN) training at NAS Whidbey Island in Washington State with VA-128. Lyle Bull was Carr's BN instructor there in VA-128—which, according to Carr, meant that "You did quite a bit flying, but also spent a lot of time in the bar."[40] Charlie Carr graduated from Whidbey in 1965 to become one of the first A-6 BNs in the Marine Corps. He then went back to Cherry Point to join the second Marine A-6 squadron, VMA (AW)-533.

VMA (AW)-533 deployed to Chu Lai air base in the Republic of Vietnam in the Fall of 1967. At Chu Lai, Carr flew scores of night missions, quickly becoming one of the most skilled navigators in the Marines. For one mission against Hanoi Radio's transmitter, he and his pilot, LTC Bill Fitch, received the Silver Star—America's third-highest decoration for valor.

After flying 125 missions against North Vietnam Charlie Carr returned to the United States. Like many pilots fresh from combat, he had problems adjusting to garrison duty. "I personally got very bored with the whole thing," he explained. Charlie talked to his wife about his personal problems but she did not seem to understand.

One day, he said to his wife, "Hey, I think I want to go overseas."

"Do it at your peril," she shot back.

Not fully understanding the "money end" of divorce, Charlie accepted the orders, jumped into a VW bug, and drove from Cherry Point to Laguna Beach, California. When he arrived in California, the divorce proceedings against him were already in progress. Charlie didn't mind. "What could they do?" he thought. "Send me to Vietnam?"

Charlie Carr's second SEA tour, at Da-nang during 1969 and 1970, was a "piece of cake" but very monotonous. The bombing halt against North Vietnam during this period meant that most of his missions were easy ones into South Vietnam and Laos. Roughly 90 percent of these were against targets picked up along the Ho Chi Minh Trail in southern Laos by the Igloo White sensors. The monotony of these missions used to get to Carr, and he looked forward to diverting to the Air Force bases in Thailand. At Nakhon Phanom, he visited Task Force Alpha, the Air Force group that ran the sensor operation. He remembers listening to some of the funnier acoustic tapes. One tape captured the distinct sounds of an enemy soldier sawing himself off a tree in an attempt to remove a branch containing a sensor: "You could hear the crack and the scream." Another featured a North Vietnamese soldier happily having sex. Now blissfully single, Carr greatly enjoyed diverting to Udorn to experience the local culture. "If you had just a little time (say an hour), you could get out of the airplane at Udorn, take a left and a left and a left and you would be at the Twilight. Present yourself at the Twilight, get a rub and a scrub, and a glass of Singha for a buck. You are then so calm and relaxed after a hard mission. We used to talk about the women with neat hands. It was absolutely gratifying."[41]

Charlie's second tour ended in early 1970. He proceeded immediately to Quantico, Virginia to the Amphibious Warfare School (AWS) for six months. Although scheduled to be an instructor at Pensacola after AWS, Charlie again schemed his way onto a third SEA deployment. "I ended up calling a friend [Captain R. H. Amos] down at VMA-224, and asking him if I could join the squadron and he said, 'You're damn right.' The next thing you know I got my orders changed, although my monitor absolutely fanged the shit out of me [i.e., yelled at me]. Hell, this was a new adventure, getting to go out on a carrier."[42]

The Coral Sea Departs San Francisco: 12 November 1971

For Charlie Carr and the rest of VMA-224, simply leaving San Francisco turned out to be an adventure. At 0500 on 9 November 1971, just as the crew started returning from shore leave to the *Coral Sea*, over 1,000 antiwar protesters staged a demonstration in front of the main gate at Alameda Naval Base in Oakland where the carrier was docked. Jerry Houston, an F-4 pilot on the ship, remembered the scene vividly. "As we approached the main gate at Alameda, there were several hundred long-haired demonstrators with North Vietnamese flags; they had our flag upside down and they spit on us and called us baby killers."[43]

On the morning of the ship's departure, 12 November, 1,500 protesters again rallied at Alameda in an attempt to prevent the *Coral Sea* from sailing. When the ship finally sailed, 35 sailors stayed behind in solidarity with the protesters—but not one of them was a pilot.[44] FBI agents halted all traffic over the Bay and Golden Gate bridges to prevent any attempts at sabotage. Navigator Billy Angus's attitude typified that of the pilots of the squadron towards the antiwar movement: "I believed in the war. I was apolitical. I was there for the good times—the camaraderie, the flying, the sense of adventure."[45] Houston, a more senior officer with several Southeast Asia tours under his belt, took a slightly different view of the protests:

> All the protests were directed against the *Coral Sea*—they wanted to keep that ship from going. Goddamn, we're going out there [to the pier] with our wives and we're not that hot to go back there again. I was on my fourth deployment and Chuck [Schrader, his roommate] was on his second. Hell, you have to fight your way onto the base to go do something you're really not hot to do anyway. You kept going and did it more for each other than anything else. I thought more of the Vietnamese fighter pilots than our members of Congress. Then, we thought the protesters were weak dicks who didn't want to get killed. Now, I realize that we had no business being over there. Goddamn it, it wasn't all that fun but it was fun being a part of it. Most of the dissatisfaction at the flight-crew level was not with the war but with the way we were running it. Everybody wanted to level the country. We were not there to discuss the rights and the wrongs of the war, we don't declare war. We were paid to fight.[46]

In the fall of 1971, notwithstanding, the men who volunteered for duty were a rare breed. Marine personnel officers might have frowned on Charlie Carr for finessing his way onto the *Coral Sea,* but the reality of the situation was that the war was unpopular and few Americans wanted to strap themselves into an A-6 and drop bombs an North Vietnam. The services were lucky indeed to have a small cadre of air warriors willing to ignore the bad press and the protests and go to war.

Adjustment Problems

Upon leaving Alameda, VMA-224 faced several immediate challenges: pilot adjustment to carrier life, a CAG who did not fully support the squadron, and a weak squadron commanding officer.

During the 1960s, approximately 20 percent of Marine pilots attended pilot training at Air Force schools. These pilots tended to have some bad habits that needed to be broken. For example, they learned in the Air Force to flare the aircraft when landing—something one can never do when landing on a carrier. When a pilot lands on a flattop, he actually flies the aircraft at full power right up until the tail-hook grabs the airplane. This technique is designed to allow the pilot to fly right off the carrier, or "bolter," if none of the cables are grabbed. Needless to say, for an Air Force-trained jock this type of landing was very unnatural. As Charlie Carr put it, "Our landings were bad, we were crowding the pattern, we had terrible boarding rates at night. In fact, we almost got tossed off at Pearl Harbor, but they did not have another Navy unit to take our place."[47] Overall, despite having flown 355 simulated carrier landings on a ground field in June of 1971, followed by actual practice landings aboard the USS *Lexington* at Pensacola during July–September 1971, VMA-224 still appeared unprepared for carrier flying when it arrived at Alameda to join CAG-15 on 15 September 1971.[48]

The squadron was also unprepared for the basic procedures for operating in the confines of a ship. On a carrier, seemingly simple tasks often become elevated to a level of high art. "It took a couple of months for the maintenance people to get used to the symphony of moving planes around a carrier," recalled Angus.[49] Because the original CAG, Thomas Dunlop, viewed 224 as a nuisance, the squadron never had an advocate in the ship's hierarchy to intercede with a senior chief or the aircraft handling officer

when a bottleneck occurred on the hangar deck. To ensure adequate communication between Ready Room 5, the maintenance shop, and the electronics shop, 224 even had to install its own phone system. Tom Sprouse, the
squadron's communications officer, remembers stringing communication
wire throughout the ship with two enlisted Marines about two weeks before
the carrier left Alameda. En route to Hawaii, Sprouse received a summons
from the ship's captain, William Harris. Harris' lecture went as follows:

> Marines are all alike! They think they can drill through bulkheads, lay
> communication wire and do whatever they damn well please.
> Gentleman, this is not a battlefield, it's my ship, and you need to
> explain exactly what you did to it to the ship's engineering depart-
> ment:[50]

Standing with Sprouse during this lecture, not defending him, was the
original squadron commander, Lieutenant Colonel B. R. Stanley. Bill Stanley
was 45 years old and a very weak pilot. On take-offs he would turn across
the bow, thereby jeopardizing both his aircraft and the carrier. He would
also abort a mission for the smallest reason imaginable. Once the squadron
commenced combat operations on 15 December 1971, Stanley avoided flying combat missions as often as possible; instead, he chose to fly the less
dangerous tanker missions. His behavior absolutely infuriated Charlie Carr
and the other officers who flew the tough missions. The situation truly got
out of hand in the middle of May 1972 when Stanley approached his executive officer, Lieutenant Colonel Ralph Brubaker, and asked if the squadron
could get along without him for a while: apparently he wanted to go home
to attend his daughter's graduation. "Bill, to be honest with you, you
shouldn't go, but I think we can get along without you," Brubaker
responded.[51]

In the middle of Nixon's Linebacker campaign against North Vietnam,
Stanley flew home to Cherry Point, North Carolina. He told no one he was
there but someone spotted him anyway and reported him to the second
Marine Air Wing commander, General Tom Miller. Miller promptly relieved
him of his command. "What the hell is this guy doing here when the guys
on his ship are bombing Hanoi?"[52]

Ralph Brubaker was more understanding. "He wrote me a very nice letter after he was relieved and I read it to the squadron. Billy would have killed
himself if he had stayed out there. He was doing everything wrong under

the sun. Down in my heart, I think he went home hoping this would happen and it did. He was either going to kill himself or kill himself and his crew member."[53] Fortunately for the men of 224, CAG Sheets, along with Brubaker and Charlie Carr, not only filled the leadership vacuum but turned VMA-224 into one of the Sea Services' finest A-6 squadrons on Yankee Station during the spring of 1972.

A MiG Encounter

In contrast to Lieutenant Colonel Stanley, Sheets possessed ample quantities of the most critical leadership ingredient in military aviation—aggressiveness. An old fighter pilot by training, Sheets often requested a Sidewinder missile for his A-6 because he was determined to be the first A-6 pilot in history to bag a MiG. On 6 May 1972 he nearly succeeded.

The mission that day was to hit the Bai Thuong airfield about 25 miles west of the Thanh Hoa bridge. Sheet's plan called for a special Vulture flight of four A-6s to fly ahead of a high strike force of A-6s, A-7s, and F-4s and knock out the airfield's guns before the main Alpha strike arrived. By flying in at under 100 feet, about thirty seconds ahead of the other group, Sheets also secretly hoped to skinny in and catch a bunch of MiGs on the ground. James Ruliffson, an F-4 pilot with VF-111, argued vociferously with Sheets about the mission.

"I think this is dumb," he said. "You guys are exposing yourselves. I think you ought to put a couple of fighters in with you."

"No, we're going to do it my way."

Sheets knew there might be MiGs over the airfield that day but he believed his A-6s stood a very good chance of achieving complete surprise. Unknown to Ruliffson, Sheets had also arranged with Captain Harris to get a real-time MiG warning from Red Crown, the Navy's radar command and control on a picket ship in the Gulf of Tonkin.[54] If any MiGs were in the air that day, he would know immediately where they were and Vulture Flight would be able to avoid them. Sheets even cautioned Ruliffson to avoid the temptation to break off from the high strike force to protect the A-6s from MiGs: "Ruff, don't go chasing MiGs. If you see them, leave them alone. You're the high-group TARCAP (target combat air patrol—the planes that patrolled the skies over a ground target for MiGs) leader. Lead that strike to the target and protect them."[55]

Roger Sheets, Charlie Carr, and the rest of Vulture Flight catapulted off the *Coral Sea* at 0400. As soon as the flight crossed the North Vietnamese coastline it dropped close to the ground and spread out. As they approached Bai Thuong from about fifteen miles out, the silence of dawn was rudely broken by an urgent radio transmission: "Vulture, Mustang 1, heads up!"[56] Sheets now knew that MiGs were in the air but continued leading the mission. "I figured that we had come this far and we were spread out and low and I could see no reason for not going ahead and laying the cluster bombs along the field."[57] Sheets delayed the start of his CBU-24 drop a few seconds because he wanted to get some of his bomblets into the revetments at the far end of the airfield. As Carr recalled, when they got into the target area, he "looked up and saw two silver 21s heading northwest; they were getting the hell out of the area."[58] He then noticed a pair of MiG-17s over the airfield at 2,000 feet. The 17s dropped their fuel tanks and one of them lit its afterburner and attacked Vulture 3, an A-6 manned by Phil Schuyler and Lou Ferracane.

Ruliffson, leading the main strike force, almost peeled off into the MiG. "It was just laying there for me. Piece a' cake. All I had to do was split-S and I had a free MiG. But the last words I'd heard on deck were Sheets' saying, 'Don't chase the MiGs.'"[59] Instead, Ruliffson radioed Jerry "Devil" Houston, who was flying MiG cover that day in an F-4. Houston at first did not see the MiG, which was painted in black, white, and gray camouflage, but his RIO [Radar Intercept Officer] Kevin Moore soon spotted it at two o'clock low. The MiG was just about to pass left to right behind Houston's tail, so Houston reversed right, dropped his centerline tank, and headed into the MiG's rear quadrant.

Blinky Sheets then surprised everyone that day. Just as the MiG started firing 37-millimeter shells at Phil Schuyler and his BN, Lou Ferracane, he did a zigzag and cut between the MiG and Vulture Three. As they crossed in front of the MiG, Charlie Carr looked over at him and said, "*CAG, I sure hope you have a plan!*"[60]

"Blinky was fighter experienced, and former fighter-squadron CO," explains Ruliffson. "By this time, he knows about the MiG-17's terrible rate of roll. He's understood the tactics that by this time Top Gun and the RAGs [Replacement Air Group] were all teaching."[61] Sheets' plan was to use the A-6's superior maneuverability at low speeds to keep the MiG at bay. "Now this guy is on my right side and a little bit high," said Carr. "I've already gone from air-to-ground on the weapons panel to air-to-air. The seeker is energized and we're all set to shoot him. That was CAG's desire—to shoot the MiG down. He said, 'Hey Charlie, we'll just drag this guy a bit. You watch the MiG and I'll keep us out of the dirt.' So now I've turned into a RIO. And I've got myself all twisted around looking out the right side, and this guy's a little high on us and rolls in and starts shooting."[62]

Every time the MiG got close enough to take a shot, Sheets would do a roll and then break to change direction. The idea was either to get the MiG to overshoot them so they could take a shot from behind, or else to drag it out until it had to turn for home; Sheets would then do a 180-degree turn and shoot the MiG down. Houston, barreling toward the MiG at 600 knots (nearly twice as fast as Sheets was traveling at that point), had no idea of what the CAG was up to. All he saw was an Intruder flying in front of his target. "I was maybe 200 feet above the trees, and I called the A-6 to break. He wouldn't break, he wouldn't break, and wouldn't break. I was approaching minimum range and it was either shoot, hope you're on the MiG, or lose the opportunity, so I shot."[63]

Meanwhile in Vulture one, Carr looked over his shoulder and couldn't see Devil Houston's F-4, but he knew it was there. "CAG's unspoken thought at the time was, 'Screw Devil, we're going to bag the MiG.' We went through about two more passes and meanwhile this Phantom behind us is screaming to break, get the hell out of there, and all this sort of shit. And finally this Seventeen rolls in and shoots rockets at us. And I said, 'Atolls"; [The Soviet version of a Sidewinder]; in those days there was a rumor that they were going to configure MiG-17s with Atolls. We didn't know. CAG immediately pumped the engines back up and broke right, forcing the MiG way high, and now we're down low, and I heard 'Fox Two,'" [U.S. code for a Sidewinder launch] and I saw a missile go out and hit this guy in the tailpipe."[64]

Houston remembers that time seemed to compress when he launched that missile. "First, I pulled the trigger and nothing happened. You're supposed to have three-quarters of a second delay. I had time to recite the Gettysburg Address from the time I pulled the trigger until anything happened. At an instant like that with the adrenaline flooding your brain, the clock stops, and everything else is in ultra slow motion."[65]

"For Christ's sake," thought Houston, "It's not going! The goddamn thing's not going to go. I mean it was just an eternity, but you're only talking about a three-quarter second delay."[66]

The missile did eventually fire, blowing the tail off the aircraft and forcing the plane into a ridge. They saw no parachute.

That was the first and only MiG Jerry Houston saw in his SEA career. When he landed on the *Coral Sea*, the first thing his CO, Commander Foster "Tooter" Teague, said to him was, "Jerry, you have a choice. We can fly you every day and try to get you to be an ace or we can send you to Hong Kong for a couple of weeks and your wife can come over and meet you."[67] Jerry chose Hong Kong.

As for Blinky, Sheets and Charlie Carr, after doing a victory roll over the *Coral Sea* they too joined Houston in the VF-51 ready room for the celebration. After the celebration Kevin Moore, Houston's RIO, pulled Carr aside and said, "Hey, Charlie, don't ever let CAG do that again. Jesus Christ, man, you guys damn near got bagged."[68]

For all his skills as a pilot and as a professional naval officer, Roger Sheets never achieved the ultimate trophy of combat command in Vietnam—a MiG kill. With such a status symbol, Sheets might have risen to admiral and achieved a level of fame comparable to Robin Olds'; without it he would retire an obscure captain, with a staff assignment in New Orleans. In the Vietnam War, success at the wing level was still defined more by individual heroic acts by the leader than by the collective accomplishments of a unit.

The Mining of Haiphong Harbor: 8 May 1972

Just three days after the MiG encounter, Vulture Flight was ordered by Washington to conduct one of the most significant air missions of the course of the Vietnam War—the mining of Haiphong Harbor.

Because nearly 85 percent of the North's import tonnage flowed through the port of Haiphong, the mining option had been frequently discussed but never attempted: there was always too much fear that such an action might precipitate direct intervention by either China or the Soviet Union. What prompted the sudden shift in policy was a combination of elements. Several weeks earlier, North Vietnam had launched its Easter Offensive, and by 1 May 1972 NVA units had captured Quang Tri, the capital of South Vietnam's northernmost province. With only 60,000 American troops left in South Vietnam, General Creighton Abrams, the commander of MACV (Military Assistance Command Vietnam), faced the very real possibility of a total South Vietnamese collapse.[69]

In response to this dire situation President Nixon drafted the following memorandum to Secretary of State Kissinger: "I have determined that we should go for broke. . . . We must punish the enemy. . . . Now that I have made this very tough watershed decision I intend to stop at nothing to bring the enemy to his knees."[70] After a number of meetings between National Security Council staffers and the Joint Chiefs of Staff, it was decided that mining would be the best option in the current situation in Vietnam. Hence on 4 May, Admiral Thomas Moorer, the JCS chairman, ordered Chief of Naval Operations Elmo Zumwalt to gin up a draft for such an operation, to be code-named Pocket Money.[71]

Admiral Zumwalt chose five captains within his office to assist him with the plan. In a mere four hours (by midnight on 5 May), they finished it. Operation Pocket Money was born. Mines would be laid along the single 150-yard-wide ship channel leading to Haiphong's harbor. The mines would be set for a seventy-two-hour delay to allow the 37 foreign vessels (16 Soviet, 5 Chinese, 3 Polish, 2 Cuban, 1 East German, 5 Somalian, and 4 British ships registered in Hong Kong) to leave the port. In the end only four Soviet ships and one British ship would depart; the delay needed to be implemented nonetheless for diplomatic reasons.[72] The rest of the ships would remain at Haiphong until the war's end in January 1973.

The most critical aspect of the operation was timing. The mines needed to be dropped minutes before Nixon's televised speech to the nation on 8 May, which meant that the *Coral Sea* air wing would only have forty-eight hours to refine and implement Pocket Money. As soon as the mission order arrived on the ship from the JCS, Roger Sheets summoned Charlie Carr to the Air Intelligence center. Carr remembers being confronted by a Marine sentry with a rifle at the door—a phenomenon rarely seen on the carrier. "I knocked on the door, and Lieutenant Commander Harvey Ickle, the operations officer of VA-22 and the mine warfare officer on the *Coral Sea*, opened up the door. He had a coal miner's helmet complete with a little light on his head. I said, 'You're shitting me,' and Harvey said, 'No, I'm not.' We then started planning the mission with the CAG, using a marvelous old French map as our guide."[73]

Under Sheets' plan, A-6s would be used to drop the 1,000-pound MK-52 magnetic mines and A-7s to drop the smaller 500-pound MK-36 acoustic mines. The MK-52s were especially unwieldy. The barrel-shaped mines were 80 inches long and 19 inches in diameter. Designed to be dropped by parachute, they would then rest at the bottom of the channel until the large magnetic field of a passing freighter or warship triggered them to detonate. The magnetic sensitivity of the MK-52 could be adjusted and dead periods could be programmed into the mine's timer. The mine also could be set to go inactive after a predetermined time period. For Pocket Money, this period would be 180 days. After that point, the mines would not go off unless directly struck a sharp blow, such as by a dredging device or a large anchor.[74]

For Blinky Sheets and Vulture Flight, the challenge of dropping the MK-52 was twofold. First, the mines needed to be dropped in a very precise pattern along the Haiphong channel, making navigation absolutely critical. Charlie Carr, the lead navigator for the mission, decided he could not trust the A-6's intervalometer (the bombing computer linked to the A-6's navigation system), which automatically released ordnance over a preprogrammed target, for this critical mission. Instead, he chose to rely on his own skills and a simple wristwatch to punch the mines off.[75]

Other challenges were the MiGs and SAMs. Heavily laden with cumbersome MK-52s, the A-6s would be extremely vulnerable to enemy defenses. Detachable nose and tail cones for the mines were supposed to cut down on drag; unfortunately, the *Coral Sea* only had enough cones to equip two out of the four mines carried by each A-6. In a meeting that first night Sheets explained the situation to the admirals in charge of TF-77, the carrier task force on station in Yankee Station, and of CTF-75, the corresponding cruiser and destroyer task force. At that meeting the admirals decided to bring the cruiser USS *Chicago* to within forty miles of Haiphong, close enough to protect the strike force with its Talos anti-aircraft missiles. CTF-75 requested that Sheets keep his aircraft below 1,000 feet so that anything above that altitude could be declared hostile. "The admirals looked at me and said, 'Is that okay with you, CAG?' and I said, 'No, I want anything above five hundred feet to be declared as hostile. We'll be well below that.' I've never seen a MiG above a couple of thousand feet when they were down trying to engage so I wanted that buffer zone to be as low as possible—because when you're sitting there with eight thousand pounds of mines without cones on them, you're just a sitting duck."[76]

On the day of the mission, Admiral Jesse Greer asked if he and a couple of his staff members could sit in on the briefing "not because they wanted to nitpick but because this was a very historic event and they wanted to be a part of it." During the briefing, Sheets mentioned that the mines would be "positive armed."; once dropped, the mines would go live after a 72-hour delay and could not be turned off. As Sheets explained, "We looked at this as a one-shot deal. If we didn't get it right this time, they would put everything they had in our way on the next go-around. During the briefing, when I mentioned that the mines were positive armed I got a funny reaction from Admiral Greer. He didn't say anything, but it was just a look that came briefly over his face and then left. What I didn't know at the time but found out later is that although we had gotten approval for the mission, we hadn't gotten the final okay to go ahead and put the mines in. He knew that, but didn't say a word about it, he just let us go on. When I found that out later, I understood why he had that fleeting look of 'Oh, God!'; on his face."[77] Admiral Greer knew the risks involved in continuing the mission but decided to put his career on the line and press on.

Sheets' strike force of four A-6s and six A-7s streaked to the target at 360 feet above sea level at a speed of 360 knots. As the formation closed on Haiphong harbor, a swarm of MiGs suddenly appeared on the *Chicago* radar screens. The cruiser immediately launched a Talos missile and downed a MiG; that was enough to scare the remaining MiGs away. Sheets and company then began punching off mines at precisely 0859 local time. Two minutes later, Sheets radioed the *Coral Sea* to inform Greer that all the mines were in the water. The *Coral Sea* then issued a flash cable to the White House, telling them that the mines were in the water. Nixon, who had already begun his speech, had been speaking slowly to allow the A-6s to get out of the target area safely. With a stern face, he was describing three courses of action with the American public: immediate withdrawal of all U.S. forces from Vietnam, continued negotiation, or direct and decisive military action. As soon as he received the signal that the mines were in the water he announced, as a part of his speech, that he had reluctantly chosen the third option:

> I have ordered the following measures, which are being implemented as I am speaking to you. All entrances to North Vietnamese ports will be mined to prevent access to these ports and North Vietnamese naval operations from these ports. United States forces have been directed to take appropriate measures within the internal and claimed territorial waters of North Vietnam to interdict the delivery of supplies. Rail and all communications will be cut off to the maximum extent possible. Air and naval strikes against North Vietnam will continue.[78]

Despite the apparent strength of the antiwar movement, a Gallup poll reported that 74 percent of Americans interviewed supported President Nixon's hard line against North Vietnam. By the war's end, Navy and Marine aircraft would drop over 8,000 mines in coastal areas of North Vietnam and another 3,000 in inland waterways. The mining of Haiphong itself closed this critical port for 300 days and almost certainly influenced the North Vietnamese decision in January of 1973 to come to a peace settlement.[79] Without the use of Haiphong harbor, the NVA could not resupply its air defenders with enough SAMs to foil Nixon's December 1972 Christmas bombing campaign. Whereas on day one of that campaign the NVA had been able to fire 200 SAMs at the U.S. B-52 force, by day eleven it could only get 23 missiles in the air. In short the mining, as well as the bombing of missile storage sites, radar, and communications systems, convinced the North Vietnamese to send their diplomats back to the bargaining table to negotiate what would ultimately become the Paris Peace Accords signed on 27 January 1973.[80]

The Spirit of the Vultures

Humor was a key ingredient in keeping the morale of VMA-224 high during its long periods on the line. Inevitably, Charlie Carr was the ringleader in this department. A master storyteller and one of the wildest members of the squadron in port, Carr rarely entered the Ready Room without several jokes up his sleeve. One of his best took place in the context of a joint raid against the San Hoi bridge with A-6s from the *Constellation*. Before the joint briefing with the *Conny* crews, Carr went down to the parachute shop and had them make up a set of white headbands with a big rising sun in the middle. The whole squadron put on the headbands for the briefing. When the bridge called for them to man up, they ran up to the carrier deck, ran to the bridge, bowed three times, and then jumped in their aircraft—just like the scene in the popular 1970 film *Tora! Tora! Tora!*[81]

When everyone had returned from the mission, Captain Harris paid a visit to Ready Room 5. "Guys, that was great, it was one of the funniest things I've seen in my life, but you can't do it any more. I'll surely have sailors writing home saying I'm launching *kamikaze* raids off my boat."[82]

Another common activity among the Vultures was singing songs in the Ready Room. Roger Wilson, one of the pilots in the wing, saw himself as a future rock star and even brought a Fender guitar with him for the cruise.

Apparently he was "absolutely terrible," but his squadron mates still loved to hear him play.

During liberty at NAS Cubi Point in Olongapo in the Philippines, squadron antics often escalated. Known as the rowdiest squadron on the ship, VMA (AW)-224 often began their liberty with a lecture from the flight surgeon. "Once again," the doctor would begin, "VMA (AW)-224 has had more VD during the last in-port period than any other squadron on this ship." The entire ready room would then erupt in laughter, and urge each other to keep it up. Carr says, "I wish we could have worn a VD patch, except our CO wouldn't let us do that."[83]

Once in port, Charlie Carr and many of the other officers would quickly shed their uniforms in favor of Levis and T-shirts. After a quick beer or two in the O Club, these men would head off to Olongapo. "It was a sailor's town. Olongapo, Olongapo, how I love Olongapo. All the girls seem to come from Cebu City. We used to call them LBFMs—little brown fucking machines. If FedEx wants to hire me to be their regional manager at Cubi, I will do it: I know the territory."[84] Angus concurs: "When the ship pulled into Subic Bay, I thought I had died and gone to heaven. Olongapo was just paradise: cheap beer and cheap women."[85] A favorite drinking game played by pilots was called Smiles. In this game, a group of officers would sit around a big table with a like number of prostitutes under the table. While a prostitute performed fellatio on each officer the officers would nonchalantly sip beer or play cards, trying not to crack up; the first one to smile paid for all the girls and the beer. As Carr once said to me, "If you take every sea story about Po City and double it, you might wind up close to the truth, but don't count on it." Another pilot suggested I write a history of the Navy in the Philippines and title it "Olongapo: An Oral History."

Whereas Olongapo was the center of aviator sexual activity in the Philippines, the nexus for the squadrons' social activity was the Cubi Point Officers' Club—a place to hang out and drink, a staging ground for missions into Po City, and a debriefing center after those forays. Naturally, many humorous events occurred in this popular night spot. On one occasion, for example, Deke Burdoyne, the CAG on the *America* (CVA-66), staggered up to Charlie Carr at 0200 and said, "I'm the greatest CAG in the fleet, and can outfly Blinky Sheets any day of the week."[86] Carr, in no mood to hear his CAG disparaged in such a manner, turned around and slugged Burdoyne. Fortunately for Carr, in the Navy of the early 1970s what happened at the Cubi Point club generally stayed at the club. "I saw Deke the next day at the bar and all was forgotten.[87]

Such was not the case when Lieutenant Commander Phil Schuyler, the squadron's Navy liaison officer, got out of hand. On that night Carr had gone to town and left Schuyler, nicknamed "Beer Barrel," at the O Club with someone else. "I didn't do a good Barrel watch. Occasionally somebody would bust out the front window of the O Club. But anyway, the window costs fifty bucks so Barrel went over and got the night manager of the club and said how much is the window and the guy said fifty bucks and Barrel says here's fifty bucks, and then he promptly took a chair and busted the window out. Well, shit, he paid for the window, that was the rule, so what? Well, the next day, you know, he now has to see Captain Bill Harris for busting the window out of the O Club. Barrel is pretty much shit-faced and hung over but anyway we kind of get him brushed up a little bit, spruced up, and got him in his uniform, got him in a jeep, and off to the goddamn pier. He then went up to the bridge, where Captain Harris made him stand and wait there for a good amount of time before calling him over to his chair. He then proceeded to read him the riot act. 'Goddamn it, I would have expected this out of my Navy officers but not from a Marine.' Phil's standing there in a Navy uniform, looks down at his Navy belt buckle, and then said, 'But, Captain, I'm in the Navy.' Harris nearly fell out of his damn chair laughing."[88]

Lieutenant Colonel Brubaker, the squadron commander, didn't always find these stunts amusing. "Phil tore up the club at Cubi Point a couple of times. He was unmanageable. When he was drunk, I would often escort him to his room in the BOQ, and fifteen minutes later he would be back in the club."[89] Charlie Carr, similarly pushed the limits of his squadron commander's tolerance. "Charlie did some things that I did not approve of but so be it, we all do those things once in a while. One time Charlie gets up on a table and there's no women in the club or anything, and pulls out his wingding and urinates all over the table. Right in front of all of us. Of course they've had a couple of drinks and they think it's funny."[90] Ironically, when Brubaker was asked who he would choose to go to war with him again if given the chance, the first two names out of his mouth were Charlie Carr and Phil Schuyler.

The Beer Barrel

As the old naval-aviation saying goes, "The guy you bail out from jail the night before is the same guy you want on your wing for the morning hop." Phil

"Beer Barrel" Schuyler certainly fell into this category. The son of a truck driver, Phil Schuyler grew up in Carpinteria, California, a small town just south of Santa Barbara. He later attended college at California State Polytechnic University in Pomona on a football scholarship. Because money was always tight for this working-class youth, Schuyler transferred after two years to UC Santa Barbara near his hometown of Carpinteria, and finally to Los Angeles State, where he earned his degree in 1962. Phil, like many athletes, didn't enjoy the academic aspects of college life but needed a degree to fulfill his postcollegiate dream: an opportunity to fly with the United States Navy.

Phil Schuyler entered flight training in 1962—a period in naval aviation before the Vietnam War when the demand for aviators was low and competition for wings fierce. Of the 82 trainees who entered training with him, only 20 received their wings. As for Phil, he made it through the program but didn't have the academic scores for fast movers; instead, he ended up in the Grumman S-2, a twin-engine propeller-driven plane used to hunt and track submarines.

Because the threat from submarines was virtually nonexistent in Vietnam, Schuyler ended up flying a lot of gunfire-support missions during the early stages of the war. Stationed aboard the USS *Bennington* (CVS-20), he flew 120 such missions in the S-2. As he describes it, "We would check in with the destroyer, we would set up a race-track pattern, he would fire, we would spot the round, and then adjust his fire accordingly."[91] Occasionally, his plane would be fired on by small arms or a 50-caliber machine gun, but other than that the tour was relatively uneventful. "It was on the '67 cruise that I decided to go for the A-6. A friend said the A-6 was the way to go, it's the newest airplane we have."[92]

Phil Schuyler did his jet transition at the A-6 at Kingsville, Texas, and then went to NAS Oceana, in Virginia Beach, Virginia in December 1967 to train in the A-6 for a further six months. Shortly thereafter he deployed with VA-65 on the USS *Kitty Hawk* (CVA-63) in December 1968. Unfortunately for an adventuresome soul like Schuyler, his 1969–1971 cruise on the *Kitty Hawk* was nearly as uneventful as his first tour on the *Bennington*. Owing to President Johnson's November 1968 bombing halt against North Vietnam, VA-65 ended up flying most of its missions into Laos. "Almost every flight was a full system drop. We carried between sixteen and twenty-two MK-82 500-pound bombs. Most of the guns that fired at us were 23-millimeter. We never got hit on that cruise. I would usually fly one hour-and-forty-five-minute mission per day."[93]

Despite the monotony of the war, Phil Schuyler continued to renew his enlistment with the Navy. "I liked the people, and the flying," he explained. "Besides, the war was going on and I did not feel it was the time to get out."[94] Like Carr and Sheets, Schuyler was a natural warrior, in it for the long haul. Hence he had no misgivings about serving a third tour in Southeast Asia aboard the *Coral Sea*. The idea of serving with Marines, though, initially put him off. "I had some misgivings about the Marines at first. We had always kidded the Marines about their maintenance and how dirty their airplanes were. Once I got to know the people, I felt better about it."[95] One of the people who impressed Schuyler the most was Carr. "Charlie was the most experienced BN we had. On that cruise, Charlie finished his six-hundredth combat mission, two hundred of them in North Vietnam."[96] Schuyler would end up flying with Sheets and Carr on many difficult missions, including the 16 April 1972 SAM-suppression mission and the Bai Thuong airfield raid. His most memorable mission with these two, however, would occur on 29 May 1972.

The target that day was a railroad repair facility at Uong Bi just east of Haiphong harbor. Just two weeks before, a strike package of eight A-7s had attempted to bomb the target but aborted after receiving heavy anti-aircraft fire. None of this detered CAG Sheets. Determined to take out the target, he was convinced that a lead flight of four A-6s could fly low enough to penetrate the area's defenses and take out the SAM sites, thereby paving the way for a larger Alpha strike of A-7s and F-4s.

Almost from the mission's outset, things started to go wrong for Phil Schuyler and his Marine BN, Lou Ferracane in Vulture Three. Somewhere over the karst islands in the waters off Haiphong, the flight flew over an old French fort, and Schuyler took a 23-millimeter round in his wing. Although the round started a small fire in the wing, he chose to press on. "The target was very important, so we elected to stay with the formation."[97] As soon as his plane was over land, Schuyler dropped down low and skillfully carved his way among a series of ridges until they reached the railyard. He then popped up, released his 500-pound bombs, and took four more 23-mm rounds. Two of them slammed into his plane's left wing, the third exploded on the armor plate of the engine, and the fourth came right through the cockpit, grazing Ferracane's face and taking out the BN's radio and console. With both windscreens shattered, and dirt and paperclips blowing around the cockpit, Schuyler pressed his intercom button: "Lou, you okay?"

"Roger, I'm okay. Aircraft is flying."

"Okay, select the armament panel for the second target."

Schuyler knew that the A-7s and F-4s in the main Alpha strike depended on Vulture Flight to take out Uong Bi's SAM and AAA sites. He was willing to risk everything to dump his cluster bombs on those targets.

When he pulled up and turned for home, the CAG ordered him to reduce power. As Schuyler did so, though, a cloud of black smoke went up from his wing. He instantly thrust the throttles forward to increase power and, once clear of the SAM ring around Haiphong, did a slow climb to 6,000 feet and had Blinky Sheets, as flight leader, fly under him to check out the battle damage. On his first pass, the CAG couldn't see anything because the bomb racks and a drop tank obscured his view.

"Jettison your MERS [multiple ejection bomb racks] and tanks," ordered the CAG.

"Roger," Schuyler responded as he pickled off the equipment—probably sooner than CAG expected, because the dropped tanks nearly hit the wing of Roger Wilson and Bill Angus's A-6.

"Vulture Three, *eject, eject, eject!*" the CAG suddenly called out.

Schuyler and Ferracane looked at each other in complete amazement. They had a TACAN (radio navigation beacon) lock on the carrier 52 miles ahead of them and were completely committed to getting their aircraft back aboard ship.

"Roger, CAG. We're going to pull the power back and then get out."

"Negative Vulture Three, *eject right now!*"

Still not believing what he was hearing, Schuyler blew the canopy and ejected at 430 knots. Sheets later informed him that he could see daylight under the airplane from the trailing edge of the flap to within about four inches of the front of the wing. Apparently the tracer round from the French fort had hit a hydraulic line and started a small fire; with time, the fire had eaten into the wing like a blowtorch. Therefore, fearing that the plane would go into an uncontrollable spin if the wing sheared off—as seemed likely—Sheets ordered an immediate ejection.[98]

As an LSO aboard the *Coral Sea*, Phil Schuyler often marveled at the abundance of poisonous sea snakes and sharks in the Gulf of Tonkin. At night, he would have nightmares of landing in a large ball of mating snakes or having a shark rip his torso apart. "It would drive me nuts." [99] Hence, when he landed in the water and felt something hit his foot, his immediate thought was *shark!* Actually, it was the cover that contained his raft.

After they had been in the water about twenty minutes, a large HC-6 landed right in the middle of Haiphong harbor and picked up both Schuyler and Ferracane. After about a week of recuperation for what he thought was a sprained back, Schuyler flew seven more missions before the *Coral Sea* left Yankee Station on 11 June 1972. When he got to Cubi Point, the flight surgeons X-rayed every bone in his body—standard procedure after a violent ejection. "We hadn't been there ten minutes when the surgeon came out and told my BN that his back was okay and that it was probably just a bad sprain but that I had broken my neck so I was grounded." Schuyler's back never healed. They put him in a horse collar for a couple of months, but the bones never did reattach themselves as single unit. Schuyler today suffers from arthritis, which has grown around the two bone fragments that broke off from his vertebrae; nevertheless, he still leads an active life as a fighter-tactics instructor at NAS Oceana. For the extraordinary heroism shown during his shootdown mission, Phil Schuyler received the Silver Star.

Cowboy Angus

A kind but intense young man, Bill Angus was one of the most popular junior officers in VMA (AW)-224. LTC Ralph Brubaker, the squadron commander, praised Angus for his responsible attitude within the squadron. "If anyone ever abused another officer or got into a heated argument, Bill was the one that would calm everyone. If anyone went out and got a little incapacitated, Bill would be the one to take him home. Bill was a fine guy to have around. If anyone needed any help, Bill would provide it."[100] Charlie Carr, who often referred to him as "Billy Anguish," also respected Angus but used to tease him for his seriousness. "Bill is a neat guy but he appears to be somewhat of a hand-wringer. If you didn't know Bill Angus at all and you first met him, you would think he was a worry-wart. But he isn't."[101]

Like Carr's, Bill's background was eclectic. The son of a mining engineer, Bill lived in Caracas, Venezuela between the ages of five and ten, attended an international school there, learned to speak fluent Spanish, and developed a lifelong interest in travel and foreign culture. Tragedy, however, would interrupt his adventures in Venezuela: his father died suddenly of a heart attack when Bill was only ten years old. Two weeks later Bill found himself back in the United States, attending public school in Golden,

Colorado. Basketball and football helped Bill cope with the loss of his father, as did several trips to Europe and Mexico during his high-school years.

In 1963, Bill Angus went on to attend Colorado State University at Fort Collins, where he majored in business administration. Fearing that he would be drafted immediately upon graduation, Bill's mother offered to pay for an additional year of college in the hope that the Vietnam War would end before he graduated. It didn't, and Angus ended up joining the Marine Corps in 1968. At that time, the Marine Officer Candidate program, known as Platoon Leadership Class or simply "PLC," was one of the easiest commissioning programs to enter but one of the hardest to graduate from. The Marine philosophy was to give any college graduate a shot at officer training, then allow the drill sergeants to separate the wheat from the chaff in the grueling training cycle at Quantico.

Due to poor eyesight, Angus did not qualify for pilot training; instead, he gravitated to the NFO program. A lazy student by nature, he barely got through the academic phase of the training, but loved the flying. When he finally got selected for the A-6, Angus was in heaven. "The A-6 was an overwhelming aircraft—unbelievably sophisticated. It was possible to sit in the navigator seat, tell the aircraft where it was (activate the inertial-guidance system), and punch in the coordinates of another airfield and it would tell you how to get there and how long it would take. The computer integrated all the navigation systems on the aircraft. It took me a couple of years to become proficient with the system. You had a toggle switch that allowed you to monitor fifteen aircraft functions. The 747's cockpit is child's play compared to the A-6's."[102]

In November 1969, Angus transitioned to the A-6 in VMAT-102 at Cherry Point, and then joined VMA (AW)-332. He flew with this squadron until he learned about VMA (AW)-224 and the *Coral Sea* deployment. Naively, he volunteered for duty on the carrier, thinking it would be an opportunity for travel and adventure. "I was told that nothing was going on in SEA and we would fly the Ho Chi Minh Trail and then go to these glorious places like Australia. To me, it seemed like a grand adventure without too much combat."[103]

For Bill Angus and the other junior officers on the *Coral Sea,* the first 30 days of night missions into Laos would forever change their attitude about combat. "The first thirty days of the tour, you are in shock and fully well terrified of anything and everything," recalled Bill's wingman, Tom Sprouse. "The first thirty days, I had trouble sleeping at night and was always worried about tomorrow."[104] Neither Angus nor Sprouse nor any other junior officer in VMA-224, however, sought to avoid combat. To ease his mind about the next day's mission, Bill would spend hours planning his flight and marking up his maps with color-coded symbols for flak traps and SAM sites. "Even though I relished the flying I didn't aspire to be the last person killed in Vietnam. I did everything within my power to know what's going on and to know where things were."[105] The more Angus worked on his night navigation, though, the more missions he ended up being assigned to fly. "It's kind of a Catch-22. If you're good at it, you keep doing it. If you aren't good at it, you don't do it."[106] In contrast to fighter jocks like Olds or Sheets, Angus didn't view war as a wonderful opportunity to prove his skills or gain a thrill. Once in it, however, his pride in being a Marine pilot and a Vulture made him work hard to be a valuable member of the team—a man someone like Sheets would pick to fly with. In this sense, he was similar to Rasimus—but unlike Rasimus, Angus never learned to love the game of war.

On 11 June, the odds finally caught up with Bill Angus and his pilot, Roger Wilson. The target that day was a power plant in Nam Dinh, the third-largest city in North Vietnam. Four planes were scheduled to fly that day, but two aborted, including Carr and Sheets' plane. Charlie Carr, who had planned the mission, believed that large 2,000-pound bombs represented the best type of ordnance for knocking out the target. Carrying these bombs, though, meant that Vulture Flight would have to release its ordnance at 4,000 feet, an extremely high altitude well within the operating parameters of the enemy's SA-2 missile. Tom Sprouse, who flew Angus's wing with Al Albright as his BN, recalled that the plan was for the two planes to fly in side by side and drop the ordnance simultaneously on the target. "It was just going to be one pass so we were side by side. He was maybe five or six hundred yards to my right. As we were in the run, out of the corner of my eyes, I saw this flash on the right and I was just to the release point, so I released the ordnance and looked over and Angus's aircraft was just tumbling. It went into the edge of a lake. We circled around and couldn't see any chutes or survivors. In the meantime we were getting tracers everywhere. We took two or three hits from 7.62 millimeter AK-47 rounds."[107]

When Tom Sprouse returned to the *Coral Sea,* he reported both men dead. The next day, Hanoi Radio announced that they had captured the pilot of the A-6 that had been shot down over Nam Dinh. In truth, however, they had captured not the pilot but his BN, Bill Angus. Sadly, Roger Wilson did not survive the bailout. Sprouse would not learn the fate of either man until he saw Bill Angus walk off a plane at Travis Air Force Base in March 1973. As for Angus, he doesn't recall any part of the mission from the time the AAA or SAM hit him until he ended up in the Hanoi Hilton fourteen hours later.

For the men of VMA (AW)-224, their odyssey in Southeast Asia was almost over. By 12 June they would be enjoying drinks at the Cubi Point O Club, perhaps followed by a rendezvous with a Filipina bar girl later on the evening. Eight days later, on 22 June, the squadron would briefly return to Yankee Station for six days, but no aircraft would be lost. Overall, the 44 pilots and BNs of VMA (AW)-224 flew more than 2,800 sorties over Southeast Asia with a loss of just four aircraft—an excellent record given the intensity of the air war in the spring of 1972.[108]

The odyssey of Bill Angus, however, would continue within the walls of the Hanoi Hilton. No one would know whether Angus was alive or dead until operation Homecoming, the general POW release in 1973. His mother—who had tried so hard to keep him out of harm's way but who was extraordinarily proud of his Marine commission—would die during his incarceration, leaving him with no immediate family to return to when he stepped off that aircraft at Travis AFB in March of 1973.

Admiral James Holloway, the commander of the Seventh Fleet in 1972, once referred to Roger Sheets and Charlie Carr as one of his "best A-6 crews in Southeast Asia."[109] It could also be said that Vulture Flight comprised the finest collection of A-6 crews in SEA during the same period. If it did not, the unit would not have been chosen to mine Haiphong harbor—one of the supreme achievements of U.S. naval air power over the entire course of the war. What few historians of the conflict realize is that this unit consisted mainly of Marine aviators, who came to the *Coral Sea* poorly prepared for carrier operations. That they performed so well thoroughly debunks one of the great myths of airpower history: the myth that only naval aviators can perform well in a carrier environment. The story also shows how a motley assortment of rather unmilitary types can perform well beyond anyone's expectations in combat. True, these men were professionals in the sense that they were all officers and volunteers, but they were not professionals to the same degree that an Annapolis or West Point graduate is a professional.

None of them possessed regular commissions or viewed the Marine Corps as a career, although a few managed to stay in long enough to make it one. They were reserve officers serving in full-time positions, with very little hope of promotion or advancement. That they gave America a maximum effort in an unpopular war is difficult to understand. Charlie Carr and Billy Angus, though patriotic, did not think of the flag when they strapped into an A-6; they thought of doing a good job for the pilot sitting next to them, the Vulture flight, the squadron, and to a certain degree the Marine Corps. These men were clearly imbued with a fighting spirit that enabled them to transcend their inadequate training and reserve commissions to form one of the finest units of the war.

This spirit is partly the result of the incongruous Roger "Blinky" Sheets and his remarkable leadership. It is ironic indeed that this former enlisted man and fighter pilot would go on to become one of the most famous A-6 pilots and commanders of the war: a more egotistical wing commander might have stayed with fighters in the hope of getting a MiG, but Sheets put his MiG-Killing aspirations aside to help a squadron clearly in need of instruction and support. That he almost got a MiG at Bai Thuong reveals just how skilled Sheets was as a pilot. But Roger Sheets' skills went far beyond the stick and rudder of the cockpit. Unlike Robin Olds, this man had the absolute confidence of all of his superiors, from Captain Harris on up to Admiral Holloway. Perhaps his more humble origins are partly responsible. Sheets' father was not a flag officer as Olds' was, nor did Sheets attend a service academy or even a college, for that matter. Instead, he learned about authority by rising through the ranks as an enlisted sailor, and grew up with a chaplain and line officers rather than with aviators—factors that gave him a more cautious outlook on authority than Olds.

More significant than his relationship to his superiors, Blinky Sheets, despite his awkward appearance, knew how to inspire his Marines. He took time to educate the Marines on carrier operations and made sure they received fair treatment from their Navy colleagues. He also built esprit de corps with the Vulture logo and slogan. When he pointed to that vulture poster at the end of every ready room briefing and said, "Gentlemen, *let's go kill something!*" his men knew that he meant it. Like the aviators of the Eighth Wing, the men of VMA (AW)-224 knew that their leader was the kind of guy you wanted with you in a dark alley: Sheets had fangs and knew how to use them.

The spirit of war and the spirit of the kill are inextricably linked. Sheets knew this and knew how to transform fear into bloodlust. He also knew how to inspire men like Angus, who did *not* have a strong bloodlust, to fly and fight to the utmost of their abilities. He accomplished this end by emphasizing the status of "being a Vulture" constantly in speeches, and made the men of Squadron 224 push themselves hard to earn this special status.

CHAPTER 4

BAGGED

The POW Experience

Hoa Lo Prison, Hanoi: 12 June 1972

"The last thing I remember about my shootdown was standing next to Tom Sprouse on the flight deck before the take-off," recalled Bill Angus.[1] Bill's ejection was so violent that he would not regain consciousness until fourteen hours later in one of the four cells of "New Guy Village," an area located at the southern corner of the Hoa Lo prison in Hanoi. When he awoke, he found himself in a masonry cell painted in dull white with green doors. A lone 30-watt lightbulb dangled from the twelve-foot ceiling; ventilating holes in that ceiling produced the only fresh air in the room. Dressed only in underwear, Angus awoke to find mosquito bites up and down his legs and arms. His bed consisted of a block of concrete with leg irons on one end and a thin straw mat for a covering.

For the next three days two NVA officers interrogated Bill extensively, occasionally hitting him in the stomach, ears, and back of the head when his attention wandered. By 1972, the North Vietnamese no longer practiced much torture on American prisoners but they still punched prisoners and kept them in isolation, in a half-hearted attempt to glean intelligence and destroy the spirits of their captives. Officially, American prisoners were supposed to follow the 1955 Code of Conduct for members of the U.S. armed forces. Article V of the Code stated that a prisoner was "bound to give only name, rank, service number, and date of birth," and "that he would evade answering further questions to the utmost of his ability." In practice, Bill Angus and most others followed a 1967 modification of the Code, called

"Plums." A code word similar to "jewels," Plums stood for little jewels of knowledge. These were policy statements issued by Colonel John Flynn, a senior officer at the Hanoi Hilton, which augmented, expanded, or substituted for the Code of Conduct. Plums required a pilot to take physical abuse and torture before acceding to specific demands, but it did not expect a man to die or to seriously jeopardize his health and safety. They also called for "working with the camp authorities for the improved welfare of all and ignoring petty annoyances." However, there would be no early releases, no appearances for propaganda, and any "flexibility or freelancing would be subordinated to the need for unity and discipline."[2]

The North Vietnamese interrogated Bill Angus every day for three days and then once every third day for the next four weeks. His food consisted of pumpkin soup (chunks of pumpkin in a tasteless broth), a small loaf of French bread, and warm milk or tea brought in once a day in the morning. During that entire time, Angus had no idea where he was or if any other American prisoners were in the jail. After four weeks his interrogation ended, and the Vietnamese moved him to a similar cell in the "Heartbreak Hotel" section of Hoa Lo. Built by the French some seventy years before, the Hoa Lo complex, or "Hanoi Hilton," was large enough to accommodate 400 prisoners and contained several distinct areas, which prisoners traveled through during their POW odyssey. Heartbreak Hotel consisted of eight one-man cells and a bathing cell, just off the main courtyard of the camp. Just to the west of Heartbreak was Camp Unity—an area of large multi-person cell blocks. Eventually, Angus would end up with fifteen other Americans in Room 5 of Camp Unity, but for the next four days, he lived alone in the Heartbreak Hotel.

Soon after his arrival in Heartbreak, Angus was awakened by tapping noises. Across the hall, an Air Force major named Bill Talley was attempting to communicate with Angus, using the POW tap code that had been taught to him at the Air Force survival school at Stead AFB in Nevada. Angus, however, did not know that code; his Marine survival training at Cherry Point did not include it in the curriculum. As a result, Talley had to fill Angus in on the details of the code quickly when the guards were away. Talley explained to Angus that each tap indicated the position of a letter on a matrix of five rows and five columns, from the letter A, signaled by one tap for the row and one tap for the column, to the letter Z, five taps for the row and five taps for the column. The letter K was dropped from the matrix in favor of C, leaving only the twenty-five letters necessary to fill the matrix.[3]

Once Angus learned the code, he began to receive news about the other POWs in the complex: the names, ranks, and shootdown dates of the other officers in the prison. In return, he provided his fellow inmates with the latest news from the States, including information about sports teams and the stock market. The stock market, incidentally, was a hot topic among the POWs because many were making excellent money in investments. Angus learned that as a POW, his entire monthly check of $1,300 would go to a tax-free military account with a guaranteed 10 percent yield. "I remember one of the FOGs [fucking old guys] saying, 'God, I hope this war never ends!' I looked at this guy and said, 'God almighty, are you crazy?' and he said, 'No! Shit, I'm making all this money!' One guy said he was making $20,000 a year tax-free just on his investments (about $80,000 in 1999 dollars), and some came home to accounts worth over $100,000."[4] Angus himself would return to a tax-free account worth $15,000—a sizable sum in 1973. A joke circulating around the camp—that turned out to be true—was that the military had even decided to pay each prisoner $5.00 a day as a food and quarters allowance for time spent in prison in Hanoi.

To pass time in camp, Angus used to jog in place and do push-ups and sit-ups. He also wrote a sports journal. But the most fun he had in camp was performing raunchy skits about Filipina prostitutes with J. B. Souder and Ted Sienicki. "Our group as it evolved was a composite. You had the ultra-serious thinkers. It seemed to pass that Sienicki and I were the funny, fun-loving guys."[5] One of Ted's, J. B.'s, and Bill's favorite topics of discussion was women. These men fantasized that when they returned to the States, the women there would be falling all over them at the Officers' Club. "We thought the POW status would have great sex appeal—it could be played like a violin."[6] According to Souder, a reporter at Clark AFB in the Philippines asked a young bachelor POW just after his release about the POW's fantasies while in prison. In typical pilot style the POW responded, "A beautiful blonde with a bottle of Champagne in her hands." Apparently, an enterprising young Air Force public-affairs officer (PAO) at Travis, AFB, California, saw the report and went into San Francisco to round up forty young women interested in dating the bachelor POW. When the ex-POW landed at Travis, the PAO took him to a bus. Inside it were the forty women, each with a bottle of Champagne in her hands. As the legend goes, the PAO then said that the young man could choose any woman on the bus to for a date "with the implicit understanding that the woman he selected would take him to a hotel and screw him silly."[7]

For Bill Angus and other POWs captured after the death of Ho Chi Minh on 3 September 1969, life in the Hanoi Hilton, while certainly not luxurious by any stretch of the imagination, was bearable. Although Angus eventually lost 20 pounds, suffered from severe boils, and even had a bout of malaria, he never endured the torture or the long periods of isolation that the POWs captured earlier in the war experienced. It was the pre-1968 shootdowns who really fought and won the war of resistance against the North Vietnamese. It was these men who endured long-term solitary confinement, torture, beatings, and forced confessions until 1969, when the North Vietnamese generally abandoned such practices. Lieutenant Colonel Robinson Risner, the senior imprisoned Air Force officer for most of the war, lived in solitary confinement during most of the 1965–69 period and damaged his voice by gargling with lye soap before making a taped confession. The North Vietnamese had intended to compel Risner to confess that the U.S. Air Force had committed war crimes against the Vietnamese people. Commander James Stockdale, his Navy counterpart and a future vice-presidential candidate, pounded his face black and blue with a 50-pound mahogany stool to disfigure it for a similar taped confession. Both men were willing to risk permanent physical damage to thwart North Vietnamese efforts to extract propaganda from them.

Other pilots risked their lives in heroic escape attempts. Major George "Bud" Day, USAF, despite a broken arm and a twisted knee, managed to escape from his captors near the DMZ. During his two-weeks as an evader, he was wounded by both American bombs and Vietcong bullets. He eventually made it into South Vietnam before being recaptured and severely tortured. Air Force captains John A Dramesi and Edwin L. Atterberry escaped from the "Zoo," a former film studio turned prison at Cu Loc on the southern edge of Hanoi, on 10 May 1969 by climbing a wall. They made food bags and stashed high-energy items in them such as raw sugar. They covered their faces with skin cream that matched the Vietnamese complexion and wore black peasant clothes, surgical masks of the sort peasants wore on the street to prevent the spread of disease, and Vietnamese-style conical hats, made from the straw of the mats that covered their beds in the Hilton. They even carried baskets on bamboo shoulder poles to further enhance their disguise. Atterberry, an experienced telephone lineman before the war, shorted the electric wires running along the top of the wall, and the two men were gone before the guards got the searchlights back on. Despite their extraordinary preparations, the two men were captured a few miles from the Zoo the next day. The Vietnamese beat Atterberry to death in Room 5 of the Zoo and tortured Dramesi in Room 18 for an extended period of time.[8]

During these early years, the most common form of torture involved the use of ropes. This treatment is described in gruesome detail by POW Al Stafford, a Navy A-4 pilot.

> Several guards arrived, carrying ropes and straps, some of them stained with blood. Beginning at the shoulder, they wrapped my arms, carefully and patiently, tightening each loop until the rope would not take any more tension, then throwing another loop lower, and then repeating the process, until my arms were circled with loops of rope like ceremonial bracelets. When I thought that the pain was as bad as it could be, the guards forced my arms together, behind me, until the elbows were touching, then tied them together. Then my arms were raised toward my head and pulled by a long rope down toward my ankles, which were lashed together. I was being bent into a tight circle. I was passing out, now, then coming to and blacking out again. Without actually deciding to, I started answering their questions.[9]

Stockdale, who endured rope torture with a broken left shoulder, described the process in terms similar to rape. "The guard put a bare foot on my right (thank God) shoulder and mounted my back as my head slumped toward my knees."[10] The guard then placed his foot directly on Stockdale's bowed head and pressed it against the bricks in the floor between the calves of his legs. Everything then began closing in on Stockdale, " . . . the tremendous pain of my lower arms and shoulders—the claustrophobia—the hopelessness of it all."[11] After Stockdale finally relented, the guard "dismounted and I raised my head as he methodically started loosening the arm bindings. I'd never felt such relief in my life, even as the blood surging back into my arms induced its own form of throbbing pain."[12] By the end of his stay in Hanoi, Commander Stockdale would be tortured fourteen more times with ropes by the same guard, nicknamed Pig-Eye.

Many of the other early shootdowns clearly suffered to an extraordinary degree in Hanoi; their stories are well documented in various POW memoirs such as Stockdale's *In Love and War,* Risner's *Passing of the Night,* and Dramesi's *Code of Honor.* Less is known about the experiences of the 236

U.S. airmen shot down after the death of Ho Chi Minh in 1969. These men were called FNGs (fucking new guys), and their tales, because of their less dramatic nature, have been eclipsed by the more dramatic stories from earlier in the war.

Because virtually all the Americans held in North Vietnam were pilots and aircrew, the POW experience formed an essential part of the fast-mover experience in Vietnam. At least 801 Americans were incarcerated in various Communist jails in North Vietnam. For these men, their entire world was transformed with the pull of the ejection handle. First, most suffered a variety of injuries from the violence of the 1960s Martin-Baker ejection seats; broken bones, burns, shock, etc. Second, in a hair-raising fraction of a minute these men were thrust out of a comfortable air-conditioned cockpit into a hot, steamy, hostile countryside teeming with peasants who would just as soon kill them as see them transported to Hanoi. Why was the North Vietnamese population so hostile to U.S. pilots? Because in some cases American bombs from the air had damaged or destroyed their property and killed or injured their close friends and family members—and even if not, these peasants were continuously subjected to virulent political indoctrination about such destructive events. If a pilot made it to Hanoi, and most did, he would find his living conditions to be in stark contrast to what he had just left. He had been living in an air-conditioned trailer or stateroom with clean sheets, hot food, cold beer, and good laundry service, but he would now find himself in a hot mosquito- and rat-infested cell, with a slop bucket as a toilet and prison pajamas as his only clothes. Worse still for a busy pilot, his routine of flying, maintenance, and administrative duties would be replaced by hours and hours of dead time.

Yet despite being violently thrust out of a busy routine and a comfortable lifestyle, most American pilots survived in captivity and did not seriously violate the Plums. In fact, only eighteen or so officers, led by Navy Commander Walter "Gene" Wilber and Marine Lieutenant Colonel Edison Miller, actually made sustained, damaging propaganda broadcasts for the North Vietnamese, and most of these men were ultimately disciplined by the POW leadership and "brought back into the fold."[13] Not surprisingly, all of these collaborators were FOGs captured during a period of sustained North Vietnamese torture and extortion. With the FNG group, collaboration proved less of a problem than philosophical and personality conflicts with a few of the senior FNG officers. Not having experienced the hardships of the earlier years, many of the younger POWs found some of the senior

American leaders in Hanoi to be overly cautious and bureaucratic, and agitated for a "tougher" stand against the guards. The crowded cells at the Hanoi Hilton during 1972 tended to exacerbate these conflicts. Although in the end Stockdale's "unity over self" dictum and the pilots' strong desire to maintain professionalism in strained circumstances ultimately kept the cocky younger POWs from committing any serious violations against the chain of command, the 1972 period in POW history was marked by more tension and conflict in the ranks than were earlier periods.

Ted Sienicki

Bill Angus described Ted Sienicki as "one of the wildest guys I have ever known in my life: he was tremendously talented, self-confident, and fun loving; he was a stud!"[14] Half working-class New Jersey and half Ivy League, Ted was born in Elizabeth, New Jersey in 1948, and spent most of his childhood in Irvington, a factory town populated mostly by immigrant workers. Ted's father, a second-generation Polish-American, worked as a shipping clerk at the Monsanto Chemical Corporation and was proud of his immigrant heritage. According to Ted, "I was from a family that kind of knew our background—our background was fighting Russians for a thousand years, basically."[15]

Ted Sienicki grew up speaking Polish at home, and "English with a horrible New Jersey accent" outside the house.[16] In high school, he ran track and graduated near the top of his class in 1965. His outstanding academic record and board scores won him admission to Brown University in Providence, Rhode Island. During his senior year at Brown in 1969, Sienicki worked as a youth home-life supervisor at the Rhode Island Training School for Boys, a prison for offenders under the age of 21. His job involved supervising 20 prisoners during an eight-hour shift. "They locked me in a building with twenty kids and at the end of the eight-hour shift if I came out alive they were happy."[17] What impressed Sienicki most during his tenure at the prison was that the prisoners feared most by the guards were the ones thought to be unpredictable. The guards might fear a shoplifter more than a murderer just because they believed he was crazy. One threat from a "crazy" prisoner might be enough to compel a guard to quit his job.

Another aspect of prison life that fascinated Ted Sienicki was how unpredictable and volatile life behind bars was. One day at the high-security juvenile prison, for example, he decided to take some of the kids out to the back yard. There were a couple of two-by-fours lying around and one of the kids picked one up and said, "Hey, let's use this and we'll kill Mr. Sienicki." The boy was trying to be humorous—but unknown to him, a guard saw him lift that stick and "before I could say shit, about twenty state troopers came out with batons and beat these kids to a pulp. And I tried to stop them. The thing that impressed me the most is how quickly a situation can change in a prison."[18] When Sienicki eventually found himself behind bars in Hanoi, such knowledge of prison psychology would prove very useful indeed.

Whereas many of his classmates from more privileged backgrounds at Brown decided to flee to Canada or feign a medical ailment to secure a draft deferment, Ted Sienicki's patriotic upbringing prevented him from avoiding the draft even though he had no "burning desire" to enter the military after college. "I believed in the draft," he explained, "because it kept the military close to the people. I was willing to sacrifice some of my personal freedom to uphold the citizen-soldier ideal."[19]

Unfortunately for Ted, his new wife Christine Getz, a high-school sweetheart whom he married on 10 August 1968, did not share this ideal. Fearing that a draft call would lead to a long period of overseas separation, she believed that enlistment, while requiring a one-year separation for a Vietnam tour, would be less stressful than the two years of separation required by the draft. Ted simply said "Okay" to her demands and filled out the first recruitment postcard that arrived in his mailbox. "That's why I went into the Air Force," he explains. "If it had come from the Marines or the Navy, I would have gone into that."[20]

With his extraordinary academic talents, Sienicki aced the Air Force qualification test and secured a slot in a pilot-training class at Randolph Air Force Base in San Antonio, Texas. Motion sickness, however, terminated his pilot career in short order, and he soon ended up at Mather AFB, California, in the navigator program. "I set the world's record for getting sick in airplanes; I threw up about ten times a flight."[21] Sienicki still vomited from time to time in navigator school, but he scored exceptionally well on his tests and was picked up for F-4s at George AFB in Victorville, California.

Sadly, two weeks before Ted Sienicki's graduation, tragedy struck: his young wife Christine came down with leukemia and died within 20 days in the medical center at Travis AFB, Texas. By the time Ted had finished burying her he had lost 35 days of school. The Air Force changed his assignment from F-4s to C-141s. Devastated from recent events and anxious to fight for his country in fast movers, Sienicki successfully lobbied for the F-4 WSO position he originally received just before Christine became ill. His Air Force personnel officer readily agreed to this plan, and he finally overcame a string of bad luck by being selected for F-4 RIO training in 1971.

Ted Sienicki breezed through the F-4 program at George and immediately requested a transfer to Southeast Asia. He told the scheduling officer, "I want to graduate in the morning and be in Vietnam in the afternoon. Don't give me any goddamn time." Distraught over the loss of his wife, he did not want to dwell over his loss during a long leave period. "I wanted to quit wasting my life and just go to Vietnam." The Air Force did not take into account Sienicki's personal needs and gave him 40 days of leave anyway. During this time, he helped sail a friend's boat from Acapulco to San Diego and basically "drank beer for thirty days."[22] He also served as the yacht's navigator—a job much easier in a 6-knot sailboat than in a 600-knot fighter plane.

After his sailing trip, Sienicki headed to Fairchild AFB near Spokane, Washington to undergo survival training. As would be expected of a former prison employee, Ted Sienicki loved survival training. "I learned quite a bit in the lectures; I learned, for example, if you ever get shot down, you are not a pilot, you are not a navigator, you are not whatever you were, you're a goddamn evader. I learned that lesson very well."[23] Sienicki also learned the six or eight different roles that interrogators often assumed with inmates. In fact, when he got to Hanoi, he said, "It was like replaying Fairchild: I had Vietnamese guys playing the same role and I almost laughed in prison."[24]

At Fairchild AFB, Ted Sienicki set a camp record for time spent in the "black box": a small holding chamber that resembled an oversize coffin, with no light and very poor ventilation. "I was very uncooperative and they can't really tolerate uncooperative people when they're only running the camp for a couple of days, so naturally they have to have some kind of techniques to get you to cooperate—the box kind of shuts you up for a while."[25] It may have shut Sienicki up but it certainly did not scare him. During the first day of his training he escaped; however, he made the mistake of following instructions and calling the camp to inform them that he had successfully evaded capture. "That was my dumbest move, because they said, 'You're going back and you can't tell anybody you escaped.' That was really annoying. I would have stayed out there and grabbed a nap!"[26]

Following survival training at Fairchild, Sienicki went through a one-week jungle survival school at Clark AFB in the Philippines. There he learned about snakes, jungle plants, and other aspects of jungle survival. For his final exam, the Air Force dropped him in the middle of the jungle and ordered him to evade indigenous Negrito trackers for as long as he could.

Ted Sienicki finally arrived in Ubon, Thailand, in February of 1972. This was a quiet time in the air war: most missions were bombing runs against lightly defended supply targets along the Ho Chi Minh Trail in Laos. After fifteen missions "boring holes" through Laotian jungle in standard F-4D bombing missions, Sienicki volunteered for fast FAC [forward air controller] duty with the Wolf FACs—a more challenging assignment that involved far greater exposure to enemy fire than did the standard F-4 bombing missions. According to Ted, even though he was a junior navigator the Wolf FACs accepted him "because he was the only one dumb enough to apply."[27] The last seven planes lost at Ubon before Sienicki arrived had been fast FACs.

The fast FAC program was the Air Force's solution to forward air control in a high-threat environment. As slow-moving OV-10s began to be shot down over Laos and near the DMZ in North Vietnam, the Air Force began using fast movers to mark targets and call in air strikes. A typical FAC mission lasted three hours and was roughly the equivalent of ten ordinary missions. An F-4, carrying white phosphorus smoke rockets, would fly low over a high-threat target, mark it with rockets, and call in another F-4 to bomb it. A fast FAC had to be extraordinarily precise to mark a target at high speed with an unguided rocket. After several strikes had been called in on a single target, the mission could also get very dangerous. Sienicki, however, did not mind the increased danger. "It actually was a lot of fun on a good day. Getting shot at a lot, and having them all miss, is a lot of fun when it's done right. That sounds very flip, but it really is a lot of fun. Not so much fun when you're doing it, but a lot of fun when you're done."[28]

With his extensive vocabulary, Ted Sienicki had no trouble describing minute ground features in the Laotian jungle to other fast movers that were flying 18,000 feet over the target with only a few minutes' worth of gas in their fuel tanks. He also had no trouble communicating with pilots from diverse service backgrounds. "Some guys are showing up off a carrier, some are showing up half hung over, some have something else on their mind," recalls Ted. "You don't know what the hell's on people's minds when they show up. You really don't even know what kind of ordnance they have."[29] Being a fast FAC, in short, demanded creativity, patience, and tremendous verbal skills.

Ted's Sienicki's favorite mission was supporting troops in contact with the Vietcong (VC) or North Vietnamese Army (NVA). "When there were Americans on the ground, it's a goddamn, no joking, scenario. All of a sudden, all the make-believe war was off. You essentially had a real job."[30] The unpredictability of a close-air-support mission also thrilled him. "The thing with troops in contact is, nothing that you're told necessarily turns out to be true. Troops north of the smoke or south of the smoke. I mean everything could be a lie, and you really have to be flexible."[31] He vividly remembers talking to desperate Army NCOs or junior officers who had no idea how to guide a fast mover to a target. "All these guys knew was that they were being overrun and desperately needed our ordnance on the target."[32] In these types of situations, Sienicki would instruct his pilot to make an initial run over the target and drop just one bomb. This way adjustments could be made if the pass was long or God forbid, short—meaning that it had impacted on friendly troops. Unfortunately, the initial run also gave the VC/NVA more time to adjust their anti-aircraft fire. No matter; Ted Sienicki "lived to hang it out for the grunts on the ground."

He also lived to fly and fight. In fact, during his entire tour as a Wolf FAC, he never took a day off to go to Bangkok, nor did he get deeply involved with either American women or Thais. "I had some girlfriends, on and off kind of, but I didn't have any kind of relationship."[33] Therefore, when Dave Yates, his pilot, invited him to go to Bangkok on leave to meet women, drink beer, and shop, Sienicki politely declined, claiming he "hadn't gotten his fill of flying yet." This proved to be a very poor decision on his part. Survival in the Wolf FAC business depended a great deal on teamwork. With Dave as his pilot, Sienicki knew the nuances of his flying and did not need to communicate much in the cockpit to get him to put marking rockets directly on target. By going on leave with Yates, he might have kept the team together a bit longer. Instead, he ended up flying his last mission out of Thailand with an unfamiliar pilot, Tim Ayres.

On 3 May 1972, almost everything that could go wrong for Ted Sienicki did go wrong. First, the two aviators flew the F-4E rather than the D model that day. A new aircraft with radar-homing-and-warning gear completely different from that on the D model, the F-4E compelled Ted to focus more on operating unfamiliar equipment while flying than on looking out for AAA and SAMs. "I used to sit and read that dash one [manual] on the E-model because I always wanted to fly an E-model; I had been reading for the last couple of months, on and off, and I could figure out how to tune the missile and stuff like that, but no one had ever taught me and no one ever cared. That's how haphazard war is. No one ever asked me!"[34]

The second challenge of the day involved timing. Normally, F-4s launched at 0530 to arrive over a target just as the enemy gunners were waking up. On 3 May, however, the large number of aircraft assigned to the mission delayed the take-off time to 0730. Sienicki distinctly remembers telling Ayres, "We're not going to wake them [the enemy] up because they're going to sleep about an hour longer and then they're going to wake up and say, 'Let's have breakfast, there's nobody here.' So they're going to have breakfast in thirty minutes, then they're going to say, no one's here yet, why don't we go sit by the guns and wait for the stupid fuckers."

True to his predictions, that's exactly what happened. Ted Sienicki and Tim Ayres flew into a barrage of fire on their first pass over a SAM site in Route Package One, and took a hit immediately. The airplane broke into two parts; Ted and Tim were in the front piece, with no wings. Both parts were fireballs, tumbling end over end, and the pilot and the backseater pulled their ejection handles simultaneously.

Before each flight, Sienicki always set his seat for "command eject." Once enabled, a seat set to the command-eject configuration would eject both the pilot and the navigator in the event that the navigator pulled the ejection handle first. Sienicki believed that by activating this feature, he would never accidentally punch out early. "I knew that if I ever ejected, I was not going to be an early ejector, I knew I had that in my temperament."[35] Still, when he reached down between his legs to pull the D-ring ejection handle, he still felt compelled to recheck the command-select-valve to confirm he was also ejecting the pilot. As the front half of the F-4 tumbled through space, Tim Ayres likewise reached down the left side of his seat, struggling with the intense G forces to find that ejection handle. Sienicki complains, "I couldn't *find* it; I couldn't see it; and I brought my hand back and I said, 'Well, he's going to have to trust me,' and I pulled the handle and the whole time I was going up the rail I was saying, 'I broke his back: I broke his back!' I could just picture him not being ready to eject."[36] As it turned out, Tim Ayres, who also had his seat set for command eject, had the exact same thought as his own seat was going up the rail.

Regardless of who pulled the handle first, the ejection did not come a moment too soon. Ted Sienicki's parachute canopy filled with air and swung just once before he slammed into terra firma. During May of 1972 Route Package One, an area of North Vietnam near the DMZ, was teeming with North Vietnamese troops heading south to participate in the Easter Offensive. As Sienicki touched down through a hail of bullets, he remembered a headline he had recently read in the *Stars and Stripes,* "30,000 NVA Invade South," and thought to himself, "Yep, there's thirty thousand gomers; I can see them all."[37]

Although terrified, Ted Sienicki never lost his determination to evade capture. He landed in an open area about the size of a football field in broad daylight. No one could have missed him yet. Sienicki remembered hearing a story in survival school about a kid from Kentucky who managed to hide from the survival instructors in an open field simply by covering himself with grass and dirt. Even though there were NVA soldiers a mere 20 yards from where Ted had landed, he still threw himself into a bush as soon as he got his chute and helmet off. The scrub bush provided virtually no cover, but he improved his position by covering himself with leaves and hunkering down. He thought to himself, "These guys are going to find me as soon as they get near me."[38]

They didn't. A motley group of troops, no two dressed alike, swept through the area but failed to see Sienicki. Firing rifles of every caliber these troops, wearing sandals, black shorts, black long pants, half uniforms, and pith helmets, went sauntering though the area laughing loudly and bantering among themselves. "Son of a bitch, this is *not* like in the movies," Sienicki thought to himself. "Nobody is sneaking around thinking that there was a war going on. This is like a fraternity fire drill."[39]

The soldiers walked up and down the field seven times and still could not find him. He chuckled to himself. "Maybe they won't find me."[40] He figured that if he could just keep hidden until nightfall, he could hike to the DMZ in a couple of days.

All of sudden, one of the soldiers stepped on Sienicki's leg and the game was over. The startled soldier jumped back and started yelling, and soon Sienicki found himself being pulled out of the bush by a mass of soldiers. The group grew to about 75 people, all trying to punch and kick him. He knew that the most dangerous period of captivity for an American pilot is immediately following capture. Lacking the discipline of prison camp guards, irregular troops and armed peasants would just as soon kill a pilot as hand him over to regular NVA troops. Most had been on the receiving end of a bomb run or had friends or family members killed by American aircraft. As a result, they had no love for U.S. pilots, whom they commonly referred to as "Yankee air pirates."

As the soldiers pummeled him, Sienicki rolled into the fetal position and tried to ride out the beating as best he could. At one point, a soldier tried to smash his head with a rifle butt, but another soldier got in the way and ended up getting conked in the process.

While all this was going on, the one thing going through Ted Sienicki's mind was, "'None of this really hurts; nobody has gotten a full shot on me without being deflected by somebody else.' But I felt like I was going to be ripped apart if this went on much longer."[41] Ted probably got hit a hundred times during his initial capture, but none of the blows were full, straight-on shots. The melee finally ended when an NVA regular officer started barking orders at the crowd to cease and desist. Surprisingly, the irregulars paid attention and the beatings ended.

The first thing the NVA officer did was order the troops to strip off Sienicki's boots and G-suit. But both his boots and G-suit were secured by zippers—something very alien to these peasant soldiers. The troops tried and tried to pull off his boots but to no avail. Finally, the officer motioned to Sienicki to remove his boots; he wanted him to be barefoot so he couldn't easily run away. For added assurance, the officer ordered the men to put him in leg irons.

During the next nineteen days, Ted Sienicki and Tim Ayres (who was captured a few thousand yards away) endured a slow truck ride over poorly-maintained dirt roads. Ayres did not have a bowel movement for the next ten days, and Sienicki for fourteen. Worse yet, the bumpy ride caused Sienicki's coccyx to penetrate through the skin of his rear end. Although Sienicki and Ayres were forbidden to speak with one another, they did so at times, when no one was looking. This communication allowed them to "get their stories straight" for the next phase of their POW experience, interrogation.

Ted Sienicki's tactic for his interrogation was to play dumb. "I was twenty-four, but some people told me I looked like I was sixteen; I really looked young. I decided that I was going to be talkative, kind of giddy, and try to look stupid. That was my ploy."[42] Unknown to Sienicki at the time, Vietnamese culture equates age with knowledge, so his ploy worked very well. The Vietnamese would ask him questions about his mission, squadron, and aircraft, and he would gin up nonsensical responses to any serious questions posed. For example, he often complained to his captors that he was suffering from hepatitis and could not eat the food. "I acted like I was totally concerned with my own health and always tried to push the subject to something else."[43] At one point, Sienicki's interrogator got so frustrated with him that he pointed his finger and yelled, "Your military knowledge is very poor!"

Sienicki did his best to look insulted, and remembered saying, "What the hell did I do now? I'm really hurt." But inwardly he was smiling. His ploy clearly seemed to be working.

Soon after his interrogation, Ted Sienicki became a tap-code communicator and quickly developed a reputation for being a very aggressive POW—an attitude which set him at odds with his Camp Unity room commander, Lieutenant Colonel Joseph Kittinger. By the time Sienicki arrived in Hanoi, the American POWs in the Hanoi Hilton were organized as the "Fourth Allied POW Wing." At the top of the chain was Colonel John Flynn, code-named Sky, in Room 0 or Rawhide. Colonel Robinson Risner acted as deputy commander, and the other O-5s and O-6s in Rawhide comprised the wing headquarters staff, with Commanders James Stockdale and Jeremiah Denton heading up Operations, and others assigned Intelligence, Plans, etc. Below the wing level were squadrons with commanders, deputy commanders, and department heads, as in a regular Air Force wing structure. Kittinger commanded the Room 5 squadron, a "tough" group of FNGs who Stockdale and Denton believed "were in Unity instead of the Zoo because the Vietnamese judged them to be poor candidates for propaganda."[44] Within the Room 5 squadron, each officer was either designated a department head or assigned an administrative function. For example, Lieutenant Commander J. B. Souder, a Navy F-4 RIO from the Coral Sea, acted as the squadron's medical officer and Ted Sienicki as communications officer. It was Sienicki who received and decoded the incoming message traffic tapped through the walls from "wing" headquarters, and it was in this position that this aggressive young junior office came into a philosophical conflict with his POW squadron commander, Lieutenent Colonel Kittinger.

Colonel Kittinger had gained recognition early in his career as the "first man in space," when he ascended in a hot air balloon to 96,000 feet on 2 June 1957. Later in 1960, he broke another high altitude balloon record, traveling to 102,000 feet before bailing out in a high pressure suit. He descended four minutes and 38 seconds, reaching a speed of 614 miles per hour before his parachute's drag chute finally slowed his descent. The same parachute would later be used by astronauts in the event of an ejection. In Vietnam, Kittinger served three tours before being shot down. Some of the navigators in his squadron, the 555th, deeming him an adventurous type, sought to avoid flying with him, fearing that his overwhelming desire to become an ace would end in disaster. There were even bets placed as to which navigator would get killed flying with him. True to unit predictions, only a few days after his first victory with the 555th, Kittinger was shot down on 11 May 1972; fortunately, both he and his navigator, William Reich, survived. Reich was released with Kittinger on 28 March 1973.

Once imprisoned, Kittinger went through a transformation. In an attempt to gain information on new laser guided munitions being employed by the Air Force during this period, Kittinger's Vietnamese captors took him to a little building in the countryside, shackled him, and performed rope torture.[45] This torture session made such a profound impression on Kittinger that when he returned to Heartbreak he would not even communicate with Americans in neighboring cells for fear of receiving additional torture if caught. According to Sienicki, who was also at Hearbreak during this period, Captain William Schwertfeger "tried to enlist Kittinger as the Heartbreak SRO, but Kitt was totally unresponsive. We spent hours trying to get Kitt to look into the corridor, so he could communicate with us, and never succeeded to any usable degree. I remember when I finally saw Kittinger's face—it was a look of extreme horror."[46]

The horrible memory of torture remained with Kittinger throughout his stay in North Vietnam and made him into one of the most acquiescent SROs in Hanoi. When Sienicki suggested during an aircrew meeting that Room 5 refuse to stand up when one of the enlisted guards, named "Silas," entered the room, Kittinger immediately vetoed the idea. "I don't know what the hell he got threatened with," recalled Sienicki, "but he came back from a meeting with the Vietnamese camp commander about the issue and ordered everyone to stand up for the guard, and we said, 'we don't want to do that; why don't you do this: when he comes in, we'll sit down, and then you call us to attention and we'll stand up.' We did not want to give up the authority in our command structure and here's our commander and he's willing to give it up.'"[47] Ultimately, Kittinger and the room reached a compromise. The room would come to attention when either he or the duty flight leader gave the order, but would then sit on their bed boards while the Turnkey actually did his head count.[48]

Petty crises with the Silas and the other guards continued during the summer of 72. One involved communications. Ted Sienicki and First Lieutenant Ken Wells, USAF, were the fastest communicators in Room 5. "Ken and I won out of the 40 guys in the contest to see who could do it the fastest," explained Sienicki, "and no one ever came close, because we practiced the shit in real life, sometimes 6–8 hours a day. To communicate to the guys who were there 5 years or longer, which is what we were doing, you had to be very good, because these guys were very, very skilled and it was like a baptism by fire, because it wasn't just how fast you could move your hands, it was the set of abbreviations that had come to be in use."[49] It was also the level of risk that a communicator was willing to take to get his message across. When it became evident that the tap code was ineffective in reaching the Fogs in Room 3, Sienicki and Wells began yelling messages out a small window in the toilet to a group of Fogs who were listening from one of the rat holes at ground level down the alley from Room 5. Silas caught them in the act two weeks later and decided to take away Room 5's afternoon outside periods until late October.[50]

The situation became even more tense in September when the Vietnamese tried to get various rooms in Unity to visit the "War Crimes Museum" in downtown Hanoi. One by one the rooms resisted the trip, but only Kittinger and the Comm team knew of their resistance because Kittinger did not allow the team to share messages with the room. "We were bound by his order not to tell anybody, but we knew goddamn better than anybody what the messages were, because we were the ones standing there, looking through the hole in the brick, getting the messages, and then later transcribing them for him."[51] After the Wing Deputy Operations Officer, Lieutenant Colonel Robinson Risner, issued an order that "no one would go to the War Crimes Museum," Ted could not take it anymore. At the 1700 air crew meeting that day when Kittinger asked if anyone had anything to say, Sienicki spoke up:

> I got something to say. Five days ago they tried to take Risner's room down to the War Crimes Museum, and they've been trying to take other rooms since then. Tomorrow they're going to come for us, and I think we should have a plan because, for starters, none of the others went. I think they're going to come in and try to intimidate us, but I don't think they're going to shoot anybody. I think we just ought to

either lock arms, or do something so that they cannot physically carry us through the door.[52]

Kittinger just glared, and would not allow any discussion over Ted's question. Sure enough, the next evening the Vietnamese called the senior officers out of the room one by one "as though it were a routine quiz." Kittinger announced that the selected individuals were merely being moved to other rooms. The Vietnamese, though, did not want the POWs to bring their bed rolls with them—the usual routine when a prisoner was being moved to another room.[53] Most of the individuals selected were senior officers and flight leaders, who truly believed they were being moved to another room, despite some evidence to the contrary.[54]

As soon as they saw the bus and a large contingency of Vietnamese guards, with flak jackets, helmets, and weapons, surrounding it, some began to have an uneasy feeling about where they were headed. Darkness and a lack of street lamps, however, prevented them from gaining a fix on their location as the bus wove its way through downtown Hanoi. The bus stopped in front of a large building and the Vietnamese shepherded the POWs into a room with a large 4 by 12 foot table in the middle of it filled with sundries: tea, cookies or candy, and cigarettes. "We had been told by the FOGs," according to Souder, "to take all of the goodies we wanted in situations like this because it would not constitute accepting special favors—just taking advantage of the opportunity to get some goodies for nothing in return."[55] Souder, Kittinger, and the others took seats and began to eat. The Vietnamese then explained that they were there to see the museum, and ordered the group to file into the museum. Kittinger stood up, but Navy Commander Ronald Polfer hesitated. "Ron had this quizzical look on his face like he knew we'd been duped and was mentally formulating what to do," remembered Souder.[56] As for Souder himself, he opted for passive resistance. "After repeatedly coaxing me to get up, the guard pushed me a little and I exaggerated the force and fell onto the floor. The next guy did the same, and the next, and the next, right on down the line."[57] A wrestling match between the guards and the POWs ensued as the guards attempted to manhandle the Americans into the museum. Major Bill Talley, a big Air Force flight leader from Oklahoma, wrestled two guards to the ground, before Kittinger finally ordered him and the others to proceed into the museum.[58] Polfer believed this order "was appropriate because they were going to be forced to view the museum no matter what." Still, some POWs continued to resist by looking away from the displays in the museum, which consisted of U.S. survival equipment, defused bombs, pictures of bomb damage to residential areas, and "horrible pictures of body parts and dead babies."[59]

Because of this and other disagreements between Kittinger and Ted Sienicki, Kittinger gave Sienicki a low OER (officer evaluation report) after his release because of his "attitude problems." Although Sienicki eventually managed to earn his wings and become a successful F-111 pilot, the Air Force never promoted him above the rank of major.

Such a decision was a terrible loss to a service desperately seeking leaders with integrity. Lieutenant Sienicki had upheld the highest traditions of the United States Air Force in many ways. He demonstrated his enthusiasm for flying and fighting; he stubbornly refused to give in to his captors' demands and thereby aid them in their propaganda war against the United States; and finally, he showed extreme compassion towards his fellow POWs.

For example, during the Christmas bombing in December 1972 Ted, although ill with malaria and shaking uncontrollably for weeks on end, volunteered to take care of bedridden B-52 crews being held in New Guy Village. During that terribly cold winter of '72, Ted and several other junior officers petitioned the guards every day to let them into the room with the sick B-52 crews. "We want to go in there and take care of these son of a bitches. These guys are sick. They're going to die!" Sienicki would tell the guards.[60] Finally, the Vietnamese relented, and Ted, J. B. Souder, and First Lieutenant Ralph Galati, a USAF F-4 RIO, were allowed to enter the room. What these three radar intercept officers discovered horrified them. "First of all, these guys smelled like shit," explains Ted. "They really did. They were bad, and they had such bedsores—I didn't know at the time, but I found out later—they had entire areas on their body as big as grapefruits that looked like holes in their back where the flesh had just rotted from not being moved enough in bed. Some of the guys had been unconscious for thirty days."[61] One man, Captain Thomas Klomann, USAF, had hit his knees ejecting downward in a B-52. Huge chunks of his knees were missing, and his calves were swollen up like balloons. Another, Technical Sergeant Roy Madden, had pus leaking from one of his broken legs.

With little medical training, Ted Sienicki; and J. B. Souder did their best to treat these men. They massaged each man's entire body to get his circulation flowing and to reduce the spread of the skin boils and ulcers. They also lanced many of the ulcers with flame-sterilized razor blades. But far and away the most heroic act of medical attention was performed by the chief medical officer in the room, J. B. Souder. Apparently Thomas Klomann, who was so delirious most of the time that Ted nicknamed him "Spaceman," hadn't produced a bowel movement since arriving at the Hilton, and his anus had expanded, opened up, and completely dried out. As J. B. described it, "It looked like a piece of sun-dried horse shit."[62] J. B. requested a board from the guards with a large hole through it. Klomann was then placed sitting upright on the board. While Sienicki distracted him with small talk, Souder crawled underneath the board, and proceeded to dilate Klomann's anus by rubbing the walls of it with his fingers and hot water. "I used to talk to doctors at the hospital," recalled Souder, "and I once asked them how they dilated a woman's vagina during pregnancy. They told me they did it by rubbing the sides with their fingers. Since the anus is a sphincter muscle similar to a vagina, I figured I could employ the same technique with Spaceman." It worked, and gradually J. B. managed to get his entire hand inside Klomann's anus and start cleaning it out with hot water that the guards had provided. "I then lit a match and took a look inside. What I saw was a gray, hardened, golf-ball-shaped thing that was blocking the passage from Spaceman's large intestine, so I reached in and yanked it out."[63] With this blockage cleared, Klomann could now pass fecal-matter out of his system and a serious medical problem had been solved through J. B.'s ingenuity.

Prior to his service in Hanoi, Souder had been given no formal medical training whatever; all of his knowledge came from reading books and talking to doctors. "When I first became a medical officer, I couldn't fucking believe that no one would treat a wounded prisoner if treatment involved getting near a pilot's genital area or asshole. I was disgusted with this behavior. 'If you haven't seen an asshole before, go fucking look at the mirror,' I would tell these guys."[64] The Navy formally recognized J. B. Souder's medical service in Hanoi with a Bronze Star; in reality his compassionate actions should have been recognized with a Distinguished Service Medal or higher. "It doesn't matter," said J. B. "One of the guys who I gave massages to repaid me with a martini for every massage I gave him. The guy kept track of the martinis on a piece of paper in his wallet, and it took him ten years to finally repay the debt."[65]

After about two weeks of constant attention, with no visible improvement in the condition of the sick prisoners, tension began to mount in the room. J. B. Souder decided to act. He walked up to Ted Sienicki just as Ted was finishing spoon-feeding one of the guys. When the guy, barely able to speak, struggled to ask Ted to wash his teeth, J. B. proceeded to tear into him.

"What the fuck do you think you're talking about? Do you think we're going to brush your teeth? Who the fuck do you think we are?"[66]

Ted Sienicki's jaw dropped. The B-52 guys were in bad shape and he was willing to do anything to help them, however ugly.

"J. B., what's up? I'll be happy to brush his teeth," he later asked out of earshot of the wounded men. J. B. looked up at him.

"These guys are dying, and we've been in here for four, five days, maybe two weeks. Look how long we've been taking care of them. Are these guys getting better?"

Sienicki stopped and thought about it. "Well, they're not getting better."

"They're not getting better because they're expecting us to take care of them. They don't have the fighting spirit. Some of these guys are losing it."

J. B. was right. Ted and his fellow navigators were nursing these men to their deaths. Roy Madden, the tech sergeant, got the message loud and clear without so much as an explanation from either Ted or J. B. When Ted went to feed him some pumpkin soup, he grabbed the bowl and said, "Give me that goddamn soup! I can eat that myself. I don't need any help."

From then on, every time this badly injured airman had the chance, he insisted on doing things for himself. Slowly, Roy's spirit began to pervade the room, and the health of the B-52 crewmen began to improve. Thus, the lowest-ranking enlisted man in the room helped a group of officers to pull themselves together emotionally and begin to heal. Sadly, Roy's leg infections turned to gangrene, and his leg needed to be amputated soon after his release. At a State Department ceremony for the POWs, Sienicki saw Madden in a wheelchair, with one leg, and walked up to him. Madden looked relieved to see his comrade.

"Oh, man, I am so drugged up; I can't recognize anybody; I was looking for you. I'm so glad to see you. Can you tell me when the Commander in Chief enters the room? I want to make sure I'm standing." Ted Sienicki's last memory of this heroic NCO was seeing him struggle to stand up on his crutches as President Nixon and Secretary of State Henry Kissinger entered the State Department auditorium. "I never saw him again," Sienicki lamented. "That was a misty period in my life."

Another of Ted Sienicki's last memories of POW life occurred after the Paris Peace Accords had been signed between Henry Kissinger and Le Duc Tho on 25 January 1973. In a twilight interval somewhere between captivity and freedom, the living conditions of the POWs improved measurably and they were given much more freedom to roam the camps and speak to one another. One day, Sienicki walked up to a truck parked out in the common area and began talking to a new group of prisoners being brought to the Zoo. A guard approached him and started to berate him for violating camp rules against communicating with new prisoners. Sienicki told him, "I'm tired of being goddamn locked up! The war's over. I don't want to be treated like this any more!"[67]

The guard then ordered Sienicki back to his barracks. Sienicki, in no mood to have a good attitude towards him, spat at the guard's feet—a big insult in the Vietnamese culture. At that point the guard looked as if he was going to come over and hit Sienicki, who decided to employ the trick he had learned at the Rhode Island Training School for Boys. "The best thing I could do was let this guard think I'm crazy. I'm standing there with Bill Talley and a couple of other guys so I knew these guys would not let this thing get carried away."[68] He immediately lunged toward the guard saying, "I'm going to kill you, you son of a bitch!" Needless to say, three or four guys restrained him before he actually got to the guard.

"I wanted them to know that they needed to be afraid of us too. That's all. Because the guy who you are most afraid of in prison is the guy you think is crazy."[69] Sienicki's trick worked. The guard left the scene without saying a word.

Roger Lerseth

In contrast to Ted Sienicki, Roger Lerseth grew up in a distinctly middle-class, middle-American world. The son of a supermarket manager in Spokane, Washington, Roger, born in 1946, was two years older than Ted. He graduated from West Valley High School, and made up his mind very early on that he wanted to fly jets with the Navy. Since the University of Washington in Seattle had a naval ROTC unit he applied there in 1964, and graduated in 1969 with a degree in economics and an ensign's commission.

During his initial physical screening for flight training, Lerseth discovered that his eyesight disqualified him from becoming a pilot. Discouraged but still wanting to fly, he chose the Naval Flight Officer (NFO) option, and set his sights on the A-6 Intruder. The A-6 was truly a team aircraft. Often, in combat or while flying at night or in bad weather, the pilot could not survive without the assistance of his NFO navigator. In the A-6, an NFO could literally project flight instructions to the pilot via the pilot's Visual Display Indicator monitor. Therefore, when Lerseth arrived at Pensacola, he created a special cover page for his notebook that read, "THINK A-6!!!" Much to his pleasure, his dream came true. When he graduated with his navigator wings, Lerseth was shipped off to VA-75, an A-6 squadron based at Naval Air Station Oceana in Virginia Beach, Virginia.

VA-75, known as the "Sunday Punchers," was not Lerseth's first choice for a squadron. As a Washington State man, he originally requested duty with an A-6 unit at Whidbey Island, Washington, in WestPac (Naval Forces, Western Pacific). But VA-75 turned out to be everything he could have hoped for in an A-6 unit. On his first Mediterranean cruise in 1971, he enjoyed the delights of Cannes and Palma, and was looking forward to visiting Rota, Spain on a second such cruise in 1972, when life took a different turn. The North Vietnamese had just launched their Easter Offensive, and VA-75 was emergency deployed in April aboard the USS *Saratoga* (CV-60) to Vietnam to assist in the defense of South Vietnam.

Roger Lerseth ended up flying his first SEA mission as NFO in SEA on 18 May 1972 in defense of An Loc. Located in Binh Long province only seventy miles from Saigon, An Loc was the site of a major battle between besieged South Vietnamese troops and North Vietnamese and Vietcong soldiers. On 11 May the North Vietnamese launched a major attack against the town, but were repulsed by South Vietnamese Fifth Division and American airpower, including B-52 strikes. For Lerseth, the whole episode seemed "surreal."[70] From his aerial vantage point, he could see North Vietnamese tanks rolling along the road to Saigon and civilian airliners taking off from Tan Son Nhut Airport, all in the same view. Lerseth also remembered the surprise in the voice of the Air Force OV-10 FAC pilot when he radioed to tell the FAC that his flight of four A-6s, each with 18 bombs under its wings, could loiter over the target for an hour. This FAC pilot was accustomed to F-4 aircraft, which literally had only minutes of fuel left when they arrived, and had trouble figuring out what to do with the massive firepower of the Navy A-6s.

Roger Lerseth's first night mission against North Vietnam occurred around the end of May against the power plant and fuel-tank farm at Nam Dinh. As he recalls, "It scared the piss out of me."[71] The night was pitch black, and Lerseth was confident going into the target because he had a radar fix on it even before getting over land. Everything went smoothly until 30 seconds from the target, when the North Vietnamese suddenly opened up with intense barrage fire. They knew exactly where Lerseth's plane was headed, based on his land position and azimuth. "My God, is this what it's like?" he asked himself. "Everything looked like it was coming towards you like the starry-night screen-saver on Windows."[72] Roger tried to ignore the flak by concentrating intensely on his radarscope. Nevertheless, when he got back to the carrier, he was shaking and still scared to death.

Eventually, though, Lerseth began to understand the North's defenses, and his fear "became a lot more manageable."[73] He flew a total of 96 missions before getting shot down; he earned five Distinguished Flying Crosses, twelve Air Medals, and a Navy Commendation Medal with a combat V for his achievements. As a Navy mine-warfare-school graduate, he also flew numerous mining missions to augment the initial mining done by CAG Sheets and the pilots of VMA (AW)-224 off the *Coral Sea*.

In late August of 1972, just days before Lerseth would be shot down, the *Saratoga* left the line for well-deserved R&R at Naval Air Station Cubi Point in the Philippines. Rather than spending their time in the strip bars of Olongapo, he and some of his squadron mates invited their wives to meet them in Manila. The VA-75 squadron commander, however, warned the men against such a plan.

"It ain't appropriate, friends, for your wives to follow you to war. They don't belong here."

Lerseth responded with the arrogance that comes from just having flown a string of tough combat missions. "Excuse me, sir, you know it's my R&R, and I would rather spend it with my wife than alone. Thank you for your concern, but you really can't tell me I can't do that."[74] Later in Hanoi, he would greatly regret making this remark to this commander. Far from simply trying to prevent the wives from witnessing the libidinous behavior of the squadron in Olongapo, this skipper had serious military reasons for not wanting any wives to journey to the Philippines. In the event that one of the men got shot down, the squadron, as Navy custom demanded, would have to give up an officer for five days to escort the widow back to the United States.

The sixth of September of 1972 was an unusual day for Carrier Air Wing Three on the *Saratoga*. Rather than attacking a single target on this day, the wing split up and attacked multiple targets, including the Kien An airfield south of Haiphong and several targets within Haiphong. A four-plane division of A-6s led the 34-plane Alpha strike force and were ordered to hit the airfield, a forward staging base for North Vietnamese MiGs. Each plane carried ten 1,000-pound delayed-fuse bombs—perfect for cratering a runway.

On this day, Roger Lerseth flew in the number three plane with Lieutenant Commander Don Lindland, the VA-75 operations officer, in the pilot's seat. The A-6 on Lindland and Lerseth's wing would be flown by a new replacement pilot, George "Duck" Hiduk. Hiduk had shared some concerns about his inexperience with Lerseth before the mission, and was not particularly enjoying his Vietnam education. To cheer him up, Lerseth let out his traditional loud whimper (begun months earlier to lighten the tense atmosphere of the briefing room before Alpha strikes), in the flight briefing when the CAG announced the targets for the day. "I must admit," explains Lerseth, "that the whimper was not always a performance. There were definitely times when it reflected a heartfelt, primal urge to get the hell out of Dodge."[75]

On the way up to the carrier deck, Lerseth put his arm around Hiduk and said, "Duck. You'd better watch out. It's duck hunting season up North."[76] Duck struggled to laugh.

The launch went off without a hitch and Lerseth and Don were soon heading toward the Alpha Strike rendezvous point just south of the Do Son peninsula. Lerseth's radar homing gear picked up the North Vietnamese Fansong radars, and he quickly began to prepare for battle. He tightened his oxygen mask, lowered his helmet visor, checked his belt, and made sure his ejection seat was armed. "While I honestly never expected to ever have to leave the Intruder other than by the ladder on the flight deck, those traditional coast-in rituals seemed to help my mindset as we entered the badlands."[77]

Ace 3, the call-sign for Lerseth and Lindland's aircraft on that day, hit the coast exactly on schedule. Lerseth's pulse shot up ten points as he armed the bombs. He then clicked his intercom. "Don, your pickle is hot."[78]

Lerseth started picking up the Singer Low indications on his RHAW (Radar Homing and Warning) gear, an indication that somewhere near Haiphong a North Vietnamese officer had just switched his Fansong radar from search to track. Lerseth's A-6 was now being "painted" intermittently by enemy surface-to-air missile radar. Because the target area was obscured by low-lying clouds, Deke Bordone, the strike leader as well as the CAG, led the A-6s in an arc around the planned roll-in point in an attempt to acquire the target visually. Meanwhile, Lerseth punched off a couple of bundles of chaff (strips of metal foil) to try and confuse the Fansong radar that appeared to be painting them. The CAG then called: "Ace One is in," indicating he had found the target and begun to roll in. Lindland followed close behind and Lerseth continued to focus on the instrument panel.

Someone then transmitted a warning call on the UHF radio: "Got an Ace hit. Get out."[79]

Just prior to this call, Lerseth had felt a jolt that pulled him off his seat. He looked out the right side of the canopy and noticed gray JP-5 fuel streaming out of a two-foot hole in the wing. Lerseth informed Don Lindland, "We are the Ace in question," and told him to pickle the bombs and head for the coast.

Lindland pickled the bombs and turned to head home, then felt another bump. The A-6 nosed into a 60-degree dive and began to shake so badly that Lerseth could no longer read the instruments. "I watched Don fighting to get control of the aircraft, which wasn't happening, and tried to check the instruments, which because of the vibration I couldn't read," explained Lerseth. "I was along for the ride. It felt like forever."[80]

Roger Lerseth's frustration was soon rudely interrupted by an explosion, followed by a tremendous rush of air. Don Lindland had just ejected, leaving Lerseth alone in the cockpit with a flopping control stick. "It was clearly time to leave the womb. Just the same, I had a residual glimmer of hope to get the airplane to the Gulf."[81] As Lerseth struggled to read the instruments, he noticed the ground coming rapidly towards him through the windscreen. That settled things for Lerseth. "I straightened up in the seat, reached for the face curtain, and pulled."[82] Lerseth would later learn from other pilots that his plane had been hit by explosions from two SA-2 surface-to-air missiles. Incidentally, Ace 4, flown by Duck Hiduk with Bob "G-Man" Miller as his BN, also got hit by the same SAM that day, but they managed to nurse their crippled aircraft back to Da Nang. The radio traffic generated by the dual emergencies greatly confused rescue efforts.

The Rescue Combat Air Patrol (RESCAP) F-4 lead called out, "Okay, two-one-one's got two good chutes . . . "

"Ace Four, you still okay, Babes?" radioed the A-7 flight leader, Commander Chip Armstrong.

Deke Bordone, the A-6 lead, then broke into the chatter:

"Say side number of aircraft down please?"

Duck in Ace 4 finally responded

"OK, ahh . . . five-on-six . . . We've got a hit . . . We're feet wet now."

"Who had the two good chutes?" Bordone persisted.

The E-2 command-and-control aircraft then interrupted.

"Someone reported two good chutes . . . What aircraft was that please?"

"Two-one-one had a tally-ho on two good chutes . . . The people are [in] good shape . . . two miles east of the airfield . . . due east of the airfield," the F-4 RESCAP lead finally reported.[83] But there was nothing that could be done now. Roger Lerseth and Don Lindland were too deep in enemy territory for a successful extraction.

The force of the ejection knocked Lerseth completely out. Looking back at the ejection 25 years later, he concluded that he shouldn't still be alive. The GRU-5 Martin-Baker ejection seat was not designed to get a crewman out of an A-6 going straight down at the speed of sound. As he regained his consciousness during the bailout, though, his only thought was, "Oh, shit."[84] He tried to grab the parachute risers to maneuver the parachute, but he couldn't raise his arms. He then tried to grab the radio in his survival vest, but soon learned he had no survival vest. "It was gone. So were my helmet, mask, gloves, boots, and sidearm."[85] Worse yet, He couldn't reach his chute risers, and noticed that his left leg was "literally flopping in the breeze."[86] He later learned that he had a shattered left femur, a fracture of both the left tibia and fibula, and hyperextended ligaments of the left knee. He also had severe cuts on his hands from going through the Plexiglas canopy; a compression fracture of the right tibial plateau, point fractures of both elbows, and a dislocation of the left elbow.

He felt no pain until he landed on a rice paddy. On his back on the paddy, reeling in pain and with his legs lying at unnatural angles, Lerseth was thankful. "I originally thought during the parachute descent that the leg was severed. Once on the ground, I decided that anything that hurt that much certainly still had to be attached."[87] His thoughts were soon interrupted by the sounds of yelling, screaming, and shooting. While waiting to be captured, one last thought entered his mind. Although he knew at this point that a rescue was completely out of the question, perhaps if he could just activate his emergency beeper and homing device, he could let the Navy know he was still alive and avoid being classified as MIA. Lerseth could see a lanyard hanging out of his seat pan and pulled it, thinking it was attached to the beeper. It was not. Instead, it inflated his rubber raft. He laughed. "The North Vietnamese are going to think I plan to row my way out of the rice paddy."[88]

A Navy F-4 from VF-31, flown by Lieutenant Commander Gene Tucker and his RIO, Lieutenant Bill Kemp, made two passes over Lerseth, taking an extraordinary amount of AAA fire in the process. "While I was ecstatic that they and the rest of the rescue guys were pressing every limit to get us, I was also afraid that they would try too hard to make something happen that couldn't."[89] A confluence of North Vietnamese soldiers and civilians soon ended the rescue attempt. Suddenly, Lerseth remembered that he had an empty holster with no gun. Thinking that this item might raise suspicion, he struggled to bury the holster and bandolier in the mud with his operable right arm. At this point, the Vietnamese still couldn't see him because he was lying so low, but they could see his parachute 20 yards downwind and seemed to be firing at it. When a bullet sprayed mud in Lerseth's face, he figured the game was up and raised his right arm in the air. All shooting stopped.

A 13- or 14-year-old boy in shorts and bare feet approached Lerseth with a broken bottle. After a brief moment of hesitation, he started smashing Lerseth's head and face with the bottle and screaming at him in Vietnamese. "The only thing that saved me at that point, because I couldn't defend myself, was the militia. The guys in the khaki militia uniforms finally pulled him off."[90] The mud around Lerseth was red from his blood. The bottle had cut his face apart, blocking vision in his left eye, and his hands were still bleeding from the bailout. The North Vietnamese methodically cut away his flight suit, and then six men carried him over to the road. "Every move was excruciating," Lerseth remembers. "The procession out of that rice paddy was the worst experience of my life. I would gladly have blown myself away if I could have put my hand on a weapon. I really wanted to die."[91]

Eventually, the Vietnamese gave him a shot of something, but the painkiller did little to ease his predicament. Roger Lerseth's trip ended in an open-air hut, and his pain began to subside a bit once he was placed on a bed. An older Vietnamese woman approached Lerseth and began to talk to him in Vietnamese. Sensing some empathy in this woman, Lerseth indicated that he was thirsty. The woman soon returned with a cup of very hot tea. In the midst of this chaotic and violent day, Lerseth was moved by the maternal compassion of this elderly peasant. "She sat with me and gently patted my shoulder while we all waited for the next event to occur."[92]

NVA troops arrived shortly in a light military truck and transported him to a hospital in Haiphong. There several Vietnamese attempted to interrogate him, but he passed out shortly after the session began. The only thing Lerseth remembered from that session is that several Caucasians of unknown nationality observed the entire interrogation but did not mutter a word, even though Lerseth attempted to communicate with them in French, Norwegian, and German.

When he awoke, Roger Lerseth found himself in an operating room; someone was trying to put a mask on his face. He again passed out. When he finally awoke for the second time, he found himself on a crude wooden bed with a rice sack for a pillow. He looked up. Staring at him were two beautiful Vietnamese girls. "'Well, Jesus,'" Lerseth says he thought, "'I've died and gone to Vietnamese heaven.' I then turned my head a little bit to the left and saw a guy with an AK-47 standing there and I realized that I hadn't quite made it yet."[93] The doctor who examined Lerseth in post-op was Vietnamese and didn't speak a word of English. However, Lerseth later learned from doctors in the States that the North Vietnamese surgeon had done a fairly decent job of inserting a rod in his leg to line up the shattered bones. The only problem with the operation was that the surgeon had cut through too much of Lerseth's muscle and had inserted too small a rod, designed for someone of Vietnamese stature rather than for larger Westerners. When Lerseth finally returned to the States, it would take him six months of physical therapy to loosen up the muscles around this fracture.

Lerseth stayed in Haiphong for four days and was then placed in a covered jeep for transshipment to Hanoi. The jeep traveled to Hanoi via Route 5 and at one point even crossed a river at Hai Duong (midway between Hanoi and Haiphong), which Lerseth had recently seeded with Mark-36 Destructor mines a week before. "God, now I've just done myself in," Lerseth lamented.[94] But apparently the North Vietnamese had cleared the mines at that crossing and they got across just fine. His journey ended at Heartbreak Hotel in the Hanoi Hilton.

"I'd been through survival, escape, and resistance school, but I was still not prepared for what happened and don't know whether it's because I am naive naturally or what, but I was not at all prepared for people to be so vicious. I was not at all prepared for the isolation period."[95] Although the North Vietnamese did not systematically torture Lerseth, they kicked him quite a bit. After he defecated on the floor one day due to his immobility, they smashed his left arm cast and redislocated his left elbow; Lerseth had to reset it all by himself.

Day after day, Roger Lerseth lay suffering from his wounds on the hard ground and endured question after question about mining and the weapons systems on the A-6. "It was a typical hard sell, soft sell. One guy came in and tried to help you and another guy said, 'We know where your family is. We'll withhold medical treatment. You're a war criminal.' The standard stuff."[96]

Lerseth's young age was his only saving grace. The Vietnamese kept saying to him, "You're very young, you're very young."

"Thank you. Thank you," he would say. And it was the wrong thing to say to them, because the Vietnamese venerate age, and Roger Lerseth's youth insulted them. "Every time I said 'Well, thanks' to the age comment, they got pissed off. I eventually caught on and decided not to play that up too much, except that every time they'd ask me questions about mining and weapons systems on the airplane, I'd just say, 'I'm so young, I'm sorry, they don't tell me those things. I'm just one of the gofers. I just do what they tell me. They don't tell me how things happen.' And I think they bought it."[97]

The final stage of Lerseth's interrogation involved writing a biography about himself and his family in a book they gave him. Although the Navy had warned him against lying in survival school because lies eventually get caught, writing a thin biography became a way for Lerseth to keep his mind occupied during solitary confinement. "It became a mind game for me to create a lie I could live with. I just very slowly built up this little animated family that was nonexistent."[98]

Lerseth does not remember how long his interrogation lasted, but he does remember eventually being moved into a large 30-by-60-foot empty room in Camp Unity. "I was alone in a great big huge room laying on a wooden bed beneath a single 30-watt light bulb. They would occasionally give me an aspirin for my pain and that's it."[99] Lerseth remained quite alone for 10 days before he received contact from fellow Americans—flight-suit comrades like himself who took some real chances to get Lerseth into the POWs' clandestine system.

His first contact occurred on a Sunday morning. Prisoners in a room about a hundred feet from Lerseth's began singing gospel songs, but then lit into a unique rendition of "London Bridge Is Falling Down." Singing the tune out of their back window so that it would reverberate down to Lerseth's room, the POWs started the second verse as follows:

"New prisoner, what's your name, what's your name, what's your name? New prisoner, what's your name? Tell us please."

Lerseth caught on immediately and responded, "My name is Lerseth, Lerseth, Lerseth. My name is Lerseth, thank you very much."

"Could you spell it phonetically, phonetically, phonetically? Could you spell it phonetically? Thank you much."[100]

By the time Lerseth had done so a guard came into his room, aimed an AK-47 at him, and told him to be quiet. The message, however, was out and Lerseth's attitude changed by "five hundred percent." Although he remained in solitary for 45 days, unable to move and in complete physical and emotional pain, that Sunday communication uplifted him at a moment of profound need. "That was one of the happiest days in my life—just knowing that the other guys knew I was there."[101] When separated from their machines, even individualistic types like Lerseth can become group oriented very quickly.

Lerseth's next POW contact was with First Lieutenant Quoc Dat Nguyen, a South Vietnamese A-1 Skyraider pilot known to the other prisoners as Max Dat, who came by the window in Lerseth's door and gave him a thumbs-up sign. "At that time, he just looked like a Vietnamese to me; I had no idea who he was. He was the guy who confirmed my existence to the other POWs, and for him to come to the door was dangerous but he did it anyway."[102]

Getting into the POW system did not happen overnight for Roger Lerseth. It was a slow evolution. After recognition, the next step in the evolution involved communication. Roger Lerseth learned the tap code from an unknown American who gave him the specifics of the code in plain English through a rathole in the wall—again, at great risk to himself. However, the American who risked the most to bring Roger Lerseth into the system was an Air Force F-4E backseater named Captain Kevin Cheney. Roger met Kevin almost by accident. Every prisoner who smoked received six cigarettes a day with breakfast, but one day Lerseth's guard forgot his smokes. Lerseth mentioned that to the guard, who slapped himself on the forehead, then left the room to fetch the cigarettes. Suddenly, through the open door, Cheney ran in.

Kevin Cheney remembers the scene vividly. "Lerseth was being kept in solitary for refusing to sign a war-crimes confession so it was critical to the POW Wing to get into that room and give this guy some support and encouragement. The first thing I did when I got in the room was clean him up. Lerseth, immobilized from his injuries, was literally lying in his own excrement and stunk."[103] As he started cleaning Roger up, Cheney quickly explained the camp set-up, the chain of command, and the Plums. Then he pointed to one of the walls and said, "Look, buddy, there are people on the other side of that wall. When you can get out of this bed, that's where we are."[104] Then the guard came back in, hauled Cheney out, and beat the hell out of him. They then threw him in solitary confinement for two days.

"The beating wasn't so bad," Kevin Cheney remembers. "What hurt more was being sent to solitary for two more days. You see, I had just gotten out of solitary a few days before. Helping Lerseth out was well worth the effort. It was one of my proudest moments in Hanoi."[105] As Lerseth explains, Cheney, the unknown American, and Max "put their assess on the line" to get him into the system and lift his spirits. Knowing that other people cared about him and knew his whereabouts made all the difference in the world, and Roger Lerseth soon began to heal physically.

Eventually the Vietnamese brought him some crutches, and he began to hobble around his huge room. He looked out the window in the door and in the courtyard he saw for the first time, some Americans. Lieutenant Robert "Gull" Randall, an F-4 pilot from VF-103 and a former drinking buddy of Lerseth's aboard the Saratoga, immediately attempted to teach Lerseth the POW sign language, but Lerseth, a BN who ordinarily wore glasses, couldn't make out the signs. "Gull had to practically get next to the door for me to get the sign language."[106]

The next day, Lerseth thanked Gull in sign language and attempted to communicate some information, but Gull soon gave him the cut-off sign—an indication that a guard was heading towards them. Lerseth attempted to move away from the windows but ended up losing control of one of his crutches (a crude piece of wood without a rubber tip), and rebroke his leg. "You couldn't make a comedy any funnier than that!" he exclaimed.[107] Rather than punishing him, the Vietnamese decided at that point that Lerseth was too young and stupid to take care of himself, and moved him in with some other POWs—"Much to their chagrin, I'm sure, because I hadn't had a bath in forty-five days."[108] Eventually, forty to fifty guys would share a room with Roger Lerseth, and his life slowly began to improve.

A final high point in his POW experience came in December of 1972. Someone in the room had enough chocolate from a Care package to frost a small loaf of bread. This wee little birthday cake, in turn, was consumed to honor one pilot's one-year anniversary in Hanoi. "We were sitting around eating this little cake," explained Lerseth, "and suddenly this A-6 barreled over the compound, flying low and fast. The bombs went off, the sirens went on, the lights went out, and then the anti-aircraft fire started."[109] The All Clear soon sounded, the lights went back on, and everything was quiet again. All of a sudden, an F-111 goes ripping by in the opposite direction and the whole process starts over again. At this point all the guys in Lerseth's room started cheering and singing the Star-Spangled Banner.

"Hey, the peace thing is falling apart, but at least they're bombing again!"[110]

That time the Vietnamese did not sound the All Clear, because soon flights of B-52s started coming over and the sound-and-light show began for real. "I don't know how to explain the sound of a B-52 string going off. You could have read a newspaper, it was so light up there. When they were firing SAMs to 35,000 feet, we knew that the Air Force had brought in the big guns. It was really great to look at the faces of the guards."[111] Since Lerseth had a bad case of dysentery at the time, he enjoyed most of the Christmas bombing from the honey pot, a little wartime irony that caused the other prisoners to "laugh their asses off" during the entire show. Roger Lerseth's dysentery, incidentally, started in November of 1972 and didn't end until six months after he got home. "I was on the pot twenty or thirty times a day during the whole time."[112]

Jim and Sue Latham

Under what circumstances is it appropriate for a wife to visit her husband in a combat area? This is an age-old question that the U.S. military has been struggling with, to a greater or lesser degree, since its founding. During the American Revolution wives lived in Army camps and cooked and did laundry for the troops. When a battle commenced, these women would assist the medical corps in caring for wounded soldiers. But despite the obvious labor benefits of camp-followers, some American military leaders perceived them as an impediment to combat operations. George Washington, for example, complained in his diaries that women put unnecessary strain on his logistics system. Although wives again made appearances in combat areas during the War of 1812 and the Civil War, they virtually disappeared during later overseas wars such as World War I, World War II, and Korea because of the great distances involved and the fact that the military controlled all means of transportation to and from combat areas.

However, the advent of cheap commercial air travel changed matters considerably during the course of the Vietnam War. Army wives generally could not secure visas to travel to the Republic of Vietnam, but Air Force wives had no trouble getting into Thailand, a nominally neutral country where many of the Air Force's squadrons were based during the war. During the early stages of the war, these wives would come and visit their husbands during their leave periods and stay in Bangkok, just like Navy wives who visited their spouses in the Philippines. By the 1970s, however, some wives began to take up permanent residence in Bangkok, and by 1972 a few of the younger and more adventuresome wives even started living right off base in towns such as Ubon. One of these was Sue Latham.

Born in 1947, Sue Latham, then Sue Beach, grew up on an alfalfa farm outside of Pierceville, Kansas, a prairie town near Garden City. An average student and a cheerleader in high school, Sue left Pierceville in 1965 to attend Kansas State University in Manhattan, Kansas in preparation for a career as an elementary-school teacher. While at KSU she met her future husband, Jim Latham.

Jim, like Sue, was a Kansas native, but he grew up in Shawnee Mission, a suburb of Kansas City, and did not share Sue's rural background. The son of a pediatrician, Jim went to Kansas State with only one intent: to fly and fight with the United States Air Force. "Basically, I majored in getting out."[113] At K State, Jim enjoyed drinking beers at Kites, a popular student bar in Manhattan, with fellow Air Force ROTC Cadet Roger Locher. The two officers were commissioned together, standing side by side on graduation day at Kansas State in 1969. Little did they know on that sunny spring day that one of them would pull off the most miraculous evasion of the war and the other, an equally courageous officer, would end up in the Hanoi Hilton after making a heroic attempt to evade his captors.

While Sue and Jim had been dating steadily throughout college, they agreed to postpone marriage until after Jim's training and first Southeast Asia tour. As Sue explained, "Jim basically wanted to get that first year out of the way before he considered any future plans."[114] Sue, therefore, went back home to help out with the family farm and Jim went off to train as an Air Force fighter pilot.

During the 1969–70 pilot-training cycle, there were very few fast-mover slots for entry-level trainees. Therefore, when Latham graduated from undergraduate pilot training (UPT) at Vance AFB, Oklahoma, in March of 1970, he ended up in a slow mover, the OV-10 Bronco. The Rockwell

International Bronco, originally designed as a counterinsurgency aircraft, had become the Air Force's primary forward-air-control (FAC) aircraft by 1969. The plane measured 41 feet long and had a 40-foot wingspan. Its large bubble-shaped cockpit rested between twin booms and twin tails, making the plane resemble the P-38 of World War II fame. Although this twin-turboprop plane could only reach speeds of 281 mph, it had a combat radius of 228 miles and could carry a variety of armament: up to 3,600 pounds' worth of rocket pods, flare pods, free-fall stores (including tear gas), and drop tanks on its four wing weapon-attachment points and single fuselage point. The OV-10 could also carry two 7.62-mm M-60C machine guns in each sponson.[115] Fully loaded with rockets and painted in green jungle camouflage, the OV-10 was supposed to fly low and slow over the jungle in search of targets and then mark them with rockets for fast-mover bombing attacks. If no fast movers were available and American troops were in danger, these nimble planes might also employ their own armament to support the troops on the ground. Given their slow speed and high rate of exposure, the OV-10 FACs won a tremendous amount of respect within the fast-mover community. Surprisingly, OV-10 losses throughout the war were far lower than those of their faster jet friends: all told only 45 OV-10s were lost, compared to 334 F-105s and 378 F-4s.[116]

Jim Latham transitioned to the OV-10 in a six-month course at Hurlburt Field,[117] Florida. He then headed to Nakhon Phanom Royal Thai Air Force Base to assume duties as a FAC with the Air Force's 56th Special Operations Wing in August of 1970.[118] Latham started out flying FAC duty in the "Steel Tiger" area of Laos, an interdiction zone in the Laotian panhandle that contained several strategic mountain passes into Vietnam, including the Mu Gia, Ban Karai, and Ban Raving passes.[119] These FAC missions gave him an opportunity to familiarize himself with the plains, plateaus, mountains, and karst cliffs of this remote area, a necessary prerequisite for his next assignment, a tour with a restricted-access program known as Prairie Fire.

Prairie Fire may have been the most controversial American military operation of the entire war. It involved inserting U.S. Army Special Forces troops and indigenous Montagnard commandos into the heart of the Ho Chi Minh Trail network in Laos. These troops would gather intelligence, conduct ambushes, and even assassinate NVA officers or snatch enemy prisoners. The missions, run out of the U.S. Military Assistance Command Vietnam's Studies and Observation Group (MACV-SOG), lasted from three days to two weeks and demanded almost continual air support. As Latham explains, "We would be in contact with them by radio and if they got into trouble, we would help them break contact with our guns."[120] When things really went bad, which they usually did, Latham would also direct fast-mover strikes or even B-52 Arc Light strikes in support of the teams. In the 75 Prairie Fire missions he flew, all but two teams came out in a fire fight. The extraction efforts, in particular, usually resulted in someone getting killed or severely injured or an aircraft getting shot down. All told, more than 300 SOG troops lost their lives. However, during the apogee of the program in 1968, each U.S. Green Beret in Laos was tying down over 600 NVA defenders or the equivalent of one battalion. SOG reconnaissance teams also killed more than a hundred NVA for each American lost, a kill ratio that could climb as high as 150:1.[121]

Jim Latham received a Silver Star for his work with SOG, but he paid for his medal on several occasions when his OV-10 took small-arms fire and 23-mm and 37-mm battle damage. First Lieutenant Jim Latham didn't care. He loved the program, especially the warrior meritocracy of the Special Forces community. "I once had a situation where an HH-53 pilot who was a lieutenant colonel was flying his first mission and he just couldn't believe that I would be the mission commander over him. And the Special Forces guys who were in charge of the mission said, 'This is the way it is, pal. If you don't want to fly it, you don't have to.' But he flew it and was very complimentary when it was done."[122]

Jim Latham returned to the United States after his tour, married Sue on the front lawn of her mother's ranch, and left two weeks later for a second tour. He volunteered because that was the only way he could get into fighters. However, he knew he couldn't simply return home, marry Sue, and be separated from her for another year. "I knew that I was going back to Thailand once I got out of training, and I knew that a lot of the guys had their wives there, so we just decided to go ahead and get married and go over there."[123] According to Richard Bates, Latham's backseater, "the threat was that if they caught your wife there, you would not get credit for a remote tour. Jim said, 'Who gives a shit? I already got my remote tour.'"[124] Ensuring the survival of his new marriage took precedence over petty regulations for Jim Latham. Men like him knew how easy it was to stray in the high-pressure environment of the air war over Vietnam, and sought to distance themselves from such temptations by bringing their wives with them. Frederick Blesse, the commander of the 366th Wing in 1967, described the situation very well in his memoir, *Check Six: A Fighter Pilot Looks Back*. A married man with tremendous integrity, Blesse revealed how the circumstances of war can compel even the best men to commit acts of infidelity that would be unimaginable to these same men in peacetime. A few weeks after his roommate and best friend was shot down, Blesse returned to his trailer from a mission to find his house girl, Sunrise, showering.

> She was usually gone by the time I got back. She came out with nothing but a towel wrapped around her and stopped by my room to ask if she was in the way. God, she looked gorgeous; slim, full-breasted, beautiful in her oriental way, with a little devilish look in her eye. I held out my hand and she came over and sat down on the bed beside me. Soon the towel was on the floor and we were in bed. For the next twenty minutes that delicate creature made me forget the war and everything associated with it.[125]

Blesse goes on to admit that the hardest aspect of war for him was the "relentless way in which the total effort is maintained regardless of losses and unforeseen circumstances."[126] The emotional comfort and sexual release provided by a house girl or even a prostitute could go a long way to ease this type of stress. Many men on their second tours understood this and chose to bring their wives along to give themselves an emotional outlet while they were on duty in Southeast Asia.

When Jim Latham got to Ubon in May of 1972 to join the Eighth Wing as an F-4 pilot, he immediately joined the Wolf FAC program, a night fast-mover FAC unit. This was a "high-speed" outfit, but because of Jim's previous experience with Prairie Fire, the Wolves welcomed him into their lair. Aviation author and Wolf FAC Mark Berent wrote the following description of Wolf pilots in the February 1971 issue of *Air Force Magazine:*

> Invariably they are the loner type who likes to mix it up, get down in the weeds and find the enemy, then challenge him to come out and fight. But, like their slow-moving brethren, they must have the maturity to mix prudence with daring, to differentiate between courage and recklessness. They must have a fast eye, memory for detail, ability to control several flights of fighters at once, and an intimate knowledge of every rock, bush, gun, bypass, truck park, and trail over hundreds of square miles. They must know location and height of the black-rock

karst, and be intimately familiar with where the guns are, when they like to shoot, and what positions look promising for new sites. These are the fast movers, the jet FACs who, along with the slow movers, fly the Ho Chi Minh Trail.[127]

Not surprisingly, roughly half of the Wolves were bachelors.[128]

Sue Latham joined Jim shortly after his arrival and set up an apartment in downtown Ubon with another wife, Karen Thugs. "We lived together partly for security and partly for companionship because our guys were always gone and flying night missions. They would go to work at 22:30 and come home about 0200 and sleep during the day."[129] Although the presence of these women on base was not command sponsored, Eighth Wing Commander, Carl Miller, gave them commissary and exchange privileges and allowed them to dine at the O Club. "It was really great having her there," recalled Jim, "because we would come back at three or four in the morning and everybody would come to our house and the wives would fix breakfast and we would have a big party. I think the other guys appreciated having the women around too."[130] Sue remembered getting up several times at two in the morning and putting on a pot of baked beans so they would be ready when everybody got there at 0400.

But life was not just about parties for Sue Latham. On one night, the town of Ubon was rocketed by Communist guerrillas, and Sue had to make her way through hundreds of terrified Thai villagers to get back to the base. Sue also volunteered as a medical secretary at the base hospital; she was out in the jungle with a hospital team helping to treat Thai villagers when Jim was shot down. As Bates described her, "She was a tough ranch girl from the prairies of Kansas."[131]

Jim Latham was shot down on his sixth combat mission in the F-4. It was his first mission with First Lieutenant Rick Bates in the backseat, and as with many other shootdown stories, problems arose almost from the onset of the mission. First, Jim's RHAW gear was not functioning well, leaving them very vulnerable to SAM attacks. Second, the weather that day was very marginal, especially over the main interdiction areas in Laos. Strike commander Carl Miller vectored Jim over a group of burned-out trucks along a road in Route Pack 1. Jim and Rick decided to make one reconnaissance pass over the target before dropping their load "and that's when the roof fell in."[132] Latham was climbing out of the pass in an 85-degree left-hand turn when the plane was hit in the right wing. The impact of the explosion rolled the plane to an inverted position with the nose slightly down.[133] Latham "grabbed ahold of the controls and tried to roll the airplane upright but it responded by going into a slow left aileron roll."[134] He then looked over his right shoulder and noticed that he had no right wing. "That's when I told Rick to eject—twice."[135] Rick failed to respond, so Latham initiated the ejection when the altimeter hit 2,500 feet.

Rick Bates went out of the plane while it was upright, but poor Jim Latham went out with the plane inverted. The force of the ejection twisted his legs almost 180 degrees, and fractured bones in both legs. (Jim didn't find out they were fractured until after he was released.) He hit the ground hard and started running towards some tall grass. "That's when I realized my legs weren't working right. This guy came out of the grass holding a pipe or something. My vision was blurred and it turned out that I had a real bad cut on my eye that eventually caused me some problems later in life. I couldn't see very well so I pulled my gun out and pointed at him and he dropped his pipe and ran away."[136] Jim then turned around and started going the other way, but a large group of six to eight militia and a larger group of civilians blocked his way.

Except for the officer leading them, all of the militia members were young teenagers. The soldiers cut off his flying suit with a knife, then tied Jim's hands in front of him. They then led the aviator in his T-shirt and underwear through the crowd of civilians. "As I went along, people were spitting on me, throwing rocks, hitting me with sticks. They took me into a village and put me into a grass hut and it was mass pandemonium, total chaos. The guards kept everyone out of the hut but people were screaming outside."[137]

As it turned out Rick Bates was also in a hut in the same area, though Jim didn't know it. When darkness fell about three hours after Jim got to the hut, the Vietnamese moved him to a drainage ditch filled with excrement and trash. "That's where I spent the night, getting eaten up by mosquitoes. The next day they moved me to a bombed-out building, and started digging a hole which I thought was my grave. It was about three cubic feet, and they put me in there and covered it up with evergreen branches and that's where I stayed for the next seven days."[138] The Vietnamese then moved him to an old six-sided French pillbox. That's where he received his first meal—steamed rice and cabbage. Thereafter, he was fed this diet, along with tea, twice a day.

While Jim Latham struggled to survive in North Vietnam, his wife Sue was packing up her belongings to return the United States. She knew something was up the day she came back from the jungle with the hospital group, when the hospital commander asked her to step into his office. "I spent the night at the base that night," she explains. "I was fairly confident that he was alive. The next day I went back to the apartment and started getting things together and making some sort of a plan to leave. John Fairfield was the summary courts officer and he helped me get things together. Everything had to be shipped home. John Fairfield walks on water, you can print that."[139] The Air Force is not simply a fighting force, it's a family; like a family, it takes good care of its own when tragedy strikes.

Sue Latham was allowed to stay in Jim's room on base for the duration of her time in Thailand because she needed to be near a phone in case a rescue was launched, and also to make travel arrangements. The Air Force allowed Sue to fly to Bangkok on one of its transports. They also allowed her to call her mother and Jim's parents to inform them of what had happened. On her last day at Ubon, one compassionate Air Force officer went well beyond the call of duty to help ease her plight. Wing Commander Carl Miller summoned her to his office for what she thought would be a simple courtesy call. "I had never met Carl Miller the entire time I had been in Thailand. I assumed he was just doing the socially correct thing of calling in the wife of an MIA pilot and wishing her well on her way home."[140] Little did Sue realize at the time, but Carl Miller had decided to share some precious information with her: intelligence sources had reported that her husband was alive. "He totally confided this information with me and told me that he was for all intents and purposes putting his neck and his career on the line by telling me what he did, and I was totally amazed. I was a total stranger. I told my immediate family and Jim's immediate family when I got back because that's what he told me to do. I went over there knowing that this was not an accompanied tour and I in no way expected special treatment."[141]

While much of Sue Latham's terror and uncertainty ended after her meeting with Colonel Miller, her husband Jim's continued. During his three-week stay in the pillbox, he experienced bombing so intense that it rivaled the totality of all the previous frightful moments that he had experienced in the Air Force. Ironically, the terror came not from the Vietnamese but from American airpower. Over the next three days, U.S. fast movers pulverized a truck-storage park just outside the pillbox. "They just blew the shit out of it and almost killed all of us. In fact they did kill one of the guys in the bunker; a piece of shrapnel came in the window and cut his jugular vein. All the truck drivers would come piling in this place when there was a raid on. And there was kind of some mutual compassion because it's a terrifying experience when you have five-hundred-pound bombs dropping fifty feet away from you. You just can't imagine it until you've experienced it."[142]

At the conclusion of the bombing strikes, the Vietnamese moved Jim Latham to another pillbox. They also started to get lazy. Rather than guarding him at night, these young teenagers often chose to doze off. He immediately took advantage of the situation by learning how to untie himself quickly. Finally, on one dark night about five weeks after his initial capture, he decided to break out. He untied his ropes, crawled through the tunnel leading into the bunker, and headed down a trench towards freedom. Just as he was getting out of the trench, he explains, "I saw someone coming and I crawled back into the bunker and tied myself back up, pretending I was asleep. The guy comes in and he's a senior ranking officer, and he shines a flashlight on me. He then wakes the guards up and chews them out."[143]

The next night, Latham made a second escape attempt, but again ran into the same officer while trying to make his way down the communications trench. "It was too late for me to go back to the bunker so I just kind of squatted there in the trench like I was going to the bathroom, kept my head down, and he stepped over the trench about three feet in front of me and walked up to the door of the bunker and he didn't go in. He just walked off."[144] Latham crawled on his hands and knees through a rice paddy for mile and a half and then walked the remaining mile to the beach. "My plan was to get one of these little fishing boats and push it out in the water and go find the Navy. They probably would figure out I had escaped from enemy radio transmissions and would start looking for me."[145]

Latham had trouble pushing a fishing boat out to the open water. It was low tide and he had to struggle hard to get the heavy wooden boat over the sand flats to the ocean. By the time he got to the ocean, the sun was making

"Like a brooding hen, she squats half asleep over her clutch of eggs. . . . Sitting there, she is not a thing of beauty. Far from it. But she is my F-4." So wrote Eighth U.S. Air Force Wing commander Robin Olds about his favorite fighter. Pilots loved the F-4 for its awesome power and dazzling array of weaponry. (United States Air Force)

Colonel Robin Olds is paraded around Ubon Royal Thai Air Base, Thailand, by Eighth Wing pilots shortly after his fourth kill. This hard-drinking, irascible World War II ace transformed a lackluster outfit into one of the most formidable MiG-killing units of the war. (United States Air Force)

Eighth Wing ordnance handlers load a 750-pound MK-82 bomb onto an F-4's triple ejection rack (TERS). While the F-4 is often glorified in popular literature for its role in shooting down MiGs, the aircraft's primary mission during the war was bombing. (Robert Clinton)

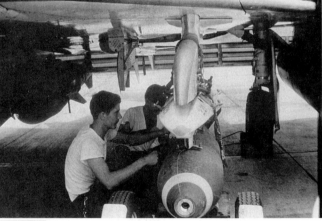

After surviving 100 missions against North Vietnam in the F-105, pilot Ed Rasimus has reason to be confident. Here he poses in front of an F-4 during his second Southeast Asia tour. (Ed Rasimus)

An EB-66 electronic-warfare plane jams enemy SAM radars as four F-105 Thunderchiefs bomb a military staging area in North Vietnam on 7 April 1966. The Thunderchief, or "Thud," was developed as a single-seat supersonic strike fighter capable of delivering nuclear weapons, but became famous in its role as a conventional fighter-bomber in Vietnam. (United States Air Force)

Commander Roger Sheets, USN, just before taking over Carrier Air Wing 9. Sheets looked like Don Knotts but possessed great charisma and inspired a fierce culture of success. (Roger Sheets)

The Vulture! U.S. Marine Corps Bomber/Navigator William "Charlie" Carr enters the cockpit of an A-6. Carr, along with his pilot Roger Sheets, participated in Operation Pocket Money–the mining of Haiphong Harbor in 1972. (United States Marine Corps)

Three Navy F-8J Crusader aircraft fly over the aircraft carrier *Bon Homme Richard.* Known as the last of the gunfighters, the F-8 was the only American fighter to rely primarily on guns for air-to-air combat. It achieved the highest kill-to-engagement ratio of any American aircraft in the Vietnam war. (United States Navy)

Captain William Angus, USMC, smiles with pride after being released from the Hanoi Hilton. Angus served with Carr in Marine Squadron 224 off the *Coral Sea* before being shot down in June of 1972. (Bill Angus)

Ted Sienicki surrounded by fellow members of the 25th Tactical Fighter Squadron at Ubon Royal Thai Air Base, Thailand: from left to right, Dave Tate, Dave Hamilton, Brad Sharp, Ted Sienicki, Ron Baxter, Scott Henley, an unidentified WSO, Kelly Irving. Shot down in May 1972, Ted emerged as one of the most aggressive newcomers to the Hanoi Hilton that year. (Ted Sienicki)

A somber Lieutenant Roger Lerseth, USN, poses for an identification photo en route to Vietnam. If Lerseth had requested a rescue after being shot down in September 1972, this photo might have been used by the extraction team to identify him. (Roger Lerseth)

A-6 Intruder aircraft of Marine Squadron 224 (VMA-224) fly over the aircraft carrier U.S.S. *Coral Sea*. One of the most advanced aircraft of the war, the A-6 could fly at night or in bad weather with its computer-assisted navigation system and carried up to 18,000 pounds of bombs. (National Archives)

Captain Roger Locher, USAF, returns in triumph to Udorn Air Base 22 days after his shootdown on 10 May 1972. Over 119 aircraft participated directly in this, one of the largest search and rescue operations of the war. Standing behind Locher is General John W. Vogt, the Seven Air Force Commander and the man who gave the final approval for Locher's rescue. (United States Air Force)

Jim and Sue Latham embrace shortly after his return from Hanoi. Latham was the only post-1968 shootdown to attempt to escape from his North Vietnamese captors. (United States Air Force)

Pirate's Bounty. John Nichols emerges from his F-8 after his 9 July 1967 MiG kill. (John Nichols)

A-4 pilot and Medal of Honor recipient Lieutenant Commander Mike Estocin, USN. Forensic evidence uncovered by the Joint Casualty Resolution Committee in the 1990s tells a very different story of Estocin's last mission than the one contained in his Medal of Honor citation. (United States Navy)

Major Robert Lodge stepping down from an F-4. Lodge was the Air Force's best hope for ace in 1972 until he was killed on 10 May. (Roger Locher)

A formation of five Air Force F-4Cs fly over the Thai countryside. The leading all-purpose U.S. fighter of the 1960s and early 1970s, the McDonnell-Douglas F-4 Phantom II could reach a maximum level speed of 1,500 mph, and carry up to 16,000 pounds of bombs, external fuel tanks, and air-to-air missiles on its centerline and four underwing hardpoints. (United States Air Force)

Air Force aces Steve Ritchie (left) and Charles DeBellevue stand beside their F-4 with five red stars painted on the air intakes, signifying the downing of five MiG aircraft in aerial combat. Captain Ritchie was the only Air Force pilot to achieve the coveted title of ace during the Vietnam War. Navigators like DeBellevue, because they operated the vital missile radar on an F-4, also received credit for aerial victories. Captain DeBellevue is one of only two Air Force navigators to make ace. (United States Air Force)

The best part of the F-105 mission was returning home. Over 333 of these planes were shot down during Operation Rolling Thunder (1965–68)—the highest loss rate of any "fast mover" during the war. (United States Air Force)

A North Vietnamese MiG-17 painted in jungle camouflage sits in front of a line of MiG-21s. Although it could barely fly half the speed of the 1,500 mile per hour American F-4, this scrappy little "knife fighter" proved to be an impressive adversary in close-in dogfights. (Collection of F. G. Rozendaal)

its away up over the horizon and he could see three guys running towards him from the beach. Vainly, Jim started to swim out to sea. "My plan B . . . was to float out there all day. I was confident I could do that. I was a good swimmer and then at night [I would] come back and get another boat. But they saw me in the water and started shooting at me. So I gave up."[146]

Recapture was hell. Vietnamese soldiers beat Latham with their gun butts and fists on his legs, arms, shoulders, and back as he lay in the sand in a balled-up position. "Then they put me on a lead rope, blindfolded me, and started running me back towards where I came from. Every time I fell down, they would beat on me. And my feet got torn up pretty bad."[147] At one point, the officer who had failed to see Jim on the night of his escape removed his blindfold and knocked him out with a Ho Chi Minh rubber sandal. When he awoke, the Vietnamese compelled him to run a gauntlet down a dike, with civilians and military lined up along both sides. "My goal was to get down there without falling down and everybody took their best shot as I went through."[148]

Back at the pillbox, the Vietnamese soldiers again kicked him and slapped him in the face for 15 minutes or so, followed by 15 minutes of rest "and that went on from eight o'clock in the morning almost continuously through about five o'clock in the evening."[149] At the end of the beatings, the senior guard held up one finger and then made a fist, meaning, "The first time, we beat the hell out of you." He then held up two fingers and ran his hand across his neck, meaning: "The second time you do it, we'll slit your throat."

"You understand," the guard said.

"Yes," Jim replied.

The Vietnamese then brought in a guy in a white coat, "who put some analgesic on my cuts, which was real fun (it hurt because I had open cuts), and looked in my mouth."[150] The Vietnamese medic then tried to pull out one of Jim's gold caps. "I bit him, so he quit that, and he went away, and then they brought in some food and cigarettes."[151] Jim did not receive any more beatings for the five remaining days that he lived in the pillbox.

The next stage of Jim Latham's POW odyssey was his three-week trip to Hanoi. "I got into the truck, and put my hand on this bare foot. It was a huge size-fourteen foot. Rick's a mammoth guy. I softly said, 'Rick, is that you?' And he said, 'Yeah, is that you, Jim?' And then they told us to shut up."[152] During the remainder of the trip, Latham and Bates began to communicate quietly with each other. Their first order of business was to figure

out what had actually happened during the shootdown and then agree on
what they would tell the Vietnamese interrogators in Hanoi.

Rick Bates then began to tell Jim about his captivity in another French
pillbox nearby. Although Bates had not been beaten nearly as much as
Latham had, the Vietnamese did subject him to a very unusual form of torture. "They had some kind of a big-ass lizard that was about two and a half
to three feet long that they captured, and they were sticking it in my face
and trying to scare me with it," he told Jim.[153] Apparently, the dark-skinned
monitor lizard was tied to a board that could be shoved in Bates' direction
from time to time. "I put up a pretty good front, but it scared the wee out
of me. I had a real bad fear of snakes, and lizards fall into that category and
it was all I could do to keep from peeing in my pants."[154]

Jim Latham and Rick Bates traveled shackled together in the truck from
roughly three o'clock in the afternoon to seven o'clock the next morning.
During much of the day they slept by the side of the road. The truck only
made two stops during the journey—a short overnight near Vinh and a
much longer stay near Thanh Hoa. Rick described the Thanh Hoa holding
area as a "kind of underground-railway stop-off point for POWs," and
claims the two of them spent 20 days there: half of that time in a barn, and
the other half in the back room of a house.[155]

It only took the Vietnamese a night and part of a day to drive the two
POWs to Hanoi from Thanh Hoa. Initially, Bates and Latham stayed in separate isolation cells in the Heartbreak Hotel. Three elderly officers interrogated the two prisoners, but according to Jim, "It was almost like they were
going through the drill 'cause they never asked any hard questions and
never put any pressure on me."[156] Rick, similarly, had an easy time. "I think
this guy was taking the Dale Carnegie course on how to be an interrogator. If you answered Question One and you gave him Answer A, he would
go to Question Two. If you gave him an answer not on his script, the line of
questioning would stop and the interrogation would be over for the day."[157]

The remainder of Latham and Bates' stay at the Hilton followed the
standard pattern. After about 10 days on 13 December 1972, the two were
moved into New Guy Village with other prisoners. The North Vietnamese
then moved everyone to the Zoo with all the other late shootdowns. "They
let me write my wife one time after I had been shot down for about two
weeks, which was a letter she never got. And then we were allowed to send
several letters, all of which were eventually received. My wife primarily lived
on her family's ranch in Kansas." Jim and Sue Latham were reunited at

Sheppard AFB in Wichita Falls, Texas in 1973, and are still happily married today. For his escape attempt, the United States Air Force awarded Jim a second Silver Star.

The total number of American POWs captured during the Vietnam War was 801, 501 of whom were pilots.[158] Some of these POWs were released early for propaganda reasons, but most (591) were released during the period from February to April 1973 during Operation Homecoming. The Operation Homecoming POWs were initially transported to Clark AFB in the Philippines. The services assigned each POW an escort officer, usually from the same branch, who stayed with him until he was moved to the United States some three to five days later. In the medical isolation ward at Clark the POWs were subjected to a variety of medical tests and intelligence debriefings. Jim Stockdale claimed that the authorities were trying to "decide whether we were nuts or not before they put us on other planes heading east."[159] Actually, there was good reason to keep the POWs in isolation for a few days. First, the POWs had critical intelligence about MIAs, which needed to be gathered and acted upon quickly to ensure that all the Americans held in Southeast Asia had indeed been released. Second, the POWs needed time to unwind and readjust a bit to freedom before reuniting with their families and friends.

For many, unwinding simply meant spending a few days catching up on news or having a regular meal at the O Club. Roger Lerseth, for instance, remembered "going down with Harry Jenkins and a group of other guys to eat dinner. We all had little slips of paper in our hand to take down to dinner and when we went to check in, they said, Okay you're all on bland diets,' and Commander Jenkins, who is about six foot six, walked over to him and said, 'I don't think you understand, son, we want steaks, and we want potatoes, and we want an American meal. You can take this bland diet and stuff it.' And the guy looked around and said, 'You're right, Sir.' So we all got steaks and the whole works."[160]

For others, readjustment meant having a few days to digest some very troubling news from home. Bill Angus, for example, thought he had everything worked out as his C-141 landed in Clark. A fraternity brother of his who flew the 141s had set up a secret rendezvous between Angus and some Air Force nurses at Clark. After this encounter, Angus planned to catch the

COD (carrier onboard delivery plane) down to Cubi Point to see his Filipina girlfriends in Olongapo. But things did not quite go as planned for him. "The day I was released was a day of some of the most incredible emotional swings of my life. I get off the 141 at Clark and I am sky high. But when I get off the bus at the hospital, a Catholic priest walked behind me and said, 'Son, I need to tell you something.' I knew right then that my mother had died."[161]

In an unpopular war, the American POWs emerged as the most celebrated heroes of the war. The media publicized their plight by airing filmed interviews of the POWs by their North Vietnamese captors, including one where Navy Commander Jeremiah Denton blinked the word TORTURE in Morse code. Throughout the war, members of the antiwar movement, including celebrities such as Tom Hayden, the founder of Students for a Democratic Society, the actress Jane Fonda, and the singer Joan Baez journeyed to Hanoi to visit the Hanoi Hilton in an attempt to promote the peace movement by drawing attention to the POWs and their plight. These peace activists failed to win much sympathy for their cause, but they inadvertently generated tremendous sympathy for the POWs.

Other individuals responsible for heightening POW awareness among the American public included the POW wives and businessman, later presidential candidate, H. Ross Perot. Beginning in 1967, the League of Wives of American POWs, under the leadership of Sybil Stockdale, began to lobby the Pentagon and the White House directly on behalf of the POWs, and soon found themselves speaking to groups around the country and appearing regularly on nationally televised news and talk shows. In 1969, Perot attempted to deliver tons of Christmas packages to the POWs but was turned down by the North Vietnamese government. He later offered North Vietnam $100,000,000 in exchange for the POWs, which was also rejected. Bowing to pressure from Perot and the League of Wives, President Nixon sent astronaut Frank Borman as a special emissary to fourteen countries to heighten awareness of the mistreatment of POWs by North Vietnam.

Although so much publicity may in the end have hurt rather than helped the plight of the POWs by convincing the North Vietnamese to hold all but a handful of them until the end of the war as bargaining chips, for newer shootdowns it demonstrated their importance to the North

Vietnamese. Latham, Sienicki, Souder, and others knew that they were valuable assets to the North Vietnamese, and as a result they felt very comfortable about antagonizing guards, refusing to participate in propaganda ploys, even escaping. Escape, though, as the Jim Latham episode demonstrates, was an exercise in futility, and generally provoked beatings. As the Denton TORTURE blinking episode illustrates, passive resistance to propaganda was far safer, and ultimately more useful to the U.S. cause, than escapes. Still, Latham's actions demonstrate that later shootdowns could be just as tough and courageous as the FOGs were.

In addition to greater perspective on the POW issue, another advantage enjoyed by the newer shootdowns was shorter isolation periods. Whereas pre-1969 shootdowns often spent years in isolation, the FNG isolation period often lasted just a few days. This meant that the FNGs were much more quickly indoctrinated into camp procedures, rules, and communications techniques than their FOG compatriots. More significantly, those in need of medical attention got it sooner and lives were saved as a result. One of the primary lessons that arise from the POW experience is the need for better medical training for combat flight crews. Bill Angus, Roger Lerseth, and Jim Latham all suffered from various injuries associated with their violent bailouts. As soon as it became clear that many pilots would be injured in this way, the armed services should have made a conscious effort to provide more medical training to aircrews. Fortunately some officers, such as J. B. Souder, took it upon themselves to gain this training; many lives were saved as a result.

The final lesson of the POW experience is that it again reveals the significance and the valor of ordinary individuals in a war without great heroes. Whereas in Korea the aces became the great heroes of the air war, the Vietnam War did not produce any aces until the final months of the war. Many Americans viewed the POWs as the most heroic individuals of the war and drew inspiration from their actions. For veterans of the air war, the lionization of the POWs has evolved into a point of contention. On the one hand, most of the former POWs take tremendous pride in having served in the "fourth Allied POW Wing" in its propaganda struggle against the Vietnamese. On the other hand many outside the POW community, and even some within it, resent the notion of a group of men becoming instant heroes just because they were unlucky enough to have been shot down. They also resent the fact that the memory of the POW struggle often overshadows many of the achievements of the Air Force, Navy, and Marine Corps in the air.

Culturally, though, the entire POW episode remains one of the most important events in the air war in Vietnam because it dispels the myth that air warriors are somehow less tough and less group oriented than ground troops. Bill Angus, Ted Sienicki, J. B. Souder, and Roger Lerseth appear rather slight in their photos, but all of these men endured beatings or injuries with courage and tenacity. They also ultimately demonstrated, albeit with a few growing pains, an ability to cast aside their individualistic aviator personas and look out for the needs of the group, whether by obeying an overly cautious senior officer or by tending to the basic and critical medical needs of their comrades. More than any other facet of the fast-mover experience in Vietnam, the POW experience reveals that this spirited collection of men could indeed act like military professionals when necessary and could, and did, adhere to the basic military tenets of organization, discipline, and the interests of the group over the self.

CHAPTER 5

A TOUGH EVOLUTION

John Nichols and the F-8 Crusader Experience

The Vought F-8 Crusader was the Navy's workhorse fighter during the Vietnam War. From 1964 to 1973, ten Navy F-8 squadrons made a total of 55 Southeast Asia deployments. These "'Saders" shot down a total of 19 MiGs and achieved the highest kills-per-engagement ratio of any American aircraft in the Vietnam War.[1] No pilot is more representative of this generation than John B. "Pirate" Nichols. One of the first pilots to enter the F-8 program, Nichols flew the Crusader for almost all of his twenty-year Navy career and ended up with over 3,400 hours in the aircraft when he retired from the Navy in 1975—the all-time record for Crusader pilots. More meaningful than hours flown, Pirate served three long tours on Yankee Station, commanded an F-8 squadron, and shot a MiG out of the sky with the aircraft's 20-millimeter cannon. His story and the evolution of the 'Sader are inextricably linked.

The John Nichols story is also the story of a naval-personnel system that pushed its finest pilots literally to the breaking point. Unlike the Air Force, whose pilots generally served a single tour of one year or 100 missions, whichever came first, the Navy compelled many of its pilots to serve multiple tours in Vietnam. This was due partly to a pilot shortage but mainly to the East Coast/West Coast organizational structure of naval aviation. If a new pilot found himself assigned to the West Coast, or WestPac as it was called, he could expect to spend his entire flying career in WestPac squadrons; a transfer to an Atlantic Coast-based squadron was unlikely even in the event of a war. For the F-8 community, the situation was exacerbated by the fact that the F-8 was the only air-superiority fighter capable of flying off the "27 Charlie" class carrier, the workhorse carrier of the war. In short, as the Navy transitioned more and more pilots to the modern F-4 during the course of the war, it still needed large numbers of F-8 pilots for its carriers—so it compelled veterans like John Nichols to fly multiple tours.

Unknown to the Navy Bureau of Personnel or "BuPers" at the time, this situation placed tremendous strain on individual pilots. Few studies of combat-related stress during the Vietnam War focus on the aviation community, but airmen were as susceptible to this condition as ground soldiers. Symptoms often described by pilots in interviews included intense anxiety and paranoia, nightmares, depression, feelings of isolation, fear, and general fatigue—symptoms which today might be associated with post–traumatic stress disorder.[2] Some aviators dealt with the stress of combat by turning in their wings or finding some other way to avoid a combat deployment, as Bill Stanley did in VMA (AW)-224. However, few pilots would admit either to themselves or to a flight surgeon that they were suffering from any of these symptoms, because to do so would be considered cowardly and would be dangerous to squadron morale. Loyalty to the squadron took precedence over personal concerns. As a result, many a Navy pilot soothed his frayed nerves after each mission with generous amounts of alcohol, an illegal substance aboard a carrier that was nonetheless tolerated by commanders and flight surgeons alike. John Nichols, however, did not self-medicate. Instead, he continued to fly missions until the war ended, and he was able to leave the Navy with honor. His experience stands out as an example of how one man endured the stress of prolonged combat flying in America's longest war, and furnishes an important window on the issue of combat exhaustion in naval aviation.

The Pirate

The son of a DuPont Corporation chemist, John B. Nichols, III, was born in South Florida in 1932 and grew up in Hialeah, Florida. John attended the first three years of high school at St. Mary's in Miami, a Catholic prep school, and then transferred to Jackson High School in Miami for his senior year to "be with his friends."[3] Like Robin Olds, John was a small kid who yearned to play football in high school, but he ended up on the bench more often than not because of his small size. Also like Olds, John enjoyed schoolyard fights. "I loved to fight and there were some times that I was so arrogant about it that I look back on it . . . I'd be trying to make out with a guy's girl sitting in a football stadium, or something, going to see a football game, and I'd just keep after her until her boyfriend wanted to fight me and then I'd go at him. I was kind of like that, I was a very aggressive kid."[4]

John Nichols left Miami for the University of Florida at Gainesville in 1952. Originally a premed student, John soon gravitated to history, both because the subject interested him more and because he didn't believe that he could maintain high enough grades to gain admission to medical school. During his senior year, John started taking flying lessons at the local airport in Gainesville for $8.00 a lesson. "I just loved it. I couldn't stop. Every time I had eight dollars, I went over there to fly Piper Cubs."[5]

Not knowing what he would do after graduating with a history degree, John began attending career fairs during the spring of his senior year in 1956. At one fair, he saw a guy in a white uniform and struck up a conversation.

"Do you like flying?" the guy asked.

"Yes, I really do."

"Well, if you want to go over to Jacksonville, we'll pay your way over there and you won't have any obligation."[6]

John Nichols absolutely loved that idea, and went over to Jacksonville for a couple of days. He passed the physical test. When he returned to campus, the recruiting officer said, "Well, they got a class for you in Pensacola if you want to do it."[7]

John leapt at the offer and never looked back.

Nichols entered flight training at Pensacola in 1956, and excelled in just about every aspect of the course, from physical fitness to instrument training. "Everything to me was easy. I never studied very hard." While his friends burned the midnight oil studying every conceivable aspect of flight, Nichols "just kind of loafed through that stuff and after a while I just knew that it was easy for me and I didn't sweat it any more."[8]

One of the high points of training for Nichols was a solo flight in a T-34 Mentor—a two-seat, all-metal, low-wing, single-engine prop plane that the Navy had just acquired for basic flight training in 1954.[9] Before soloing, John had had to endure constant "snarling" from an officer-instructor in the back seat. "Every ride was a check ride. I mean there was no friendship with these guys at all. I was scared to death of them, and I didn't realize until after I'd had ten or fifteen hops that they thought I was a real aviator."[10] Getting past the solo hurdle meant that he could finally start flying without one of those instructor monsters in the backseat.

Another high point was his first carrier landing in the T-28 Trojan—a much bigger and more powerful propeller-driven plane than the T-34. John distinctly recalled his last day of field carrier-landing practice at Naval Auxiliary Air Station, Saufley Field, a few miles northwest of Pensacola. It was a blistering hot day, and his class of seven had just completed ten practice landings and were sitting under the shade of a tree awaiting the customary briefing from the instructor. The instructor pilot stood there and, in an extraordinarily angry tone, said, "Only one of you is going to the carrier tomorrow. John Nichols is the only one ready to go."[11]

The next day Nichols fired up a T-28 and flew in formation with the instructor out to the USS *Antietam* (CV-36), the Navy's first angled-deck carrier. Over the radio, the carrier instructed Nichols to keep his hooks up for two passes until the LSO gave the "hook down" order. As instructed, Nichols made two touch-and-go landings, and then the LSO said: "Two-oh-Six, put your hook down."[12] John Nichols turned downwind, came around, and grabbed the wire with his tail-hook. "I was sitting there in the wires, looking up at Vulture's Row (an open catwalk that faced the flight deck, generally filled with observers) and thinking, 'My God, I'm here, I'm sitting on the deck!'"[13] Before John could collect himself, the flight-deck crew was giving him the "Hook Up" order and telling him to pull forward to the take-off area. A few short minutes later, the launch officer gave John the "power" signal. When John got his power up to take-off speed, he gave the officer a quick salute, and the "launch" officer returned the salute by jabbing his arm towards the deck like a fencer making a thrust. John took off and was back in the air making another pass. "It was like you're in a coma or something: it all went real swift, eight passes, eight landings, no wave-offs, no comments over the air, and I was just as high as a kite. Flying back to the field, it was just the best thing I'd ever done in my life."[14]

Back at the base, Nichols got his tie clipped in half at the Officers' Club—a Navy tradition after a pilot makes his first carrier trap. The training phase of his pilot career was nearly complete and he could begin to relax and enjoy club life. Nichols didn't drink that much, but he did enjoy the company of the local women who flocked to the Officers' Club at Pensacola on Friday and Saturday nights. "There were a lot of young women who thought naval officers were good catches, especially Southern girls. Their parents thought that that officer in the dress uniform was a welcome sight at a wedding of their daughter."[15] In fact, he met his first wife, Sherry, at a dance for naval-aviation cadets at Gulfport College. "I met her again in

Memphis and she was from a Southern family, and a pretty wealthy family, and was just wanting to get married, you know, it was just the way the girls were."[16]

John Nichols graduated from flight training in 1957 and then joined VF-174 at Cecil Field, near Jacksonville, Florida. At VF-174, a Replacement Air Group squadron, he cut his teeth on one of the Navy's newest and hottest fighters, the F-8. Only three people in his entire training class were selected for the F-8: John Nichols, William Heiss, and Dick Oliver, and of these three men only John would survive the F-8's horrendous accident rate. During 1969, 71 Crusaders suffered major accidents—one for every 1,584 hours of flying. (By comparison, Phantoms suffered only one accident for 4,140 hours.) At sea, the record was even worse: Crusader pilots could expect to have one major accident for every 678 hours flown.[17] 'Saders crashed often, for a variety of reasons normal to aircraft involved in carrier operations, chief among which were the large size of the plane and its high approach speed. Sitting way up in the nose of the aircraft with 50 feet of fuselage behind him, a pilot could easily misjudge his approach and strike the ramp of the flight deck. Making the problem even worse was the 'Sader's poor power curve. During the landing sequence, the Crusader raised the front of its wing seven degrees to enhance its stability at low speeds, but this same attitude tended to slow the aircraft down by 10 knots without the pilot being aware of it. If a pilot tried to react, his options were limited. Increasing power would add to the drag on the aircraft, causing it to lose altitude. The pilot would then attempt to solve the altitude problem by pulling back on the stick rather than increasing the throttle. As aviation author Barrett Tillman put it, "The correct procedure was frequently applied too late. On the charted power curve, airspeed was now to the left of the line showing power required to overcome drag. Once this spot was reached, the situation became irretrievable. The Crusader was now decelerating faster than application of full power could counter, and there was nowhere to go but down."[18]

For what it lacked in landing capability, the 'Sader more than made up for in the air. This sleek fighter could achieve speeds higher than Mach 1.7 in afterburner with its Pratt & Whitney J57-P-20 engine, and during its early years it set many speed records. On 21 August 1956 Commander Duke Windsor achieved a speed of 1015.428 mph in a 'Sader, thereby setting a level-flight speed record. On 6 June 1967 Captain Robert Dosé and Lieutenant Commander Paul Miller made the first carrier-to-carrier transcontinental flight in a 'Sader: from the *Bon Homme Richard* (CVA-31) in the Pacific to the *Saratoga* (CVA-60) in the Atlantic in 3 hours 28 minutes. Finally, Major John Glenn, USMC, made the first supersonic transcontinental flight on 16 July 1957 in a 'Sader: from Los Alamitos, California to Floyd Bennett Field, on Long Island, New York in 3 hours, 22 minutes, 50.05 seconds at an average speed of 723.517 miles an hour.

The Crusader also possessed something its big brother the F-4 did not have: four Colt Mark 12 cannons. Only two of the nineteen MiGs bagged by F-8s in Southeast Asia were destroyed entirely by guns, the 'Sader's 20-millimeter cannon nevertheless gave it the ability to engage in close-in, tight-turning battles with MiGs, battles that the F-4 simply could not handle. The F-8 also could carry up to four AIM-9 Sidewinders and had a tracking radar with a 60-nautical-mile range. In short, it represented "the tried-and-true approach to fighter aviation: a single-seat, single-engine dogfighter with gun armament augmented by heat-seeking missiles."[19]

Before his first check ride in an F-8, John's only jet-fighter experience consisted of 100 hours in the F-9F2 Panther and six flights in the T-33 Shooting Star—a comparatively slow Korean War-vintage jet with no afterburner. "They were dogs compared to the F-8. God, it was just a pilot's airplane! You sit in this big, roomy cockpit and the plane just responds beautifully. The quietness, the smoothness, and the power of the plane take your breath away. When you lit the burner it pushed you back in the seat, oh, man, if you weren't careful, that plane could get ahead of you because it was so powerful."[20] But it never got ahead of John. On his first flight, he did so well that his instructor in a chase plane allowed him to fly for a full hour.

Nichols' year with the Replacement Air Group (RAG) was a carefree time in his life. During the day, he flew the F-8 and at night he returned to the domestic bliss of his new wife and home. "I made around $400 a month when we were married and the first time we came to Jacksonville, we bought a house for $11,000 and I remember clearly the mortgage, interest, and taxes were $61 a month, and I made around $400."[21] As a Navy officer, John Nichols qualified for a low-interest 3 percent mortgage as well as cheap car loans, commissary and exchange privileges, and free medical care. "We bought a new car every once in a while and we had a standard of living that was equal to what I thought was middle class. I was not concerned with money at all."[22] At the time, his new bride also loved the Navy lifestyle, especially the status that came from being an officer's wife. "As a Southern girl, she loved having calling cards with her name on them, going to coffees with the CO's wife, playing bridge, and helping to organize parties at the officers' club."[23] Unfortunately for Nichols, this bliss would not last long. Long carrier deployments to the Mediterranean, and later to Southeast Asia, would soon drive a wedge between these two that would ultimately lead to divorce. These overseas periods began in 1959, when John joined VF-62 and deployed to the Mediterranean, and continued until 1973.

In fact, on his very first day of his very first cruise, John got a lesson in how hard it is to maintain a healthy marriage in the Navy from his CO, a hell-for-leather World War II fighter pilot whom John idolized. This CO, who had a famously gorgeous wife, stood up in the Ready Room for the first squadron briefing.

"Gentlemen," he said, "with the power vested in me by the Congress of the United States, I hereby declare all marriages null and void for the duration of the cruise. Wives will be responsible for their marital vows at all times. I don't care what you say to your wife in a letter, but if you mention another officer's name I will have your ass if I find out. If you go with the ladies in port, that's your business. Now, those of you who are bringing your wives to the Med, and I hope you don't, I will tell you when we're in port where I am going to be and you will *not* bring your wife there."[24] He then turned, handed his wedding ring to the duty officer, and said, "See that this is on my finger when we return."[25]

About half the men in the squadron cheated on their wives that tour, and the other half "probably would have if they had had an opportunity."[26] The everyday hazards of flying jet fighters from an aircraft carrier led to an "eat, drink, and be merry for tomorrow we may die" attitude that made moral lapses easier for pilots to justify. When combined with extended tours away from spouses, such an attitude could and did lead to frequent infidelity. In an attempt to remove this temptation from their lives, some pilots encouraged their wives to follow them around the Mediterranean from port to port—a gypsy lifestyle made possible then by a strong U.S. dollar. In those days the schedule of the Sixth Fleet was "cast in iron unless something happened, so the ship would be in Barcelona ten days, out operating with the fleet five or six, into Naples for ten days, and then worked itself all the way around to Egypt and Morocco."[27] As for John Nichols, he was simply too busy as the squadron's new LSO to spend much time with his wife during the cruise or to go chasing European women around in the *Shangri-La*'s (CV-38) various ports of call. Despite the fact that many excellent pilots engaged in carousing, such behavior was not essential for their success. For every womanizer and boozer, there was a serious near-teetotaler like Nichols who devoted himself entirely to his job. These serious-minded men could and did achieve MiG kills, but they also tended to burn out or lose their edge a bit quicker than the carousing types. The best pilots of the war, that is to say the aces, were mainly men like Steve Ritchie—men who could create some balance in their lives by enjoying the pleasures of drink or women during their down time, but who could also easily avoid these temptations while in a serious operational environment.

The Ballad of Roger Ball: John Nichols, LSO

The *Shangri-La* or *Shang*[28] as it is affectionately referred to by its crew, was one of the Navy's famous SCBC-27C or "27 Charlie" carriers—the main carrier of the Vietnam War. The 27 Charlie was a variant of the World War II *Essex*-class carrier design. During that war, the Navy decided it needed a carrier slightly smaller than the prewar *Saratoga* (CV-3) but with enough aircraft capacity to defeat any Japanese carrier in a one-to-one engagement. A total of 24 of these ships were built, between December 1942 and May 1946, all in less time than it takes to construct a single modern carrier in the 1990s.[29]

Of the original 24 ships, only six received the SCBC-27C modifications; five of these six carriers would be deployed to Vietnam between 1964 and 1973. The SCBC-27C modernization transformed a straight-deck *Essex*-class ship into a more modern angled-deck carrier. The advantage of an angled deck was straightforward: it allowed pilots to make a touch-and-go landing or to "bolter" in the event of a bad approach. On an older straight-deck carrier, if a pilot missed the arresting cables, he would hit a barricade or, worse yet, crash through the barricade into the rows of planes parked at the forward end of the carrier. With the angled-deck concept, rather than cutting power as they touched down on the deck, pilots would practice a power-on approach "that permitted them to touch down in the arresting-wire area and, going immediately to full power, to lift off again, all in the short 590-foot distance of the angled-deck landing area."[30]

Another advantage of the 27 Charlie carrier over the plain-vanilla *Essex* model was its steam catapult. The older World War II H-8 hydraulic catapult systems could deliver more than 9 million pounds of energy over a 190-foot deck, but the new Michell C11-1 steam catapults on the 27 Charlies

could generate 36 million pounds of energy. Because the early jets with their
underpowered engines required tremendous catapult momentum to launch
off the short deck of a carrier, these newer steam catapults soon became a
necessity for the Navy in the 1950s. For example, to generate enough power
to launch an aircraft at 130 knots, a carrier with the hydraulic system would
have to generate, in addition to the catapult's power, 40 knots of wind over
the deck. That meant that an *Essex* needed at least 10 knots of natural wind
plus its own maximum seagoing speed of 30 knots to achieve a successful
launch. With the newer catapult, however, a carrier could launch that same
aircraft while riding at anchor on a windless day.[31]

The final advantage of the 27C was the mirror landing system. During
World War II and Korea, the Navy relied on landing signal officers (LSOs),
equipped only with hand-held paddles, to guide an aircraft during its final
approach to the carrier. The human eye, however, could only see such a pad-
dle from less than a half a mile away. The solution to this problem was a
large mirror, concave on its horizontal axis and flat on its vertical axis. The
mirror rested on a gimbal system on the stern of the ship, gyrostabilized
to prevent it from being affected by the pitching and rolling of the carrier.
A powerful light source was beamed onto this stabilized mirror and
reflected out over the stern of the ship in a cone of light. The angle of the
mirror could be adjusted "so that the cone of light provided the optimum
glide slope for landing aircraft."[32] If a pilot kept his descending plane in the
cone of light, he would make a safe landing. To him the narrowing cone
looked like an orange spot, or "meatball." Along the top and bottom of the
"ball" were rows of green datum lights. If a pilot was too high, the "ball"
would appear above the datum lights, or below them if he were too low. The
system was later upgraded with a Fresnel lens and a colored "ball," but the
"principle of the system remained the same."[33]

———————————

Despite the many technological improvements of the 27 Charlie over the
straight-deck *Essex*-class carrier, the LSO still represented the linchpin of
the entire landing operation. Admiral Paul Gillcrist, a longtime F-8 pilot,
put it this way.

> Sometimes out there at night, when the rain is coming down in sheets,
> and you're flying into an inkwell, your only salvation in the world is

your LSO. As you ease your wheels, flaps, and hook down at a mile and a half from the ship, you know that you are now only a thousand feet above certain death and you only have enough fuel for three passes at the ship because in those days we did not have tankers. You just *had* to get aboard! Your only other option was ejection with almost no hope of rescue. And you come up to the cone of light, that meatball, and you look up and see that dim set of lights in the landing area, very faint, and that tiny little amber light to the left. You squawk out your call sign and your fuel state and on the other end John says, "Roger Ball, the deck is moving a little, listen to me." When I heard that smooth confident voice out there on a black-ass night, I could take a deep breath, and just know he would bring me in.[34]

John Nichols had been chosen to be an LSO on the basis of only one criterion: he was one of the best pilots in Squadron VF-62. His training cycle started as soon as he arrived on the Shangri-La. For two years he worked under an experienced LSO, learning every aspect of the trade. He learned to judge the speed of an approaching plane to within three knots with just his naked eye, and to sense the most subtle, minute changes in an aircraft's performance with just his ear. At first John learned to guide in the easiest types of airplane in the fleet, but he gradually worked his way up until he became qualified to bring in the most dangerous planes—the RA-5C Vigilante and the F-8U.

There are three requirements for landing an aircraft on a carrier deck: the plane has to be lined up on the right glide slope, it has to be traveling at the right speed, and it has to be at the correct altitude. Initially, the "meatball" that a pilot sees is 75 feet high by 150 feet wide but as he gets closer and closer to the deck, the cone narrows until it is only four feet by four feet in size. So the pilot is trying to fly towards this constantly diminishing "meatball" by maintaining just the right speed, glide path, and height. He can be no more than a couple of knots off in speed, six or seven feet off laterally, and a couple of feet off in altitude—or he won't make it.

The carrier landing itself is more of a controlled crash than a touchdown. In fact, Navy and Marine pilots often refer to the whole process as "sex in a car crash." At a descent rate of 700 feet a minute, the pilot *slams*, rather than touches down, onto the deck. As soon as he hits the deck, and no matter where he is, the pilot immediately goes to full power on the throttle with his left hand. If his hook catches the wire, the plane will stop; if not, he will go right into a take-off (or bolter) down the angled deck and be forced to make a second pass. Assuming that he does catch the wire, the pilot retards the throttle the moment he feels its whiplash tug. The plane will then roll back under the tension of the wire and free the hook. Then an 18-year-old sailor will charge across the flight deck into a world of danger to give the pilot a "Hook Up!" signal with his hands. Next, the sailor quickly directs the plane across the foul line to clear the deck for the next landing, which is often just seconds away. For the LSO, an airplane is in the groove immediately after it has caught the wire, so he can't look back. He must rely on other sailors to get the plane off the angled deck and reset the wire at 24,000 pounds of pressure for the next F-8 landing. He must have absolute faith in his team, because his entire focus is on that plane traveling down the groove. Finally, it is that way all day long; the interval between aircraft is continuously just seconds apart. It's the most dramatic event in modern aviation and the LSO is the most critical man in that whole process.[35]

For example, a pilot entering the groove might say, "Two-oh-three 'Sader Ball, state two-point-four." [Crusader number 203 has the ball at a fuel state of 2,400 pounds].

And John would reply, "Roger Ball, we have a little crosswind."

Immediately on the bridge everyone would jump up from their seats and the ship's captain, who would be there for all flight operations, would look over to the watch officer, who will blanch, and yell to the helmsman: "Get the *goddamn ship* turned a little bit, just few degrees."

That's how significant the LSO is during recovery operations. He's the man at the heart of the storm.[36]

Within the squadron, the LSO's power is also supreme. He's the man who qualifies all pilots for carrier duty and grades every landing. When Nichols was appointed LSO he became extremely cocky, because every time he walked into the Ready Room, the pilots paid more attention to him than any other officer. "They don't pay attention to anybody but the LSO; I don't care whether he's a commander or not, and you do not hold back because of rank even though you are aware if it."[37] Nichols would say, "Two-oh-three," not knowing who was in the airplane, and the executive officer (XO) would reply, "Here, John."

"Ex-Oh, goddamn, *really* low start. Ex-Oh, you know, you can't get up there on the ball from a start that low and make a decent pass. I was trying to get you up there early, but you didn't do it. You were climbing in the middle, and you were *never* able to get the airplane going back down, over the top, and boltered hard. I want the airplane checked, Ex-Oh, because you hit real hard."

"Okay, John."

"Now in your second pass, you came around, still had a low start, Ex-Oh, and you're not seeing the ball quick enough."

"I know, John, I know it."

When this executive officer's performance failed to improve during the course of the cruise, the CO pulled Nichols into his office and asked him, "The Ex-Oh is having a lot of trouble, isn't he?"

"Yes, sir," John responded.

"You think he will be able to be a safe carrier pilot when he takes the squadron?" (In Naval aviation, the XO becomes the squadron skipper after the CO's tour is ended.)

"No, sir."

"Thanks a lot. You're dismissed."

The CO was on the phone to the Navy's Bureau of Personnel (BuPers) as soon as John left his office. That very afternoon the XO flew off with tears in his eyes and the entire squadron waving good-bye. His career was finished.[38]

Night landings were the worst. As John explained it, "You have no depth perception; there are only these tiny, dim little lights and they seem to float from a distance in a way that disorients the hell out of you; you have no perception of movement; and yet that airplane has got to be at a steady-state and at a certain altitude and at a certain speed."[39] It's the LSO's responsibility to check your progress constantly while you're in the groove, and tell you when to add power, drop the nose, pull up, etc. And it can get more complex than that. If the mirror is broken or the deck is moving so much that the mirror is useless, the LSO must talk a pilot down. In a talk-down situation, the LSO basically steers the aircraft from the platform.

It's almost mystic, I would walk out on the deck, holding the phone and the wave-off lights and get out from behind the screen and walk toward the pilot, and I felt like I could move him with my body; it's a ballet back there. It's very difficult to speak about it because you don't even know you're doing it, but you just kind of become one with the guy in that airplane. When you're really good at that, and when they *know* you're good at it, they listen to every word you say, and they respond immediately. They know exactly what to do simply by the tone in your voice.[40]

John would virtually pull planes out of the water with the power of his voice. As a plane settled too far behind the deck of a carrier and disappeared from sight, he would callout *"POWER! POWER! BURNER! BURNER! BURNER!"* and all of a sudden the plane would come roaring up over the deck with a 20-foot sheet of flame spewing out of its tail. "Those are things that really happen out there, and ramp strikes happen, and bad line-ups happen, and broken wires happen. I've been back there when wires break and I don't even know it and the airplane's in the water and the wire is flying around, chopping the legs off sailors or killing them outright. This wire is two inches thick and it's horrible when it breaks and they do break."[41] John once recovered the entire air wing on a bad night with only the Number One wire intact.

The most legendary landing ever made by LSO Nichols occurred on 4 April 1963 in the Aegean Sea. On that day, Paul Gillcrist and Stuart Harrison launched in two F-8Es from the *Shangri-La* on a routine air-intercept training mission. Gillcrist remembered flying just south of Samos and marveling at the deep blue ocean punctuated by the "bright green of the verdant islands." "What a great day to be alive!" Paul thought, "Flying from the deck of an aircraft carrier in such a beautiful setting. What a great way to live! I wonder what the peons are doing?"[42]

Stu Harrison quickly interrupted Paul's reverie. "This is Two. I've got a fuel transfer problem."

"Two, this is One. How much fuel do you have in your feed tank?"

"Two point four [2,400 pounds]. But it's been decreasing pretty fast."

Gillcrist then made an emergency transmission to the *Shang*. "Strike, from Silverstep two-zero-four, my wingman has a fuel transfer problem. It is rapidly getting critical. Request an emergency pull forward, over."[43]

An emergency pull forward demanded that the flight-deck crew utilize every tractor on board to pull all aircraft clear of the landing area so that the distressed airplane would have maximum clearance. Inevitably, a plane or two would be damaged in such a procedure; consequently, it was only authorized in dire emergencies. A fuel-transfer problem qualified because it could cause a flameout, when the engine would shut down on final approach. There were eight fuel tanks in the F-8, and all were pressurized to feed sequentially into the main feed tank. The feed tank, in turn, fed to the fuel control, which then fueled the nozzles of the jet engine. If the fuel tanks were not providing fuel to the feed tank properly, the level of fuel in the feed tank could drop precipitously, leading to a flameout. Fortunately for

Harrison, he was only about thirty miles from the carrier when the problem arose. His strategy was to "set his throttle at idle RPM and make a straight-in descent to a safe landing before his engine flamed out."[44]

As the two planes descended through 5,000 feet, the Air Boss radioed on the land/launch frequency that the deck was ready. Perhaps they would make it after all. But, passing through 3,000 feet, Gillcrist noticed that they were too high, and Harrison didn't have enough fuel in his feed tank for a turn-around. "Fortunately," recalls Gillcrist, "Lieutenant John Nichols was the LSO on the platform that day. Although John was one of the more junior LSOs in the air wing, he was clearly the best. All I could think when I heard his voice on the radio saying, 'Paddles are up,' was 'Thank God John is waving.'"[45]

The two pilots continued their descent "fast as a fox." "Jesus Christ, one hundred and seventy-five knots," Gillcrist shouted to himself, and leveled off about a third of a mile from the ship.[46] Much to Gillcrist's surprise, Stu Harrison continued his descent. He had no choice: his engine had just flamed out. Harrison, a slightly built, balding training officer with VF-62, nursed the stick with his right hand and grabbed the under-the-seat ejection handle with his left hand. He figured he had about two seconds to decide whether or not to eject. Would he prefer to burn to death in a fireball on the deck of the *Shang* or drown in the wake of the mighty ship's screws? Harrison decided to "stay with the airplane."[47]

He gradually got the nose of the aircraft up, and the "ball" began to reappear on the lens. As the ramp rushed toward him his last thought was, "So this is how it feels to die." The F-8 slammed onto the deck and snatched the Number One wire. The flight director immediately gave Harrison the hook-up-and-taxi-forward signal. Joe Simon, the maintenance chief, then ran out to the F-8 and "gave him a two-finger circular signal meaning 'Keep your engine running.'" Stu Harrison flipped both men the bird, popped open the canopy, and got out of the cockpit. Simon grabbed Harrison just as he got his foot on the deck and screamed, "God damn you, Harrison, I told you to keep that engine running! Who in the hell do you think you are giving me the finger? I'm your commanding officer and I'm throwing your ass in hack for the rest of the cruise."[48]

"Goddamn, it, Skipper," Harrison snapped back, "the reason why I didn't keep the engine running was because the fucking thing quit while I was in the groove." He then walked away to enjoy some medicinal brandy in the privacy of his stateroom. Lieutenant Commander Stuart Harrison is the first and only pilot to ever make a dead-stick landing on a carrier. The episode barely fazed John Nichols. "Take it around Two Zero Six," he ordered Gillcrist and prepared for yet another landing.

Close Abeam: Life as a RAG Instructor

Shortly after Stu Harrison's dead-stick landing experience, John Nichols transferred back to VF-174, the F-8 Replacement Air Group (RAG) at Cecil Field in Jacksonville, Florida—this time as an instructor pilot. Before the creation of Top Gun in 1969, the Navy relied on RAG instructors like Nichols to hone the air-combat maneuvering (ACM) skills of the fleet's F-8 community. However, ACM or dogfighting during this period was more of an art than a science, and many of the Navy's top pilots were reluctant to share their knowledge with junior birdmen for fear of being beaten in training exercises—or worse, outperformed in a combat theater. John Nichols was pivotal in changing the Navy's fighter culture and transforming ACM from an art to a science. As Phil Schaffert, a pilot who attended many of Nichols' lectures on ACM, explained,

> Pilots would divulge only so much as would be nice to help the other guy, but their secrets of what they did in the air were kept secret. It was an art. John Nichols was convinced it was a science and he was able to share some things of an academic nature that other people weren't capable of and number two, did not care to. He was one of the first people who really started to convince me that there was a lot more to flying than just luck and pulling on the stick. John could use the blackboard to show you why you had not been able to get around the circle on him, or why you hadn't been able to go up higher than him—in other words, the capabilities of the aircraft. This academic approach to the performance of the airplane was something entirely new. He understood the aircraft scientifically, he had extreme situational awareness, and could translate all that into a blackboard diagram that made sense to everyone.[49]

The RAG afforded John Nichols an opportunity to dogfight with some of the best pilots in the business: close friends such as Dick Oliver and William "Beaver" Heiss. Beaver Heiss, in particular, was one of the most impressive pilots against whom John had ever squared off. A tall, laid-back kind of guy with brown hair and pale blue eyes, Beaver "was generally acknowledged to be the best F-8 aerial tactician in the Navy."[50] The two men had known each other in flight training and had served together in VF-62. Both men also frequented a very exclusive club at Cecil known as the "Close Abeam Club."

To join this club, according to Paul Gillcrist, one "had to be a very good stick-and-throttle man, have a cavalier disregard for standard rules which governed the way mere mortal F-8 pilots flew the airplane and, finally, possess a total disregard for one's own well-being!"[51] Normally, a pilot flew at 350 knots as he broke into the landing pattern at Cecil, but not the Close Abeam Club. Members of this club flew at nearly twice that speed. Club members would manually open their oil-cooler doors and allow air to flow through the louvers of the F-8's oil heat exchanger as they approached Cecil Field. The flow of air over these louvers created an awesome low-pitched moan that got louder the faster the aircraft was traveling. Close Abeamers would often break into the pattern at 600 knots with their louvers literally screaming. "It was a kind of heralding of the conquering hero," said Gillcrist. "Very macho!"[52] The Abeamer would then roll into an 85-degree bank angle and pull up to 6.5 Gs in order to kill speed for the landing. "This maneuver usually put the airplane at a position abeam of the point of intended landing—which was far too close for a prudent landing approach, hence the club nickname, Close Abeam.[53] Virtuoso stick and rudder skills were required to avoid overshooting the runway. In many cases pilots kept their throttles at idle for the entire approach to kill speed, and then at the last moment gave the engine a large squirt of power to prevent the aircraft from literally falling out of the sky during final approach.[54]

At 10 o'clock one morning Beaver Heiss and T. R. Schwartz, a guy who liked to "push things to the limit," opened their oil-cooler doors to announce a close-abeam landing. John Nichols and Phil Craven stood by the runway and watched. John heard a distinct popping sound as the Beaver's aircraft approached and saw Beaver's fuselage separate from his wing in a puff of white smoke. The engine then went into afterburner and the fuselage snapped back. (The Vought Corporation later estimated that Heiss had pulled 176 Gs in this maneuver.) The fuselage dropped like a missile onto the baseball diamond near the gate at Cecil Field—upright, with its tail on second base and its nose on third base. John Nichols raced down there in a yellow flight-line vehicle and climbed up to the cockpit with Craven and Dick Oliver. When he opened the canopy, secured the ejection seat, and undid Heiss's mask, Nichols "thought Beaver would step out of the airplane and say, 'My God, I beat that.'"[55] The airplane was intact, and Beaver *looked* completely unscathed. "The damnedest thing I ever saw in my whole life!" exclaimed Nichols. But in fact, when the wing separated from the fuselage of the F-8 Beaver's spinal cord had been crushed by the G forces. Death had come instantaneously, like a giant hammer blow. For John Nichols, the Heiss tragedy underscored his strong belief that a pilot should learn the limits of his's aircraft and never exceed them. The Navy's best pilots, the ones who would survive until retirement, took note of each training or combat accident and vowed never to repeat the same mistakes in their own flying.

Just before Nichols was scheduled to transfer to VF-191 based at NAS Miramar, another tragedy struck: he lost his other best friend, Dick Oliver. A notorious womanizer, and a skilled piano player too, Oliver pressed everything to the limit including his own marriage. He ended up killing himself flying with the Blue Angels at an air show in Canada in 1966. "Oliver was a great pilot and he made everybody gasp," Nichols explained. "When he did his solo routine he did it right above the hard deck. They wouldn't allow it today." At his funeral, an open-casket military ceremony at Arlington National Cemetery, more than thirty young women stood weeping behind his wife. Dick "was talented beyond belief and women adored him. They couldn't keep their hands off him. The guy was unfaithful all of his marriage, and you would not have blamed him because it was just the way he was and women were just attracted to him. We were convinced that he could go into the desert somewhere and find a honky-tonk with a piano, start playing it, and the women would come out of the woodwork. It was easy for him and he was always, always, always, with some woman, and he was married the whole time."[56]

Satan's Kittens: John's First Wartime Deployment with VF-191

John Nichols moved to 5922 Erlanger Street in San Diego to join VF-191 in April of 1966, and brought his wife Sherry and their three small children with him: John (seven), Gray (five), and Leigh (three). Squadron VF-191 would be John's first combat assignment and his first deployment to Southeast Asia. Although he fully understood the dangers involved in such an assignment and worried about what would happen to his family in the event he was killed or captured, he was eager to test his skills in combat and perhaps even bag a MiG. Furthermore, the deaths of his friends Dick Oliver and Beaver Heiss had hardened John Nichols to the life-and-death environment of carrier aviation. Could war be that much tougher than peace? In the end, it would be.

Before deploying on the USS *Ticonderoga,* VF-191 spent six months training at Miramar, El Centro, and Marine Corps Aviation Station Yuma in Arizona. There, much emphasis was placed on low-altitude radar intercepts of opposing aircraft. Each pilot also dropped twenty-six 500-pound bombs and shot twenty-six Zuni rockets at the El Centro range near El Centro, California in May. Nichols loved the Zunis. "They're like an eight-inch howitzer. You shoot eight of them all at once and they're so fast and hyper that there is almost no drop: it's almost pipper to .pipper. They're deadly accurate and they pulse and blow fifty feet above the ground and send shrapnel flying at Mach Five. They absolutely will decimate a flak battery. You go in on one and once you pull off and look back over your shoulder, it's gone. It's just a big goddamn explosion."[57]

On 27 July, the squadron flew back to San Diego, joined Carrier Air Wing 19, and began the process of requalifying for carrier landings on the *Tico.* Billy Phillips, an old drinking buddy of John Nichols' and the wing commander of Air Wing 19, made Nichols the air wing LSO. Nichols begged him to reconsider.

"Listen, I've really had enough of this."

"Okay, I want you to take it only so long as we are both satisfied that you have someone trained to take your job."

John Nichols ended up training a replacement by the middle of his first cruise. Now he could devote himself entirely to flying combat missions on Yankee Station—his primary goal during this period of his career.[58]

Training for VF-191 finally ended on 19 October and the *Tico* steamed to Pearl Harbor for a two-day in-port period. From there it crossed the Pacific and, after a four-day stopover in Yokosuka, Japan, headed for Subic Bay. The ship only stayed two days in Subic before transiting to Yankee Station; it commenced combat operations on 13 November.[59]

Since the MiGs were not flying that often during November–December 1966, VF-191's first line period consisted mainly of pure bombing and Iron Hand SAM-suppression missions. John Nichols' favorite mission during this period was the Iron Hand escort mission. In an Iron Hand, an F-8 fighter would escort a slower A-4 ahead of the main Alpha strike of 20 aircraft and attempt to knock out enemy SAM sites. First, the A-4 would launch an anti-rader Shrike missile at the SAM site and then the F-8 would strafe the site with 20-millimeter cannon. Nichols remembers. "I used to follow the Shrike in burner, and watch the impact. It had a Willy-Peter [white phosphorus] warhead so it made a real big flash, and since the way the SAM sites were set up with the radar in the center and the missiles and all the storage areas around it, if you got in there with 20-millimeter and just hosed it down, you could start secondaries. A lot of time we would do that and you'd see missiles squirting across the ground that we set on fire, like *great big* Roman candles. You'd get into a whole shed full of those big thirty-five-foot-long things and set fires and you'd see them scurry across the ground, go into the air and blow up—I mean it was really spectacular."[60]

The first line period ended on 17 December 1966 and the *Tico* spent Christmas of 1966 in Sasebo, Japan. It then transited back to Yankee Station on 1 January 1967 for another month-long period. The men of Air Wing 19 would endure three more line periods before finally heading back to their families in the States, and the losses began to mount. By 26 April, the day before the fourth and final line period ended, the wing had lost twelve aircraft and four pilots in combat, plus three more planes and two pilots in accidents. Most of the combat losses were caused by SAMs and anti-aircraft artillery, so the Iron Hand missions continued to be of paramount importance to the wing. And, as expected, John Nichols continued to volunteer for them.

One A-4 pilot Nichols enjoyed flying with was a young tiger named Mike Estocin. Estocin hung it out on every mission, and only a few of the Wing's F-8 pilots had the courage and skill to fly with him. A good example of Estocin's style of flying was a mission he flew on 20 April 1967, when he personally destroyed three SAM sites. During his final SAM attack of the day, Estocin prosecuted a Shrike attack in the face of intense anti-aircraft fire, despite the fact that his A-4 had been severely damaged by an exploding missile. With less than five minutes of fuel remaining he left the target area and commenced in-flight refueling, which continued for over a hundred miles. Three miles aft of *Ticonderoga*, and without enough fuel for a second approach, he disengaged from the tanker and executed a precise approach to an arrested landing. Mike, in short, was a "pure warrior." John Nichols was proud to fly with him on 26 April 1967 on an Iron Hand mission in support of an Alpha Strike against the Haiphong thermal-power plant.

John Nichols' call sign for the mission was Feedbag 111 and Estocin's, Jury 208. John's job that day was threefold: "To augment Mike's eyes, looking for SAMs; to protect him against attacks from enemy MiG aircraft; and to attack any site he hit with a Shrike, using my four 20-mm cannon."[61] The intelligence officers informed Nichols and Estocin that VN-99, a well-known SAM site north-northwest of Haiphong, would be active that day. With this knowledge in hand, Estocin and Nichols decided their exact course, altitude, and run-in headings. Nichols would fly "in a 30-degree cone, aft about 600 feet and stepped down about 100 feet from the A-4."[62] This formation, called a SAM box, tricked the SAM radar crew into thinking that it was painting a single target. When a missile was launched it would home in on the center of that target—i.e., the space separating the two planes; thus it would miss both aircraft.

Nichols and Estocin flew a pattern west-northwest of Haiphong and waited for a SAM site to go active, i.e., turn on its Fansong radar. The strike on the power plant proceeded without incident. No SAMs were fired and no radars seemed to be on.

As soon as the Alpha Strike was feet wet, John Nichols received a call from *Tico* strike control.

"Jury two-oh-eight, the strike is all feet wet. Are you feet wet yet?"

At that very moment, Mike Estocin radioed John, "Site Ninety-nine is up."

Mike lowered his nose and accelerated.

"Liftoff!" he called out, to warn John of a SAM launch. "Roger," Nichols responded, as he watched the SAM launch 20 miles ahead.

After it separated from its booster, the SAM shot above the Iron Hand and began tracking the two aircraft. Nichols tried to turn right to avoid impact, but he was too late. The missile exploded near the A-4's port jet intake, blasting the A-4 into a half-right barrel roll. Estocin regained control and pulled the aircraft upright in about a 30 degree dive heading east. Flame could be seen on the plane's belly and wingroots, but the A-4 continued to fly. Nichols immediately requested a rescue helicopter and continued to fly beside Estocin. "I flew close alongside Jury 208 and saw Mike's head lowered slightly, facing forward. He never turned or seemed to move. I switched to the guard channel but again received no reply."[63]

Nichols followed Estocin's stricken aircraft as it continued to decelerate and descend toward the cloud deck at 1,000 feet. As he entered the clouds, Nichols heard the distinctive warbling from his RHAW gear, indicating that a SAM had locked onto his plane. The SAM zoomed beneath him and exploded nearby.

"The change from bright sunlight to afternoon gloom was dramatic," writes Nichols, "all the more so against the contrast of small flames growing along Mike's wingroot."[64] This situation looked very grim as Nichols eased to the 600-foot mark. Finally Estocin's A-4 rolled to the left, but Nichols continued to stay with his wingman. Finally, when he realized Estocin was not going to recover, he leveled out and watched the A-4's wiring burn through, his two Shrikes launch, and his centerline tank punch off. The A-4 then plunged nose first into the hard ground. "I pulled up, started a hard left turn, and went to full military power. I made one 360-degree orbit, looking for a parachute. At that moment I knew the real meaning of frustration: I was alone within five miles of two MiG fields, overlapped by several missile batteries. With profound sadness I keyed my microphone and sternly told the rescue flight: 'No chance. Do not come in.'"[65]

Mike Estocin, a serious young man from Beaver Falls, Pennsylvania, was dead. At least that's what John Nichols, as corroborated by signals intelligence from Red Crown, firmly believed. For his actions that day and on 20 April, Mike Estocin received the Medal of Honor. And eventually, in 1978, the Navy commissioned a guided missile frigate (FFG-15) in his name.[66]

During Nichols' next tour with VF-191 the new Air Wing commander, Phil Craven, pulled him aside one day. "John, good news. Mike Estocin is a confirmed POW." This information apparently came from intelligence sources in Hanoi.

Nichols turned pale. "If Mike were alive in Hanoi, obviously I had missed something. Somehow I had not seen him eject from his doomed aircraft, had not seen his parachute on the enemy's turf. When I waved off the rescue helicopter, I had committed Mike Estocin to an unfathomable fate as a prisoner of the North Vietnamese. I told myself that I had done everything one man could have done. I had stayed low and slow, looking for some sign of Mike. In the most agonizing decision I would ever make, I had weighed the near certainty of one man's death against the prospect of losing several other lives looking for him."[67]

When the POWs were returned in 1973, Mike Estocin was not among them. Apparently he had died at the hands of his captors. "The burden on my conscience grew proportionately," Nichols says. "I thought of Mike every day for the next quarter-century."[68] In short, the Estocin episode gradually began to eat away at John's psyche—revealing how a single trauma can precipitate extraordinary stress for a combatant.

Overall, the entire concept of post–traumatic stress disorder (PTSD), as defined by the *Diagnostic and Statistical Manual of Mental Disorders* fourth edition (DSM-IV),

> " . . . is unique among other psychiatric diagnoses because of the great importance placed upon the etiological agent, the traumatic stressor. In fact, one cannot make a PTSD diagnosis unless the patient has actually met the 'stressor criterion,' which means that he or she has been exposed to an historical event that is considered traumatic.'[69]

Fortunately for John Nichols his suffering finally ended in 1993. The Joint Casualty Resolution Committee had recently investigated the Mike Estocin case and concluded that he never got out of the A-4, and Joint Task Force Full Accounting requested John Nichols' help in locating the downed A-4.[70] John knew then that his good friend Mike "had died a hero's death in the air, doing his duty above and beyond. He did not die alone."[71]

Pirate's Bounty: John Nichols' Second Cruise with VF-191

If the Mike Estocin episode did indeed cause John Nichols to develop PTSD, he tried to suppress it as he steamed home on the *Tico* in May 1967. Unfortunately for Nichols, his homecoming didn't help his stress, but only exacerbated it. Instead of coming home to a picture of domestic tranquility, John found his family suffering almost as much from the strains of the war as he himself was. His wife Sherry complained that every time the telephone rang during John's deployment, she and her small children thought it was the Navy calling to report his death.

At this point, John Nichols could have easily resigned his commission honorably and pursued a civilian career. Yes, he had taken the King's shilling, but he had also repaid it with a long combat cruise in WestPac. The Navy couldn't demand much more. Why, then, did Nichols allow himself to be shipped off to Vietnam for yet another tour? First, Pirate was a consummate professional who loved to fly and who could fly better than most of the pilots he knew. Second, VF-191 was Nichols' other family, maybe even his primary family, and John simply could not let his brothers down by not going to sea again. Finally and most important, he had some unfinished business to attend to. As a fighter pilot, he had spent his entire career honing his air-to-air combat skills. Perhaps this last cruise with 191 would afford him the opportunity to finally splash a MiG.

Fighter Squadron 191 underwent a training cycle between May and December 1967, and then steamed out of San Diego bound for Pearl Harbor on 28 December 1967. During this tour, the *Tico* did five line tours on Yankee Station plus a tour on the Sea of Japan in support of the *Pueblo* capture incident (18–21 March 1968).[72] It was an extraordinarily difficult evolution for the pilots of VF-191, but a rewarding one as well. During the 120 fighting days it spent on the line, the squadron conducted over 1,000 combat sorties and logged over 3,000 combat hours of flying. During coordinated air strikes with other squadrons of the Air Wing, VF-191 fired more than 300 Zuni rockets, expended more than 23,000 rounds of 20-mm ammunition, and dropped almost 100 tons of bombs—primarily in support of the Marine base at Khe Sanh.[73]

For John Nichols there were many dramatic and deadly moments. During the Tet Offensive in February, Nichols remembered one mission where his wingman Wendell Brown, a new pilot, failed to refuel during a dark and stormy night-barrier-combat air patrol. After six or seven stabs at the KA-3 tanker waiting to refuel him, Brown hit the side of the fueling basket with his probe, causing it to cave in. The *Tico* immediately launched an A-4 with a buddy-pack fuel store. With only 200 pounds of fuel remaining, Brown approached the A-4.

"Now just settle down. Take your time. Position yourself and drive it home," Nichols coached the novice pilot. "Direct hit! Beautiful!" Nichols shouted. The green light on the tanker came on, indicating that a firm contact had been established. "Pump him some gas!"

Suddenly the hose withdrew. In the exuberance of the moment, the tanker pilot had mashed the wrong button and disconnected Wendell Brown from the A-4. John screamed, Wendell screamed, the controller on *Tico* screamed. The A-4 immediately reextended the hose, but it was too late. Wendell Brown flamed out and ejected over the Gulf of Tonkin. Helicopters were sent up, but they could not find him at night in the stormy seas.

By this time, John Nichols had his own fuel problems and was ordered to divert to Da Nang. He'd been airborne now for nearly three hours and it was one o'clock in the morning. He landed in a hail of tracers, and heard the distinctive thump of rockets landing on the base as he climbed down from the cockpit. "Entering the operations office, I asked if there was any word from my wingman. Nobody knew anything about him. I took off my G-suit and harness and lay down on the floor. It felt good to stretch out, and I was content to stay there until morning. Things couldn't get much worse. This was already the worst day of my life."[74]

But it would get worse. An Air Force colonel who had come unglued from the rocket attacks on his base, roughly shook John awake.

"Is that your aircraft out front? You have to get it out of here."

"If you want it moved, move it yourself," John replied in a groggy haze.

"I will bulldoze it off the ramp if you don't get it off the field!"

"Where the hell can I go?" Nichols pleaded. "The ship can't take me. The weather is terrible all over Indochina."

"I don't give a damn. Just get out of here."

John Nichols had no choice but to suit up and try to make it to Sangley Point in the Philippines, over 800 miles away across the South China Sea. As the sun rose in front of him, John finally landed in the Philippines. With nothing in his pocket but a Geneva Convention ID card, Nichols sent a message to the *Tico* the next day; the response was, "You're where?"

This is how John Nichols' second tour began. Fortunately, things did improve: Navy helicopters picked Wendell Brown up two and a half days later in the Gulf of Tonkin, and the Air Force relieved the mad colonel of Da Nang after Nichols' Carrier Division commander sent a formal complaint to Seventh Air Force headquarters in Saigon.

John's next memory of his second tour was the *Pueblo* crisis. As tensions mounted after North Korea's seizure of the intelligence-gathering vessel, President Johnson ordered the USS *Enterprise* (CVAN-65) and the *Ticonderoga* to Korea to launch air strikes against North Korean air fields in March of 1968. The carriers were to hit seven airfields, holding more than two hundred MiG-21s, 17s, and 19s. To defend itself against this massive air armada, the Navy had only twenty F-4s and nineteen F-8s. "Nobody slept much that night. A good many farewell letters were written in expectation of the worst. . . . Yet nobody backed out."[75] At 0430 the next morning, the crews filed into the briefing room to hear the grim news. None of the usual jokes were heard. All of the pilots assigned to the strike were present. Knowing that the odds of survival were extremely thin, these men were ready to die rather than look bad. By 0500, word came down the chain of command that the mission was cancelled and everyone breathed a sigh of relief.

Events such as these were everyday occurrences for John Nichols and the other members of Air Wing 19 in 1968, but no event rivaled what happened to the Pirate on 9 July. On that day, Nichols was assigned to fly an escort mission covering Lieutenant Bill Kocar, who would pilot an RF-8G—an unarmed photoreconnaissance version of the F-8 with VFP-63. Nichols looked forward to flying with Kocar. The sky was crystal clear and visibility almost unlimited. Furthermore, Bill Kocar was one of the best F-8 pilots on the *Tico* and "his expertise was very useful even though he was unarmed."[76] As for Nichols himself, by 9 July 1968, he had 153 combat missions and over 2,800 flying hours in the F-8 under his belt. He was the best of Navy's best: a highly trained killer with virtuoso abilities.

His weapons system, the F-8E, also represented the ultimate dogfighting platform for this period, and everything on the plane would work perfectly on 9 July. For this mission, the Pirate chose to carry 600 rounds of 20-millimeter ammo in a variety of "flavors": armor-piercing, fragmentation, and tracer. He also carried only two AIM-9D Sidewinder missiles rather than the standard load of four missiles. "We thought with two of them we could always get a kill and we didn't want the extra weight. Dogfights only last a few seconds and we didn't want to be loaded down with four."[77] Nichols set his armament switches to fire Sidewinders from his stick's button and his plane's guns from the trigger.

The mission called for Nichols to escort Kocar over Vinh for a photo shoot. Bill Kocar flew at 2,000 feet above ground level, and John Nichols followed behind him in a loose two-plane formation at 5,000 feet. The two planes approached Vinh at 450 knots from the west. Gunfire erupted as the two men entered the target area but Kocar flew a straight path in order to get the best pictures he could.

At one point, Nichols looked over his shoulder to check his rear quadrant and spotted a MiG-17 closing on the RF-8 from the port side, about two miles back. He warned Kocar: "Corktip, you've got a MiG on your ass! Break left!"

Without even looking, Kocar made a hard 90-degree nose-down turn and headed for the sea. The MiG tried to follow but only managed to pull a 30-degree turn. Meanwhile, Nichols jammed his throttle to full power and pulled a 5-G turn in an attempt to get behind the MiG. Tracers flashed across his canopy from a second, unseen MiG, but Nichols gave them little thought and continued his attack. When he heard a good Sidewinder tone from the missile heat seeker, he fired his right-hand missile. "It guided and appeared to have a chance of scoring, but the Gs were apparently too much. The Sidewinder passed well outside the right-hand side of the MiG and exploded harmlessly."[78]

The MiG pilot then made a critical mistake. He lit his afterburner, giving Nichols' only other missile a perfect heat source to home in on. He immediately squeezed the missile off at minimum range; the missile went right up the MiG's tailpipe and exploded. "I'm amazed. The sky in front of me was full of small pieces of metal. But the MiG continued turning." Nichols' F-8 was now rapidly overtaking the damaged MiG, so he chopped back the throttles and popped the speed brakes—a gutsy move given the fact that there was a second MiG somewhere close behind him. "All of this is a no-no, but boy, when you got a guy in front of you the fangs kind of come out, and you just want to kill him."[79]

As he closed within 300 feet of the MiG, Nichols reached down between his knees and mashed his gun-charger button. The F-8 shuddered as compressed air drove the four bolts home on John's four cannons. "This is the most beautiful feeling. When you reach down and put the gun charging thing on, *Clunk,* and oh God, the trigger now is live and it's just quite a feeling. The whole airplane vibrates; it's a sexual feeling." Nichols was now surrounded by four "hot" 20-millimeter guns that he could control with a stick protruding up between his legs.

"I was getting *damn* close, and I just squeezed the trigger as the sight passed over the top of his airplane. It was so dramatic. I could clearly see ten to twenty explosions on the top of the aircraft, and then he just came apart in a big fireball and I let go of the trigger."[80] Nichols then banked his airplane hard to the left to fly over the pieces of the MiG, just as he would go over a banner at a gunnery shoot.

"Splash one MiG!" the Pirate called out—a call he had fantasized about making since his first day in flight school in 1956.

"Attaboy, Feedbag. You got him. Your six is clear," Kocas responded.

"The other one is up ahead," Nichols said and began accelerating. But then he reconsidered. "I don't have any more Sidewinders, and I don't even know whether I have any bullets left or whether the guns still would fire, and this has been a long day so I'm not going to chase this guy back." Better to live to fight another day than to push a bad position.

Phil Craven, the CAG, was also in the air that day and tried to find Nichols as soon as he reported the MiG contact, but John wouldn't reveal his location. (Back on the ship, John later admitted to him that he had the

MiG cornered and wasn't about to let Craven in on it.) However, when Craven heard "Splash one MiG," he called out, "Okay, you've done your job, now get the hell out of there."[81]

"*Okay*, let's get out of here," John responded.

The *Tico* knew by this point that John had made a kill, and sent a tanker out to meet him over the Gulf of Tonkin south of Vinh. Although John had 4,500 pounds of fuel remaining, enough to get him back to the carrier, he tanked anyway, thereby following a cardinal rule of carrier aviation: Never turn down fuel!

When Nichols' plane approached the ship, the captain, Norman K. McInnis, got on the horn. He congratulated him on the *Tico's* first MiG kill in SEA and asked him if he had any special requests.

"Yes, Sir. Captain, I'd like to salute your ship."

"You can do any damn thing you want."

"Two. You go right. I'll go left," Nichols told Kocar as they barreled towards the ship at 650 knots. The two planes descended to 250 feet, then pulled straight up on full afterburner, *then* did reverse aileron rolls all the way up to 50,000 feet. When he finally got the nose around and started coming back down, looking down at "God's blue ocean and that carrier, *way* down there like a little toy, and these two corkscrews of white fuel going all the way up to 50,000 feet," John "Pirate" Nichols began to ponder the magnitude of his accomplishment: a Silver Star, his name in the newspapers, and most important, a red star on his fuselage. Splash one MiG.

The next day the intelligence people came down to the Ready Room and one of the young officers asked, "You want to know who it was?"

"I don't care," John replied.

"He was twenty-six years old. His father was a schoolteacher in Hanoi. He was trained in Bulgaria and Russia and he only had 450 hours in the MiG-17."

"Okay, thanks." John Nichols then began to ponder what he had done.

We try to be tigers and yet you do go to bed at night and think about something like this. You kill a lot of people on the ground with bombs, but you never know them. This man had a name. I thought about him and I said, 'Damn, I wonder if I'd have liked him? I wonder if he always wanted to fly airplanes like I did? I wonder if he made model airplanes?' He just loved flying more than anything in the world and he thought he was a great fighter pilot. I wished he would have gotten out of the airplane. I wished I'd have killed his airplane but seen a parachute. I wished I could tell his parents that I really didn't mean to kill him. It's always a jolt to a pilot to think that there is a human being in the airplane. At first it's just an airplane that you're really striving to destroy, like you did in peacetime, but then there's a big fireball and it's gone and it hits the ground and then it suddenly dawns on you that there was a human being in there that was just incinerated.[82]

For a very small number of combat pilots the stimulation of killing another human being, similar to the "buck fever" that experienced hunters feel as deer season approaches, drives them to seek more opportunities: Robin Olds and Steve Ritchie fit into this category. However, for most pilots killing, while initially exciting, often leaves a bitter aftertaste in their mouths. John was not eager to accept the Navy's offer to go back into the combat theater soon after the kill. Despite how challenging the MiG mission was, he did not seek nor desire to kill additional pilots after he had made his first kill. This may be one significant reason why the vast majority of MiG killers in both Korea and Vietnam achieved only a single aerial victory.

A Sabbatical: The Naval War College and Have Doughnut

John Nichols left the *Tico* just five days after his aerial victory to attend the junior course at the Naval War College in Newport, Rhode Island. The War College turned out to be a welcome break for John. A student of history, he enjoyed spending time in the library reading reports about the Korean War and other historical material. In these reports, he discovered that naval aviators in Korea had not only encountered many of the same problems as their Vietnam counterparts, but also had taken time out of their busy schedules to write down lessons learned in their reports. The Korean War jet pilots, for example, were initially told that small-caliber anti-aircraft guns would not be able to hit a fast-moving jet. What they learned through experience was that the Korean gunners did not aim at any one plane as such; instead, they fired their weapons into sectors, hoping that an American jet would fly into the curtain of their fire. By plotting sectors of the sky, pilots could figure out safe routes into and out of their target zones. "Why hadn't anyone read these studies?" John asked himself. As the future commander of VF-24, John Nichols would take many lessons learned in the library at the War College and apply them directly on the battlefield.

Nichols didn't spend every minute of his time reading, however. He also flew regularly with the only other lieutenant commander in the class, Diego "Duke" Hernandez, a "water walking-fighter pilot" and the Navy's unofficial ambassador to Yugoslavia. On a Mediterranean tour, Hernandez had accidentally landed an F-8 at a Yugoslavian air-force base. Because his plane had a broken tactical-air-navigation system and the weather that day was horrible, he ended up overflying Italy and running out of gas over the Adriatic Sea. With a hundred pounds of fuel left, Hernandez decided to eject, but changed his mind when he saw a runway just ahead of him. He dropped his wheels, and landed in front of—he now saw—row after row of MiGs. Duke Hernandez handled the situation in style. "It would have killed the career of any other officer, but Duke was a great one. The Yugoslavs took him to the Club that night, got him drunk, and I know for a fact that a beautiful Yugoslav female officer strapped him on."[83] The next day, the Yugoslavians took some pictures of Hernandez and the aircraft, gave him a full tank of fuel, and let him fly off.

Duke and the Pirate used to go down to NAS Oceana, Virginia, on weekends and fly dissimilar air combat maneuvers with the Pirate in an F-8 and Duke in an F-4. "We were real good friends and good friends sometimes won't press it to the limit because you could get killed and there are certain times you know when you don't want to press it because the other guy's as good as you and you both are aggressive and you both do not want to lose."[84]

From the War College, Nichols went back to the West Coast to fly with VF-124, the West Coast RAG based at Miramar. At one point in this cycle, John traveled to the Nevada desert to assist in testing two special gifts given to the Navy by the Israeli Air Force after the Six-Day War in June of 1967: a captured MiG-17 and a MiG-21. In a top-secret program, code-named Have Doughnut/Have Drill, Navy pilots Jerry "Devil"·Houston (the same *Coral Sea* pilot from VF-51 who bagged the MiG in 1972), Foster "Tooter" Teague (another VF-51 MiG killer), Ron "Mugs" McKeown (a future double MiG killer), and TJ Cassidy (famous for his cameo role in the movie *Top Gun*) tested the MiGs against various Navy fighters, including the F-8 and F-4. The Navy flew the MiG-17 255 times. Teague and the others were amazed at the simplicity of the aircraft. Rods and push-rods operated the plane's control surfaces, rather than hydraulically powered controls. The 17 even had a stick extender to assist the pilot in making hard maneuvers. "If you really wanted to pull on it," explained Teague, "push a button and the stick telescopes up. . . . They would put their feet up on the instrument panel and just pull the hell out of it."[85]

Despite this crude control system, the MiG-17 turned better than any plane Teague and the others had ever flown. Fighting the little MiG with an F-4, claimed Ron McKeown, "was like being a giant with a long rifle trapped in a phone booth with a midget using a knife. That's really the way you found yourself. . . . You wouldn't let him get in where he could cut your guts out. You had to push him hard . . . drive him around the sky. But the big secret was to preserve your separation—approximately a mile and a half—so that you were always out of his weapons range."[86]

Foster, Nichols, and McKeown could not believe the construction techniques that the Soviets had employed to build the MiGs—rivets literally stuck out from the outer skin of the fuselage. They also could not believe how underpowered the MiG was compared to the American Phantom. "I hit the burner," Tooter Teague explained, "and I didn't feel any thrust. . . . You only got a couple hundred pounds of thrust out of the damn thing. . . . Stoke the burners on the F-4 and you're pouring fuel like a firehose with two guys holding. [Compared to the MiG-21], the Phantom was a like a goddamn barn door in the air. You survived because of its two fuel-guzzling engines."[87]

John Nichols viewed both these tests and served as the program's operations officer. Not surprisingly, he developed an intimate first-hand knowledge of the capabilities of both aircraft.[88] After the exercise, he and Devil Houston sat down together and developed a tactics manual that would later serve as the syllabus for the Navy's fighter-weapons school, Top Gun, and would help the Navy raise its kill ratio against the North Vietnamese from 2:1 to 4:1—still low compared to Korea's 7:1 ratio but an impressive improvement nonetheless.

The Final Evolution: VF-24

Getting screened for squadron command at first appeared to be a dream come true for John Nichols. Finally, he would be able to lead a squadron of fighter pilots in battle—something he had yearned to do for his entire career. But command in the end turned out to be a bittersweet experience.

When the Pirate deployed with VF-24 as its executive officer in July of 1972 (he would take command of the squadron in June 1973), his personal life began to enter a crisis: his wife, Sherry, simply was not prepared emotionally for another combat cruise, and would end up divorcing him when he returned.

As for John Nichols himself, he could feel his piloting skills begin to slip. Pulling Gs in an F-8 and making night carrier landings is a young man's sport, not a game to be played by older squadron commanders. The loss of so many friends and the whole Mike Estocin episode had also begun to wear him down emotionally. Nevertheless, Nichols went to sea in July of 1972. The Navy needed combat-proven commanders, and John was not about to let the service or his friends down. John was not alone. Unlike their counterparts in the Air Force, who flew 100 missions and then did not have to serve in Southeast Asia again unless they volunteered (which many did), many Navy pilots flew well over 100 missions north on a single deployment—and were then expected to go back and do it again every fourteen months until the war ended. As a result, a small cadre of pilots like John Nichols, Jerry Houston, Foster Teague, and Roger Sheets flew the majority of missions and took the losses. It was a very tough evolution, but no one at BuPers in Washington seemed able or willing to rectify the situation, and the tension in the Navy's air wings began to show.

Many wives got so fed up with the situation that they began to refer to themselves as WestPac widows. The WestPac widow considered her husband to be officially dead while on deployment, and freely conducted affairs with other men while her husband flew combat missions over Vietnam. John remembered running into a WestPac widow at Cubi Point in 1972. He had had to fly an airplane from the *Hancock* to the Philippines for repair. That evening he ran into the wife of one of the VF-24 pilots in the O Club. "She was there in hot pants and a blond wig. I didn't know she had a blond wig, and she wouldn't let me go. She stayed around the bar and everything and then asked me to walk her to the BOQ." On the way to the BOQ, the young woman began to complain that her husband was not sending her enough money. It then dawned upon John what she was up to. "I gave her a few bucks and left. She was disappointed and . . . it was an awkward, awkward situation."[89]

As for John's own wife Sherry, while she did not become a WestPac widow, she endured a tremendous amount of stress during John's tour with VF-24. In her position as a commander's wife Sherry, by custom, had to accompany the chaplain to inform other wives that their husbands had been killed. "You'd be there on Yankee Station and you'd lose a guy that afternoon and, so as XO or CO you're on the telephone trying to call your wife at home, and so a lot of times I would be on the telephone and I'd hear my phone ring at home and my wife Sherry would answer the phone at two or three A.M., 'Hello?' and the operator would say, 'We have a high-priority military call for you.' 'Oh, my God.' And then I'd say, 'Look, we lost so-and-so, and tomorrow the chaplain is going to be there at our house.' 'Oh, my God, no, no.' The wives went through this and I didn't know about it until years later."[90] Many of the older wives lamented among themselves that they would never have married a pilot if they had known how dangerous the job was. "These bastards," Sherry would complain to her friends. "They're going off on a job where in ten years half of them are going to get killed, and we didn't know this."[91]

In addition to tensions with their wives, the pilots by 1972 were also beginning to feel the full anger and hatred of the antiwar movement. When the USS *Hancock* (CVA-19) left Alameda in January of 1972, demonstrators surrounded the ship in little boats and some of the women stripped off their clothing and began to throw their blood-soaked tampons at the ship.[92] As the ship passed under the Golden Gate Bridge, the skipper put the ship on general quarters, fearing that a protester might drop a Molotov cocktail on the flight deck. One of the squadron commanders ran down to his stateroom, threw himself on his bunk, and cried. "It makes you cry," recalled John somewhat defensively. "It was heart-wrenching. Vicious crowds around base were shouting terrible things as our wives looked on: 'I hope they kill you!' It wasn't antiwar. . . . What we were talking about were the pro-Communists, parading with an enemy banner, hoping we would get killed, saying things like that. It wasn't 'We are against the *war*,' it's that 'We are against *you*, personally.' That's the way it was: it was not antiwar, it was pro-enemy. They were parading with the Vietcong flag and North Vietnamese flag. Those are the people I saw. I didn't see it as antiwar but pro-enemy. That's always the way I'm going to remember it because that's the way it was. They like to talk about it now in a high moral tone, but in reality it was a hatred of the people who were going out there and fighting it."[93]

What John Nichols witnessed at Alameda that day was the radical fringe of the antiwar movement. The vast majority of the movement were not allied with Third-World revolutionaries, as many nearby Berkeley members of the Students for a Democratic Society (SDS) were. In fact, in 1972 these

SDS protesters represented only a small but very vocal minority of the anti-war movement. Most Americans that year wanted to give Nixon an opportunity to achieve "peace with honor" through the Linebacker campaign. Nixon received 61 percent of the popular vote and 512 out of the 538 votes in the Electoral College in the 1972 elections, confirming Americans' support for him and his military policies.

To relieve the tensions of the 1972 cruise, most pilots took to drinking in their staterooms. "On the West Coast, when I got out there, I couldn't believe the drinking on the ship. Out in combat they drank, they got drunk at night, and had parties in their rooms. Officers would stagger down to the wardroom at 0200, and the Filipino stewards would smile at them. It was really bad."[94] In the Philippines, the drinking got so excessive that the Navy established two Officers' Clubs—one at Subic Bay for black-shoe officers and their wives, and the other at Cubi Point for those who preferred flight suits to uniforms. Aviators stacked furniture to see who could build the tallest pile, engaged in fist fights and food fights, and sang bawdy songs until the wee hours of the morning. But the most entertaining pilot drinking game was played not in the bar but in a shed behind the bar. Inside the shed was a length of track and a hydraulic catapult that propelled the nose section of an F-8 down the track at "dizzying speed." The object of the game was to catch the arresting wires at the end of the track before the nose of the F-8 slammed into a pool of slime. "To make a successful landing took a keen eye and a steady hand, neither of which was likely to characterize the occupant."[95]

After getting "knee-walking, commode-hugging drunk," pilots would file across "Shit Creek" to Olongapo to seek entertainment of a different sort.[96] It constantly amazed John Nichols that the pilots preferred Po City to any other liberty spot in Asia. One time he even polled the ship to see where everyone wanted to go and all the pilots and sailors replied, "Longapo." Why? Because there they could spend three days having sex with cheap, plentiful, and beautiful Filipina prostitutes.

John Nichols, however, never joined in these activities nor drank much at the O Club. In fact, he did his best to warn his pilots that as soon as the war ended, the Navy would take a very dim view of these goings-on. In one speech to his Ready Room before a liberty, he warned, "We're going over to the Club to have a party. I don't want any officers throwing food around. Listen, this is the way I am. This war's going to be over one day and if you don't understand what's going to happen. . . . The Navy's a real reactionary service; they're not going to put up with this; they'll wreck your career. We're going to start right now. Don't *ever* invite me to your room for a drink; I won't be there and I'll have your ass. If I find you drinking on the ship I'm going to have your ass, so you better be real careful."[97]

The Vietnam War era was coming to a close, and Nichols could see the handwriting on the wall.

––––––––––––

John Nichols tried to maintain his enthusiasm for flying and fighting throughout his final combat tour, always volunteering for the toughest missions, but towards the end of the *Hancock's* tour, in October of 1972 he noticed a subtle change in his attitude. "Nobody wants to be the last to die in a war," and Nichols was no different from any other warrior in this respect. "The last mission that I flew, I clearly remember went like this: I went up on the flight deck, and in my mind, I don't think I ever did this before, I hoped, I think I hoped, that the airplane would spring a leak after I was in it and it would be so obvious to everybody. But as I went around the airplane I handed the plane captain my helmet and I got to the left side where the Sidewinder sticks out, and I had already looked at it, it's right there by your head as you're ready to mount, and I put my foot up on the first rung of the ladder, which is quite high in the F-8. You reach up with your hand, and to get on that first step is quite an athletic move, and I grasp the handle with my hand and put my left foot way up there on the thing and I started to pull myself up and my leg wouldn't work. It wouldn't work and I couldn't straighten it so I started sweating. I was unsure. The plane captain, the enlisted person in charge of maintenance for a given aircraft, was standing behind me, and so I put my foot down and I looked around at the Sidewinder, and he said, 'Anything wrong with it, Sir?' And I didn't say anything; I couldn't say anything, and I just kept looking at the Sidewinder and he's behind me and I fooled with it a little more, like I was really looking at it. I kept saying to myself, 'Goddamn it, man, you can get up on this airplane one more time.' That's how I got in that airplane that time. I just didn't want to go. And I was a man who never would say that to anyone, but that was the *only* time that happened to me. I was out there for my third tour. That was my last mission; I knew it was going to be the last mission."[98]

VF-24 returned to the United States on 3 October 1972, and then did a two-month WestPac tour again on the *Hancock* in May and June 1973 before finally heading home for an extended shore period. The Navy offered to extend Nichols' command for two years so that he could assist the squadron's transition to the F-14 Tomcat, but by this point he had had enough. "I was disgusted with the way the war had been handled, and I was disgusted with the Estocin episode. I had agonized over thinking that I had left him there to rot in some prison camp and I was sick at heart. My marriage had dissolved and I just didn't want it any more." Although John Nichols was selected ahead of many of his peers for captain, he passed it up and got out.

Nichols wasn't alone. Constant shortages of carrier-qualified F-8 pilots throughout the war meant that the same pilots flew mission after mission over Vietnam with very little prospect of relief. Morale for Navy pilots hit an all-time low as the Vietnam War ended; many of its best sticks simply cashed their chips in and got out.

What remains so impressive about John Nichols and other naval aviators is their willingness to put aside their concerns with the war as well as their personal problems for the good of the squadron. For some, emotional outlets such as alcohol and prostitution took the edge off the war, but for more socially conservative officers like Nichols, there was no easy escape from the everyday stresses of war. For him, the only way out was to fly and fight until the war ended—a task which his body almost refused to let him do. Many historians criticize the Army and the Air Force for their one-year individual tours of duty, which made Vietnam an individual as opposed to a group experience, but in naval aviation the reverse problem existed. The Navy experience suggests that prolonged group exposure to war can be just as unhealthy as short, individual tours of duty. The lesson of Vietnam is that the best approach to sending men to combat is a combination of the Army/Air Force and Navy rotation policies: send men to war in groups but for limited time periods.

CHAPTER 6

OYSTER FLIGHT

The Air Force Top Guns of 1972

Udorn, August, 1972

One of the few high points of John Nichols's final Vietnam War cruise occurred in August 1972. The chief of staff on the *Hancock* called Nichols to his office and said, "We have a request for F-8 pilots to fly with the Air Force and teach them tactics. Just be tactful."[1] John flew to Udorn, and broke Air Force rules by approaching the field at 600 knots in his F-8. After being chewed out by the general and ignored the next day in the briefing room, Nichols proceeded not just to beat the Air Force team at tactics but to "slaughter them."[2] The Air Force decided to fight John and his wingman with four F-4s. The Air Force pilots wanted to use the superior speed advantage of the F-4s to get beyond range of the F-8s and "knock them down" with radar-guided Sparrow missiles. But things didn't quite work out that way. Nichols and his wingman spread out in a loose two-plane formation while the USAF pilots flew in a standard four-plane formation at a constant speed of 450 knots. This made it easy for Nichols to outmaneuver them. "The sight that remains in my mind from this experience," he recalled, "is the pitiful spectacle of four super aircraft in front of you, all tucked in close finger-four, pulling a level turn. An Atoll fired anywhere in range would find itself in the position of the proverbial mosquito in the nudist colony. It would hardly know where to begin."[3] John thought he would be killed in the O Club that night, he was so cocky.

After another similar day in the air with USAF jocks, Commander John Nichols finally stood up in the briefing room and began to take control of the situation:

Now listen, I was an instructor on both the East and West Coasts; I helped devise the tactics that we call loose-deuce and I think we are some of the best tactical pilots in the world; and I think we've proved it in this war so far—our kill ratio is higher than anybody's has ever been. I was sent here to try and impart some of this to you. Now, I've watched for two days and you have really not looked very good in the air. I can understand why the MiGs are killing you guys. And I'm trying to help you, so I'm not going to sit here silently any more. Horizontal turns aren't going to work any more, we fight in the vertical plane, we fight going straight up and straight down. When you turn that F-4 in a horizontal turn, I'll go straight up and straight down inside your turn and sit there on you forever. You've got to learn to fight in the vertical. You've got to learn to get out of the four-plane pattern and be flexible. You've got to give responsibility to your wingman to maneuver independently of you. You see how we independently maneuver without a word to each other. We can look at the fight and see who has got the best chance against the bogey and all it takes is, "I got it," and the other guy pulls up and gets out of there, and says "You've got it." We swap the lead back and forth. We are big enough in the Navy to let an ensign lead the flight with his commander in a dogfight, because we want to kill the enemy. We can fight out of phase with each other. We don't fly in formation against other airplanes, we fight out of phase. You're going to learn to be a yo-yo; I'm going to make you a yo-yo.[4]

The senior officers in the room just stared at John Nichols with a gloomy look in their eyes, but the junior officers were grinning. They were "happy as hell," Nichols says, because finally a senior commander was telling their superiors what they had always known: a flexible approach to aerial combat based on maneuvering might allow the Air Force to beat the odds and produce an ace by the end of the war. Pilot Steve Ritchie and his backseat navigator Chuck DeBellevue had taken a more flexible approach to air combat recently, on 8 July, and achieved two MiG kills as a result. As Nichols put it, "These junior officers knew what we were speaking was the truth. They wanted to learn this. They knew it worked."[5] Sadly, it had taken the loss of one of the Air Force's brightest stars, Robert Lodge, to convince the Air Force leadership to allow Ritchie and DeBellevue to take a looser approach to air-to-air combat.

The MiG Killers

Less than 1 percent of all fighter pilots ever achieve an aerial kill. In the Vietnam War this percentage was even lower, due to North Vietnam's reliance on anti-aircraft guns and SAMs for air defense as opposed to MiGs. All told, the Air Force only managed to shoot down 137 of the elusive MiGs during the entire Vietnam War.[6] Clearly, the MiG killers of Udorn were a special breed of fighter pilot, different in many respects from the line pilots who flew bombing missions with the Eighth Wing at Ubon. Who were these aviators and why did Udorn develop a critical mass of them by the spring of 1972?

The man most responsible for turning the 432nd Wing into the Air Force's premier MiG-killing outfit in 1972 was Major Robert Lodge. Born in 1941 to a Borden executive and a schoolteacher in Hempstead, Long Island, New York, Bob Lodge entered the Air Force Academy in 1960 and became known as "Mr. Aerospace Power" to the cadets of the Academy's Second Squadron. The "fastest slide rule in the West," Bobby's "highest ambition," according to the Academy yearbook staff, was to own an "IBM electronic brain complex."[7] After graduating fifth in his class in 1964, Lodge went on to pursue an M.S. in astronautics at Purdue. Bob, however, wanted to be more than an engineer; he also wanted to fight and fly. He underwent pilot training at Williams AFB, and then flew 100 missions north in the F-105 out of Takhli Royal Thai AFB in Thailand.

After an experience like Takhli some pilots might have been content simply to return to the States, start a family, and travel from one training assignment to the next. Not Bob Lodge. Fascinated and absorbed by the war, Bob lobbied the USAF hierarchy for a second tour in SEA. As his backseater Roger Locher put it, "Bob never had a girlfriend, to my knowledge; he was a heavy-thought type of guy, always focused on killing Communists."[8]

Ralph Wetterhahn, one of Lodge's instructors at the prestigious Fighter Weapons School at Nellis AFB, remembers Lodge clearly. "Lodge was kind of a loner, and didn't seem to be a particularly friendly guy, but not an unfriendly guy either, just real intense!" During the academic phase of the training, Lodge continually barraged Ralph with questions, trying to "suck everything he could" out of his brain. It was Lodge's eyes, though, that made the most powerful impression on this young instructor. "You remembered certain people, and I remembered him because he had what I call hunter eyes. Other guys, they look like they're out there to get shot down; not him."[9]

After he had completed the course at the Air Force's premier fighter school, the Fighter Weapons School at Nellis AFB, Lodge's quest would be fulfilled. The USAF transferred him back to Thailand for a second tour, this time as the wing weapons officer of the 432d Wing. At Udorn, Lodge immediately began to develop a plan to transform the 555th Squadron, or "Triple Nickel," from an escort squadron to a specialized counter-air team. He worked around the clock studying recent intelligence on MiGs and "refining techniques and tactics."[10] According to future ace Steve Ritchie, he was "the brains behind the entire situation." Not only did he petition Seventh Air Force for the MiG-killing mission, he also secured Combat Tree-equipped Phantoms for the Nickel, and hand-picked the pilots who would fly these scarce assets.

On 21 February 1972 all of Lodge's hard work began to pay off. For a month prior to this date, the North Vietnamese MiGs had been shadow-boxing with Udorn's F-4s over Northern Laos. The MiGs' tactic was to penetrate Laotian air space just deeply enough to scare away all the night bombers over the Ho Chi Minh Trail. After studying the situation intensively, Lodge convinced Seventh Air Force to allow him to run night MiG combat air patrol (MIGCAP) missions over Northern Laos with the new Combat Tree Phantoms. Lodge reasoned that with Combat Tree he might be able to bag a MiG with a long-range Sparrow missile shot against a low-flying target—especially if he kept his aircraft low as well.

It all came together perfectly on the night of 21 February. At 2123 local time, Lodge's WSO, Roger Locher, picked up a MiG "out of the weeds" on the Tree equipment. Lodge immediately got a clearance from Radarman First Class Billy Bunch aboard the Red Crown ship to go for a beyond-visual-range shot. The MiG-21 was heading straight toward Lodge at a combined velocity of 900 knots. "I fired three AIM-7Es," reported Lodge in his after-action interview, "the first at approximately eleven nautical miles, the second at eight nautical miles and the third at six nautical miles. The first missile appeared to guide and track level, and detonated in a small explosion. The second missile guided in a similar manner and detonated with another small explosion, followed immediately by a large explosion in the same area. This secondary explosion was of a different nature than the other two missile detonations and appeared like a large POL [petroleum, oil, lubricants] explosion with a fireball. . . . No detonation was observed for the third missile."[11] But the battle did not end there. The MiG that Lodge and Locher had killed had been the bait of a trap. Two other

MiGs suddenly appeared and attempted to pursue Lodge and Locher's plane back to Udorn. They followed the F-4 for 30 nautical miles but never got close enough for an Atoll shot. "That's something the F-4 could do really good," said Locher. "You could outrun anything without having to use the afterburner, down at low altitude."[12]

The 21 February 1972 kill was the first Air Force aerial victory since President Johnson had enacted his March 1968 bombing halt and had scaled down the Rolling Thunder campaign. It not only ushered in the final phase of the air war in Vietnam, it elevated the hopes of the Air Force leadership at Seventh Air Force and in Washington that with Lodge the Air Force might indeed produce an ace in its longest and bitterest war. From that day onward, every effort would be made to give Bob Lodge the best missions, equipment, and people to fulfil this most elusive dream.

If Lodge was the brains behind the Nickel, then Captain Richard S. "Steve" Ritchie represented the unit's life drive. Eventually Steve, not Bob, would become the Air Force's first Vietnam War ace. Bob was a distant and cerebral guy; Steve's personality verged on the flamboyant. The son of an American Tobacco Company executive from Reidsville, North Carolina, Ritchie bore a striking resemblance to the actor Robert Redford and was rumored to have had the prettiest Thai girlfriend at Udorn.[13] Steve, an avid football player in high school and college, possessed a jovial, jockish attitude that made him one of the most spirited members of the Nickel. During his very infrequent downtime, he would visit downtown Udorn, with squadron mates, to enjoy a good Thai meal, some local music, and beer. According to Squadron intelligence officer Captain Clara M. "Patty" Schneider, you could smell Ritchie a long distance off because of his Old Spice cologne.[14] "My buddy Woodstock and I mentioned to him several times that he really shouldn't use it because if he got shot down they'd be able to smell him a mile away, and his answer was, 'I hope I don't get shot down.' And fortunately for him, he wasn't, but that was just how cocky he was. He wasn't going to go by the rules."

Robin Olds sums up Steve the best: "He is brilliant. He is good looking. He is dedicated. He is everything that we wanted. But he thinks he is God's gift."[15]

The "brilliance" of Steve Ritchie that Olds alludes to is partly in his piloting skills. Like Lodge, Ritchie graduated from the Air Force Academy in 1964, flew a full combat tour in Southeast Asia prior to 1972 (195 combat missions), and attended the Fighter Weapons School. But whereas Lodge excelled as a tactician and a thinker, Ritchie not only possessed an understanding of the weapons system, but also had strong stick and rudder skills. Graduating first in his Undergraduate Pilot Training (UPT) class, Ritchie initially flew F-104 Starfighters before transitioning to the F-4 in 1968. That same year, he transferred to Da Nang and helped establish the first F-4 fast Forward Air Controller (FAC) operation in Southeast Asia.

On one mission, Ritchie's overenthusiasm for the fast FAC mission almost killed him. He and his backseater, Bob Hoag, were marking supply targets along the Ho Chi Minh Trail near Tchepone in Laos, an area where the local Pathet Lao enjoyed torturing to death pilots unlucky enough to be shot down. On this day, Ritchie felt so bulletproof after making ten marking passes over a target that he decided to make one last strafing pass before heading home. "I armed the gun [SUU-16 gun pod]," he explained, "and rolled in and my backseater, Bob Hoag, said, 'I really wish you wouldn't do this.' And I, probably being a bit overconfident because I'd flown over 140 missions by that time and had not been hit, said, 'No sweat, Bob, we're in out of the sun.' Which means the sun is blinding the gunners. Well, just about the time I was ready to squeeze the trigger, I heard a very loud bang, and the airplane shuddered and felt like it was coming apart. Bob said, 'We're hit, you son of a bitch! I told you!' So he's screaming and hollerin' at me and I'm pulling off the target, hollering 'Mayday! Mayday! Mayday!'"[16] Ritchie's F-4 had taken a 37-mm nonexplosive shell in the right engine. It came in the air intake and went through the engine, but it failed to damage any of the F-4's vital organs or cut any fuel or hydraulic lines. As a result, Ritchie managed to pull the engine to idle and nurse his crippled craft back to Da Nang. "Everything settled out," he recalled. "The engine ran in idle; it was pretty rough but it ran. So I didn't shut it down and all the engine instruments stabilized. We were extremely fortunate. Unbelievable, unbelievable luck!"[17]

Clearly, Steve Ritchie was an extremely gifted young pilot, but he still needed to exert more self-discipline with respect to the Fast FAC mission if he was to survive another combat tour in Southeast Asia. Fortunately, his work as a Fast FAC pioneer combined with glowing performance reviews won him admission to the Fighter Weapons School at Nellis AFB. At Nellis, Ritchie began to refine his piloting skills, first as a student in 1969 and later, from 1970 to 1972, as its youngest instructor pilot. Several of Ritchie's shootdowns, including his final kill on 28 August, bore direct similarities to syllabus missions he flew at Nellis. "My fifth MiG kill was an exact duplicate of a syllabus mission, so I had not only flown that as a student, but had *taught* it probably a dozen times prior to actually doing it in combat."[18]

Steve Ritchie also had the opportunity at Nellis to teach air-to-air tactics to a fellow academy graduate and the man who would ultimately be his commander again in Thailand, Bob Lodge. It was Lodge who ultimately convinced Seventh Air Force personnel to assign Ritchie to the 432nd Wing in 1972. Lodge knew that Ritchie liked to play hard, but he also knew that when it came to flying airplanes Ritchie had very few equals. Ritchie worked hard and played hard. Like a professional golfer intent upon keeping his edge, he never went more than two or three days without flying. He also worked feverishly on the ground preparing for missions. It was not unusual for him to put in 18-hour days when he was on the flying schedule. Ritchie, in short, had the same type of dedication to the mission that Lodge had. Even more important, Lodge knew that Ritchie shared another key personality trait with him: an intense desire to engage the North Vietnamese in aerial combat. If that meant killing enemy pilots, he had the capability to do so. Ritchie did not enjoy killing; however, if the mission required him to kill, he would put any natural aversion to murder aside and perform the mission.[19] Only one of Ritchie's five kills escaped certain death, "I only saw a chute after the first kill," he remembered.[20]

The French pilot and writer Antoine de Saint-Exupéry once wrote, "Fighters don't kill, they murder." Air-to-air combat represents the most intimate type of killing that a pilot must confront. It requires him to fire upon another pilot just like himself, often from the rear and by complete surprise. The results of the bloodletting also become apparent immediately: a parachute, maybe, but more likely a crash or a fireball.

A highly illustrative example of Ritchie's capacity for extreme but highly intelligent aggression occurred in his youth, when he played football for Reidsville High School. In the locker room one day, a 200-pound fullback started making fun of Steve and ridiculing him in front of his teammates. "It was the type of situation where I either had to fight him or give up. And I gave up. I knew he would have ripped me a new asshole. And so I gave in."[21] But he didn't give up. He went on a weight-training program, got stronger, and went from 160 pounds to 190. Two years later, in 1960, he went to the Sweet Shop in Reidsville to enjoy a milkshake with some friends, and the same 200-pound fullback came over and started bullying one of his friends. "I got up to walk away from him and he jerked me around. I'd had enough; I laid into him and he never got a shot off. I just fired into his face with my fists five or six times, knocked him to the floor, jumped on him and just started beating him, holding him down and beating him until they pulled me off him. And two years earlier, he had pulled my bluff."[22] In these episodes, Steve employed many of the same basic tactical principles that he would later use to become the Air Force's first Vietnam War ace: (1) It is better to live to fight another day than to press a bad position; (2) Always employ maximum surprise in an engagement; and (3) Don't quit the fight until you are absolutely certain that your opponent is destroyed.

In a study of its aces, the Air Force determined that a background in schoolyard fighting is part of the profile of an ace.[23] Ironically, while cocky and loquacious about his pilot skills, Steve Ritchie could turn suddenly close-mouthed when it came to the subject of aggression and killing. Killing "is just like sex," Army psychologist Dave Grossman argues, "because the people who really do it just don't talk about it."[24] Ritchie and Lodge never spoke of their desire to fight the enemy, but like secret sharers, each knew intuitively that the other man had the urge to do so. Lodge understood that Ritchie could and would pull the trigger when necessary—a trait not every pilot possessed. As Grossman explains, both "would not misuse or misdirect their aggression any more than a sheepdog would turn on his flock, but in their heart of hearts" they yearned "for righteous battle, a wolf upon whom to legitimately and lawfully turn their skills."[25] Both lived to knock down the "schoolyard bullies" of the world, and both spent an inordinate amount of time planning for such righteous struggles.

On 10 May Steve Ritchie and Bob Lodge would form the fighting nucleus of Oyster Flight. Lodge would be flying in the lead shooter position of the four-plane flight and Ritchie would serve as his alternate. Since there were no other Fighter Weapons School graduates at Udorn in 1972, Lodge needed to recruit skilled pilots from the ranks of the line fliers stationed there to fill the remaining positions in the flight. Age and rank made no difference; only skill and the desire to kill counted. John Markle, a 25-year-old first lieutenant, was on his first flying assignment out of flight school when Lodge chose him to be part of Oyster Flight. "We took some of those young kids along because we had to," explains future ace Chuck DeBellevue, "and you would handpick them, and pick out the best of the crop to mold and fly in the flights."[26]

A native of Hutchinson, Kansas, and the son of a Swift & Company salesman, John Markle had no idea he would join the Air Force until he met a recruiter at the student union of his college during his senior year at Fort Hays State in Hays, Kansas. "I wanted to go to Vietnam," claims Markle, "and the Air Force recruiter got to know me well at the student union, and the rest is history."[27] Markle attended Officer Training School at Lackland AFB in 1970, and went on to UPT at Laughlin AFB in Del Rio, Texas. Much to his surprise, he excelled as a pilot, graduating near the top of his UPT class. Once at Udorn Markle volunteered for more difficult missions, such as night MIGCAPS over Laos, and began to get noticed by Lodge. By 10 May, Markle had over 78 combat missions under his belt and appeared ready for the challenge of flying over the most heavily defended skies in the world.

Another young flight-suit officer from the prairies of Kansas was Captain Roger Locher, Bob Lodge's exceptionally talented GIB (guy in the back). A native of Sabetha, Kansas, Locher grew up on a farm and as a child spent a lot of time hunting. "I enjoyed tracking coyotes through the snow," Locher recalls, "because it involved putting the shoe on the other foot, and seeing the world through the angle of the coyote." Coyotes evade pursuit by taking off in a straight line and then circling back around a stalker. By hunting coyotes, Locher learned basic escape-and-evasion tricks that would prove very useful to him later on, in the jungles of North Vietnam.

Locher attended Kansas State University in 1965, majoring in food science and food management. Food science turned out to be less intriguing than Air Force ROTC, and Locher ended up pursuing an Air Force career rather than a job as an animal-feed specialist. Barred from pilot training because of a refractive-vision error just outside the 20 x 20 limit, Locher chose navigator school instead. "Then the word was, do a good job being a navigator and reapply to UPT, because they took so many back after you'd been an officer for a while, so there was hope, a light at the end of the tunnel."[28]

Historically, the Air Force regarded navigators as second-class citizens. Throughout the post–World War II period, very few command or even staff positions were open to navigators. In 1953, for example, 2,400 pilots held command positions compared to only fifteen navigators. No navigator during the 1950s expected to rise above the rank of major. To make matters even worse, a segregation system existed in many base operations areas whereby navigators were forbidden to enter certain "pilots only" rooms.[29]

Fortunately for Roger Locher, in the 1960s the Air Force navigator program gradually began to improve. In 1963 additional staff positions for navigators opened, and they increased with the onset of the Vietnam War. Locher entered the program late enough in the 1960s to also attend the new navigator school at Mather AFB near Sacramento, California. This school, which had begun operation in 1965, emphasized flying much more than did the older programs at Connally AFB and Harlingen AFB, both in Texas. By the end of his undergraduate navigator course, Locher would have over 255 hours of flying time under his belt, and over 30 hours of lead-navigator experience.[30]

Locher graduated from Mather in November of 1969 and then trained as an F-4 weapons-systems officer (WSO) at Davis-Monthan AFB in Tucson, Arizona. From there he went through the global survival course at Fairchild, and then off to Udorn. He served at Udorn from September 1970 to the summer of 1972, and flew 410 missions before getting shot down on 10 May. Steve Ritchie claims Locher was "the best backseater in SEA."[31] Why did he spend so much time at Udorn?

From the first day he entered the Air Force, Roger Locher had only one goal—to fly fighter aircraft. During the 1970s, the USAF would reconsider navigators for pilot training every six months until they turned twenty-six and a half. In theory, all a new navigator had to do was to take a physical and submit the paperwork to his unit's headquarters. In practice the Pacific Air Force, always short of skilled navigators, compelled new weapons systems operators (WSOs) to serve at least a couple of years before accepting them for undergraduate pilot training (UPT). Locher saw it differently. "Oh, thanks for your application, for being such a great American, for trying to do this. However, you haven't spent two and a half years as a navigator to realize the expenditure of training time, so buzz off."[32] Knowing full well that a safe assignment in America or Europe would not impress the personnel mafia, Locher chose to stay on at Udorn. "It was easier to stay and improve where I was than it was to go somewhere else and have to reestablish myself from scratch."[33]

Though Locher didn't know this at the time, there was another very good reason for him to stay at Udorn: her name was Captain Clara M. Schneider, or Peppermint Patty (P²) as the guys called her at Udorn. Patty came from the small farming town of Vergennes, Illinois, and immediately became friends with Roger Locher because they shared a similar rural, middle-American upbringing. Patty recalled that her friend Jenny Osterman, an intelligence officer nicknamed "Woodstock" after the girl in the horn-rimmed glasses in the film *Woodstock,* introduced them. "Woodstock and

I happened to be out by the front door where you go in to Intel, and Roger came along so she introduced us, and I said, 'Oh, where you from?' and he said, 'Sabetha, Kansas.' And I said, 'I know where that is.' Because when I was stationed at Omaha, I went right past Sabetha on my way home to southern Illinois."[34] This was in September 1971, just before Roger was due to take leave. It would be almost a full year, three MiG kills, and one bailout later before these two officers would actually begin dating. But their friendship blossomed immediately.

Her relationship with Roger Locher notwithstanding, Captain Schneider was not a camp follower looking for her MRS degree. The wing relied on her to supervise enlisted photo interpreters and decide which targets should be recommended for attack the next day. During rescue efforts, Schneider would stay up all night laboriously sifting through mountains of data trying to identify all SAM and AAA sites near the downed pilot. She would then brief the pilots and navigators early in the morning on these threats, and only then catch a few winks of sleep. Her diligent and conscientious work saved lives.

Patty Schneider entered the Air Force during a period of remarkable change for the women in blue uniforms. In 1967, the Air Force made a firm commitment to increase the WAF (Women in the Air Force), and to place these women in nontraditional military occupational specialties (MOS) such as intelligence.[35] This move was influenced not only by the feminist movement but also by the personnel demands of the Vietnam War. Even with this push, the 762 female officers serving in the Air Force at the end of 1967 represented only 0.6 percent of the officer corps.[36] Schneider was still very much a pathbreaker—especially given her choice of intelligence as Military Occupational Specialty (MOS). The only other occupation specialties available to women at the time were supply, personnel, and administration.

After graduating from Officer Training School at Lackland in 1967, Schneider attended the seven-month intelligence school at Lowry AFB near Denver. This school proved challenging. "I hated the PI [photo interpreter] portion of intel school, I couldn't see much. 'As you can plainly see, we have here such-and-such . . .' the instructor would say, and I'd get so frustrated, I'd think, 'I can *not* so plainly see!' And just about the time I'd get my stereoscope in stereo he'd say, 'And now we'll go on to the next frame.' So fortunately I did not work as a PI for most of my career. I was in Air Intelligence, which meant that I worked directly with the aircrews, briefing and debriefing and that sort of thing on the threats and stuff."[37]

Schneider graduated from Lowry in August 1968 and immediately volunteered for service in Thailand. "I was just so excited," she recalls. "I was with Seventh/Thirteenth Air Force Headquarters, which was actually a detachment to Seventh Air Force and Thirteenth Air Force." Schneider's first tour lasted from November 1968 until May 1970. Because only limited quarters for women existed on base, she lived off-base in a bungalow shared with two other women officers. Unlike the pilots, she had neither air conditioning nor a convenient Officers' Club near her quarters in which to dine. She instead lived off the economy, using local taxis as transportation (25 cents from anywhere in town), and purchasing food from street vendors and local Thai eateries.[38] "I don't think I did that much cooking, because it was real cheap to go to restaurants and you could get a filet mignon, a good-size one, for about two dollars, so we ate out a lot, and of course when I was at work . . . well, I was always on a diet, so we had what they called the Banana Lady sitting outside the gate of our compound at work and I'd get two bananas and a couple boiled eggs somewhere in the morning and that was my lunch."[39]

Patty Schneider worked twelve hours a day, six days a week. Completely committed to her work, she decided early in her tour not to date. "I kind of stopped dating my first tour because every time I'd have a specific date with somebody I'd end up having to work"[40] Instead, Patty preferred relaxing with the unit. "Our whole unit would go downtown to some place that had dancing until two o'clock in the morning."[41] She enjoyed sipping a Singha beer or a Seven-and-7 and listening to the marvelous Thai cover bands that played for the patrons at the downtown Udorn clubs. Like the guys, she also enjoyed Thai massage.[42] "Where I got my hair done they had a steam room and a massage and the guys would jeer at me when I mentioned getting a massage, because of course their idea of a massage was completely different from my idea of a massage; this one was a legitimate massage for helping your body relax."[43]

To relax, Patty Schneider also enjoyed visiting Chuck DeBellevue and Roger Locher in their quarters. They "had an air-conditioned room and I'd go over there sometimes to eat or write letters, stop on my way to the Club."[44] Schneider debriefed these guys every day and got to know them like family. "I had had an ID bracelet made with my name on it and navigator wings and a lieutenant colonel, I can't remember who it was in the command post, saw it one day and he said, 'How come you have navigator wings on that?' And I said, 'Because most of my friends are navigators, because they are the ones I debrief.'"[45]

Whereas the navigators accepted Schneider as part of the team, the pilots often treated her arrogantly. One even failed to report taking AAA fire. At the bar that night, Patty heard the guy say to his buddy, "Oh, yeah, I got shot at such-and-such a place today, be careful there." Schneider got up in the briefing the next morning and lambasted the pilots: "'If you don't tell Intel, we can't tell everybody else, so don't just come home telling war stories at the bar. If it really happened, tell it when you debrief.' But a lot of times their attitude was, 'Oh, they don't know where the threat is because it's moved by the time they get the message traffic.'"[46]

Like Steve Ritchie, Roger Locher, and Bob Lodge, Patty Schneider also volunteered for a second tour to participate in the unpopular war. Why would someone volunteer to return to a war that neither the American government nor its people seemed committed to win? For Schneider, it was the camaraderie with the people in her unit, people like herself from conservative and often rural areas of the country who were completely committed to the Air Force and its war, regardless of what others felt. "I was always a very shy person and I really came out of my shell at Udorn. I enjoyed being involved in something that I thought was meaningful."[47]

One of the people who made the war meaningful for Patty was her buddy Chuck DeBellevue, Roger Locher's roommate. Described by Patty as the most "down-to-earth" man in the unit, Captain Charles DeBellevue, flying as Ritchie's backseater, would eventually become America's top ace of the Vietnam War, with six MiGs to his credit.

Chuck grew up in the small agricultural community of Crowley, Louisiana. The son of a rice-mill manager who was a reserve Army major, Chuck never wanted to do anything in life except fly for the Air Force. However, a series of tough breaks early in his career almost kept this future ace out of the cockpit. First the Air Force Academy rejected him, so he ended up in an ROTC unit at the University of Southwestern Louisiana in Lafayette. Next he washed out of pilot training at Craig AFB in Selma, Alabama. DeBellevue, who ultimately earned his pilot's wings after the war, claims that his instructor at Craig never allowed him to solo.

DeBellevue himself still doesn't understand why, but this "ragin' Cajun" from USL refused to give up on the Air Force. He opted instead to attend navigator school at Mather AFB in 1969 and went on to F-4 Combat Crew Training at Davis-Monthan AFB in Arizona. The Mather program was "designed to take a kid out of college and teach him how to navigate in a transport airplane. They taught us basic map reading and then we went into radar work, using the radar to land navigate, and then we went into day celestial, using the sun, and then night celestial, using the stars, and then we went into water work, using pressure patterns."[48]

But DeBellevue didn't want transports; he wanted fighters. Fortunately for him, the Air Force had just begun to convert F-4 backseat slots from pilot to navigator billets. Although, unlike that of Navy F-4s, the backseat of the Air Force Phantom had a stick, a throttle, and rudder pedals, the Air Force finally recognized in 1969 that putting two pilots in a fighter plane created too much friction: both wanted to fly, land, and take off, and the backseat pilots consequently became demoralized. Navigators, on the other hand, were thrilled to be given the opportunity to avoid transport or bomber duty and help crew a front-line fighter. DeBellevue jumped at the chance to attend the first F-4 Combat Crew Training class that had no pilots in it.[49]

At Davis-Monthan, he learned the rudiments of the Weapons Systems Officer discipline, but he got very few hours of air-to-air practice. "The first time I saw a dissimilar airplane in close proximity to mine," he remembers, "was a MiG-21 south of Hanoi, and it was behind me—and that shouldn't have been the first time I saw a dissimilar airplane."[50]

Despite this "dogshit training,"[51] Chuck DeBellevue arrived in Udorn in October of 1971 prepared to kill MiGs. He got this preparation from a year and a half spent with the 335th Tactical Fighter Squadron at Seymour-Johnson AFB in North Carolina. At Seymour, he "really learned how to fly the backseat of an F-4" and ended up his tour there giving check rides to new second-lieutenant pilots. At Udorn, DeBellevue initially flew with a variety of pilots on fast FAC missions into Laos. "We were just flying with anybody. It was a fairly close-knit squadron, and it didn't matter too much for the air-to-ground work."[52] However, as the Nickel got more involved in the counter-air role, he started flying more with the Lodge/Locher team, and by 10 May Chuck DeBellevue had over 120 missions under his belt—a paltry number compared to Roger Locher's 420 but still enough to make him the second most experienced navigator at Udorn.

Oyster Flight

On 8 May, the day before the mining of Haiphong harbor, the team of Lodge, Locher, and Ritchie, and DeBellevue got its first opportunity to draw blood. They were on a MIGCAP mission near Hanoi, and their flight call sign on this day as well as on 10 May was Oyster. The Navy's radar control, Red Crown, vectored Oyster flight into a two-plane formation of MiG-21s. Although Locher had a radar contact at 40 miles distance from the flight, too many friendly aircraft were in the area to risk a long-range shot. After closing to within two miles of the target, Lodge ordered Locher to break radar lock on the lead MiG and lock onto its slower-flying wingman. In air-to-air combat speed is life. One burst of afterburner could have saved the MiG from destruction, but its pilot probably never even saw the flight of four F-4s blazing toward him from the rear at over one and a half times the speed of sound. Lodge harnessed the F-4's speed advantage to get within 4,500 feet of the MiG. He then ripple-fired two AIM-7E Sparrows, which slammed into the tail of the MiG and blew it into a tremendous fireball. By some miracle, the MiG pilot ejected from this inferno; the F-4s passed his distinctive yellow parachute while exiting the scene.[53]

For a man whose sole purpose in life was to kill Communists, 8 May was a rare moment of triumph. The usually reserved Bob Lodge performed a victory roll over Udorn! He also took time out of his frenetic schedule to celebrate with Roger Locher. On the night of 9 May, Bob and Roger "went to one of the Thai places near the gate, and Bob ordered rock lobster, his favorite meal."[54] This dinner would be a rare moment of relaxation for Lodge in an otherwise tumultuous period of mission planning, briefings, and combat. His seriousness made him difficult to get to know on a personal level, but with Locher, a brother-in-arms, he could let down his guard a bit. During one long night mission over Laos when nothing was going on, Bob made a sobering confession to Roger: he, Lodge, simply knew too much about the F-4 and the air-to-air mission to risk being captured and interrogated. "I would rather die in a thirty-foot hole in the ground with an engine up my rear end than to be a prisoner of war," he told Roger.[55] Major Robert Lodge would gladly sacrifice his own life for the Air Force and his comrades in arms.[56] "Bob was just that kind of guy," recalls Locher.[57]

At 0330 the next morning, the pilots of the 555th squadron began to file into the Officers' Club for breakfast. The large numbers of officers eating meant only one thing—a major mission in the offing. At the 0400 briefing, "you could hear a pin drop on the floor, it was so quiet," remembers DeBellevue.[58] Locher recalls the distinct odor of Ritchie's cologne wafting through the air of the room, tightly packed with hypertense aviators. "It was an anxious day, all right," recalls Markle, "because most of us had never been up to the Hanoi area."[59] Lodge informed his seven Oyster flight brothers that their job would be to fly vanguard MIGCAP for a 120-plane strike against the Paul Doumer bridge and the Yen Vien railyard. The Paul Doumer bridge, or the "Doomer" bridge as pilots called it, was the most important bridge in North Vietnam. It spanned the Red River, carrying the only rail link from the port of Haiphong to Hanoi. Any strike against it was sure to meet with considerable MiG opposition. The tenth of May also represented the kick-off date for Operation Linebacker—Nixon's plan to punish North Vietnam for its 1972 Easter Offensive against the South.[60]

Lodge planned to bait any potential MiGs with a four-plane flight from the 13th Squadron, 432nd Wing, code-named Balter. Balter flight would fly high at 22,000 feet, slightly ahead of Oyster Flight, and try to lure MiGs into a head-on attack. Meanwhile, Oyster Flight would remain low at 2,000 feet and only reveal themselves to the MiGs at the last moment, thus closing the jaws of the trap.[61]

By 0830, the entire strike package was in the air and streaming towards Hanoi. At Tan Son Nhut AFB, in Saigon, the Seventh Air Force commander himself, General John Vogt, Jr., monitored the flight in Blue Chip, his command center. A giant situation map, constantly updated by staff officers and NCOs, revealed the precise locations of all strike aircraft. Information received had already revealed that Balter 2 had aborted because of an electrical problem, Balter 3 could not refuel, and Oyster 4, flown by Lieutenant Tommy Feezel, had suffered a radar failure. Nevertheless, although combat ineffective, Feezel decided to stick with his brother pilots to provide them with an additional set of eyes.

At 0823, Oyster Flight received its first warning from an EC-121 radar plane over Laos, code-named Disco. "Oyster, Disco. Activity bearing zero-five-zero i.e., 050 degrees, with Hanoi, known as Bullseye, being the geographical center of the compass ninety-six [miles] your position."

Two minutes later, Chief Radarman Larry Nowell of Red Crown, the Navy's radar control on a picket ship in the Gulf of Tonkin, reported four separate contacts: "You got one at three-four-five at fifty. You got a bandit at zero-one-five forty-five, a bandit at zero-five-seven fifty seven, another bandit at zero-eight-one at ninety . . ." [remainder of transmission is garbled].[62]

A pilot had to have a mind like a steel trap to keep up with data like this streaming across the electromagnetic spectrum. Lodge not only kept up but flew his airplane and planned his flight's attack pattern. He had two goals: to keep his flight between the MiGs and the strike force, and if possible to cause some bloodshed in the process. Therefore, when Radarman Nowell called out at 0942, "The closest bandit I hold is zero-two-two at sixteen," Lodge dropped his centerline fuel tank, turned to meet the MiG almost head on, and descended to 3,000 feet, with the other members of his flight quickly following. Lodge's plan was to hide in the weeds until the last possible moment, let all the MiGs pass, and then pop up and blast a MiG from the rear quarter with a Sparrow.[63]

Things got very quiet at this point. No words needed to be said. Everyone knew what to do: check weapons, spread out to provide better visual coverage of each other's vulnerable six o'clock position. A few moments later, Steve Eaves, John Markle's backseater, shattered the silence: "Oyster Two has contact!"

"Oyster One has a contact zero-five-zero for fifteen."

"Oyster Three is contact, Bob!"

"Right, we got 'em!" radioed Bob.

DeBellevue (Oyster 3 Bravo) then got a hostile IFF return from his Tree equipment, indicating that his target was indeed a MiG.

"He's squawking MiG! . . . He's squawking MiG! . . . Stand by to shoot!"

Lodge elected to snap up from 2,000 feet and try to get a front quartering shot at the first MiG, which was now at an altitude of 13,000–16,000 feet, roughly fifteen miles out, and closing at 1,150 miles per hour. When the MiG got to within eight miles, Lodge fired a 500-pound Sparrow. The missile smoked out of the Phantom, accelerated to 1,800 knots, but then suddenly exploded before reaching the MiG. Lodge then fired a second missile; five seconds later its 66-pound warhead smashed into the MiG's wing and detonated in an orange explosion. "I continued my climb," recalled Locher, "and five seconds later saw a MiG-21 with the left wing missing, trailing fire. With pieces falling off it, the out-of-control aircraft passed a thousand feet to the left side of my aircraft. The pilot had already ejected."[64] Forty-five seconds had elapsed from radar contact to kill.

Almost immediately after this kill, Markle took a shot at the Number Three MiG in the four-plane flight. The first missile's rocket motor never ignited; presumably it just fell off the pylon.[65] "I observed the second missile climb slightly and turn right approximately fifteen degrees. Soon after missile launch, I visually identified a MiG-21 passing from my left to my right."[66] Markle's reaction to seeing the missile hit home was recorded on his voice cockpit recorder: "Oh right! . . . Now! . . . Good! . . . Wooohooo!"[67]

"Oyster Two's a hit!" Markle radioed.

"I got one!" Lodge answered

"Roger, he's burning and he's going down at one o'clock," interjected Markle's backseater Steve Eaves of the Locher/Lodge kill.

The third kill of the day quickly followed. Ritchie and DeBellevue turned with the MiGs and fired two AIM-7E's at the fourth MiG in the flight from about 6,000 feet. The first missile appeared to fly under the MiG but the second detonated in the rear quarter of the plane, causing another fireball.[68]

For DeBellevue, what once was a squawking radarscope was now an aerial victory, but neither he nor Ritchie had much time to savor their triumph. While they were focusing on their kill, the first MiG in the flight had swung right to get at the rear of the Phantoms. In doing so, it nearly collided with Oyster 1. As Locher remembered, it was "one of the prettiest airplanes I've ever seen."[69] The small delta wing had apparently just been polished the night before; it glistened in the sunlight as it passed just 25 feet from Locher's cockpit. Bob Lodge, always one to push the limits to get a kill, decided to ease back on his throttle and let this MiG gain enough distance to take a Sparrow shot. "There he was, burner plume sticking out, the shiniest airplane you've ever seen," recalls Locher.[70]

Roger Locher then made a fatal error. He reached down, pulled out his super-8 movie camera, and began shooting, hoping to capture his fourth MiG kill on film. Aircrew would often shoot movies for fun, but generally not during air-to-air combat. "My flight commander and I would sometimes take a camera with us," claims DeBellevue, "and when we were coming off target I'd be taking pictures of the bombs going off. I'd get pretty relaxed doing this stuff, as long as nobody's shooting at you."[71]

But such was not the case on 10 May. Just as Locher and Lodge came within Sparrow range of the MiG-21, John Markle shouted on the radio, "Okay, there's a bandit . . . you got a bandit in your ten o'clock, Bob, level!"

Two MiG-19 trailers suddenly emerged from the weeds. The tables were now turned.

"*Bob, reverse right, reverse right, Bob! Reverse right!*" Markle yelled again.

Lodge, completely fixated on the target in front of him, failed to hear the warnings. Locher, who might have seen the MiG sooner if he had not been making a movie, did hear the warning, but by then it was too late. A few seconds after Markle's warning, Lodge launched the Sparrow and then "One or two seconds later, wham! We were hit. I looked and saw the MiG [the MiG-21 in front of them] separating away. I thought we had midaired because that was exactly my interpretation of how a collision would feel. We both said 'Oh shit!' but my 'Oh shit!' was because the guy in front was getting away."[72] One of the other pilots described the scene like an aerial firing squad: "The MiG-19s looked like they were flying formation on him, just hosing the hell out of him."[73]

"The next thing I knew," recalls Roger Locher, "we were decelerating—I think the right engine had exploded. We ended up doing some really hard yaws to the right."[74] The aircraft then flipped over and went into an inverted spin. To keep the fumes out of his lungs, Locher set his mask to full oxygen, and then took a quick look at the altimeter. "'Hey, Bob,'" he said, "'we're passing eight thousand feet. It's getting awful hot back here, I'm going to have to get out.' Bob looked over his right shoulder and said, 'Why don't you eject then?'"[75] Locher went out upside down. "I don't remember seeing anything, but I sure remember hearing stuff. I could hear the wind blast, and *whacko:* right when the parachute opened I could see that the parachute was rotating just about every three seconds in a three-sixty rotation. Two MiG-19s went past, looked like they were pulling up; I thought maybe they were going to come around and hose me down. I did a four-line cut to stabilize my chute so it would go straight, instead of going in a circle."[76] Locher crashed through forty-foot-high jungle trees and finally landed on the ground. Five seconds before, he was a proud F-4 navigator on the verge of getting his fourth kill; now he was a hunted animal on the verge of being captured and forced to spend the remainder of the war in the Hanoi Hilton.

While Locher was floating down in his parachute the other members of Oyster Flight searched the area for any signs that the two airmen might still be alive. "We watched the F-4 go down," Tommy Feezel said, "but all we could see was a black pall of smoke. We kept looking for chutes but we didn't see any."[77] Neither Feezel nor anyone else in Oyster Flight saw Locher's parachute. Locher, once on the ground, looked for Lodge's chute through the trees but did not see it. He thought of going down to the crash site to search for his friend's remains but quickly realized that it would be pointless. Lodge's F-4 "burned for a long time and may have been spread out over a wide area in the jungle."

Final confirmation of Major Robert Lodge's death would not reach Roger Locher until 1977. That year, Lodge's parents placed a call to Roger Locher to let him know that the Central Identification Laboratory at Hickam AFB, Hawaii, had positively identified Lodge in a shipment of MIA remains turned over to the U.S. government by the Vietnamese. "I did not ask his parents what kind of shape his remains were in, nor did I request a report for the Central Lab when I was stationed in Hawaii," Locher laments. "It was probably just two or three pounds of bone splinters, not a whole lot more."[78]

Steve Ritchie, in an oral history recorded shortly after the event, pointed out that target fixation could be a problem even for an experienced crew like Locher and Lodge. "They let MiG-itis get them shot down. Also, Rog wasn't paying attention in the backseat. He was taking movies when he should have been looking around."[79] DeBellevue was a bit less critical. "You have to realize that we were asking people to go into the most heavily defended area in the world every day, and we were also telling them that if they get into a tight spot, they're on their own. . . . So when you start doing that you realize that your only survival is because of you. After so many missions you get kind of cavalier about it."[80]

Whether one defines it as a cavalier attitude or "MiG-itis," Roger Locher and Bob Lodge had clearly become so absorbed in the killing process on 10 May that they lost track of reality: their basic survival instincts were eclipsed by blood lust. Lodge, in particular, had no other life to live, no wife, no child, not even a girlfriend or a hobby. Killing was his only passion.

Picking Up the Pieces

Steve Ritchie was different from Bob Lodge; where Lodge's obsession with flying and fighting was all-encompassing and total, Ritchie's was more balanced. As much as he wanted to achieve excellence in the air, Ritchie enjoyed life just enough to prevent his warrior ethos from completely overwhelming his basic instinct to stay alive. Just two days before 10 May, he could have gotten a kill but chose instead to disengage rather than "push a bad position." On this day, soon after Lodge got his first kill, Mike Cooper got behind the second MiG in the element and unloaded all of his AIM-7s and AIM-4s at the bogey. Astonishingly, he missed. Cooper then cleared Ritchie to move in and take a shot. Ritchie, low on fuel, and with a MiG chasing him about a mile and a half to his rear, opted to retreat rather than fight. "I made a decision to disengage instead of trying to achieve firing parameters on the MiG that was in my front quarter . . . I was out of fuel and I had a MiG in my six o'clock. That was not the time to press and try to get a MiG at twelve o'clock. In fact, two days later, that killed Bob Lodge."[81]

With Bob Lodge and Roger Locher now MIA, Steve Ritchie and Chuck DeBellevue all of a sudden became the Air Force's most experienced F-4 team at Udorn. "When they got shot down," claims DeBellevue, "we were left without anybody who could lead the missions up north." Colonel Charlie Gabriel, the wing commander, looked at all the pilots in the wing and realized that Ritchie was his best stick. Ritchie, in turn, asked DeBellevue to fly permanently as his backseater. "We'd flown together a couple of times," Chuck says, "enough times to know each other and had liked the way each other handled things, so we got teamed up after that."[82] This was an extraordinarily unique situation: two captains leading flights in a wing, commanding numerous majors and lieutenant colonels. All of the U.S. Air Force's hopes of getting an ace in Vietnam now rested on two young blond men from America's rural South.

None of this had sunk in yet. Steve Ritchie's only concern on the night of 10 May was with his downed buddies, Bob Lodge and Roger Locher. While flying back to Udorn, Ritchie radioed ahead a code to alert the base to the loss. That night, he carefully went over the mission tapes with Chuck DeBellevue and Patty Schneider. When a pilot ejected, he could activate a radio beacon carried with him in his flight suit to let other members of his flight know his location for rescue purposes. No one in Oyster Flight had heard a beeper from Locher, but a tape from Harlow Flight revealed a weak 30-second beeper transmission on the Guard frequency (a channel reserved for emergency transmissions). The transmission had occurred at 1006, twenty-two minutes after Oyster Lead went down, and eight minutes before Harlow lost one of its F-4s. Patty Schneider knew this beeper had to be Roger's. The two had never dated, but Roger Locher was her best buddy. "We always seemed to end up together at parties and he would usually walk me to my barracks. When I had good or bad news from home he was the first one I told. I decided when he came back he wasn't going to get away from me again."[83]

It would be a long wait. For 22 days, nothing was heard from Locher. Patty remembered crying every day but never at work. After work she would visit Chuck DeBellevue, and often cry on his shoulder. Chuck didn't mind. "It was tough going back to the room," he said. "I was his summary courts officer, had to go through all of his stuff, and I kept putting that off and putting it off, I didn't even want to do that." At one point Patty told him to just leave Roger's stuff in his locker, but Chuck, a consummate professional, patiently sifted through his friend's personal belongings, looking carefully for anything that might be embarrassing. "As it turned out I didn't have to worry about it . . . he had a layaway ticket for a turntable or tape deck or something, the payment was due on it, so I had to go take that off layaway for him, talk to the PX about it." Roger Locher had left no bills, no diary, no secret love notes, no *Playboy* magazines, nothing.

———————

As soon as Locher crashed through the trees, he unharnessed his parachute and tried to release his survival pack from his chute harness, but his sluggish fingers slowed his efforts. "There are two little straps that say 'Pull' on them, to remove the rubber survival bag, but I could not make it work. And the harder I tried the worse it got."[84] He abandoned these efforts and began to move up a wooded hillside. His intent was to make like a coyote and do a large circle around the crash site, in an attempt to throw off any trackers. But after five minutes, his body began to act strangely. He could hardly breathe, he felt dizzy, and he started to see spots in his eyes. "That's when I realized, 'Hey, this is shock, man!' So I laid down and put my feet higher than my head and sucked air for about five minutes. When I got my breath back, I sat up and drank a pint bottle of water; I had two of those on me."[85] Good Air Force survival training enabled him to recover quickly from this potentially life-threatening condition and continue with his evasion.

It was during his time in shock that Locher had transmitted his beacon signal to Harlow flight. He thought that he had said, "Oyster-1 Bravo, I'm on the ground, I'm all right," but in truth he broadcast nothing: he forgot to press the mike button on the radio, and only a beacon signal went through, the one Patty Schneider was pinning her hopes on. Locher would not achieve contact with rescue forces for 22 days, and he did not make much effort to do so; he believed that he was too deep in enemy territory for a successful rescue. His plan, instead, was to march 90 miles west, cross the Red River, and then attempt to contact rescue forces. The terrain he needed to cross, he knew, consisted of rice fields and small villages, not a jungle ridge like the one he was on.

His first contact with hostile force came only hours after touchdown. At 1200, a group of soldiers came up the hillside, firing their AK-47s and yelling as they went. From his hunting experience, Locher knew that they were trying to flush him out of hiding like a scared pheasant, so he covered himself with brush and laid still, trying not to get "goosey." He told himself, "Breathe shallow. Don't give yourself away."[86] Locher sat and sweated for six hours in this position before he finally felt safe enough to move.

The next day, he again had a close call, this time with local village kids. They came within thirty feet of him but he did not budge, nor did he try to shoot any of them with his .38 revolver. "You don't kill kids or civilians no matter what country you're in," said Locher later, "because villagers will kill you on the spot for doing that."[87]

On the third day, Roger Locher hit an emotional low point. Rain-soaked and with leeches sucking blood out of his neck, he pondered his predicament. "I haven't moved more than a mile in three days. But I have escaped them so far."[88] That day, he turned on his radio and listened to the words of a downed pilot several miles to the south. The pilot ordered his friends to strafe him; he had decided to die rather than face capture. "I thought if they couldn't be rescued from there, what chance would I have? That was a dark time, my lowest psychological point."[89] To boost his spirits, Locher would think about his family and friends in Kansas. "You can be your own worse enemy, you feel so bad for yourself, 'Oh, woe is me, I'm in a bad spot, geez.' I think you could talk yourself into not waking up. And occasionally I'd find myself in a position where I'd have to fire myself back up, think about something positive."[90]

Locher knew he would probably starve to death before getting far enough west for a rescue. He had landed between growing seasons, so besides the two Pillsbury Space Sticks in his flight suit, and "water sandwiches" he obtained from jungle streams, he found very little food. During the twenty-three days he spent on the ground, he only ate three pounds of food: jungle fruit, plantains, and weeds. He could have shot gray squirrels but he was afraid of catching parasites from uncooked meat, and he could not risk making a fire. His most memorable meal consisted of taro root, a potato-like tuber with razor-sharp starch molecules that will slice your throat up unless the root is properly cooked. "I thought this ought to be like a raw potato, slice it and eat it, but that almost did me in. It got my tongue swollen up, and I had to put my fingers down my throat to keep from suffocating."[91]

Locher's routine consisted of hiding during most of the day, sleeping at night, and traveling during the dawn and dusk hours. He stayed away from trails and slept on the ground, using mosquito netting to protect his face from bugs. With every passing day, he found it more and more difficult to make headway. In 12 days he put only seven miles between himself and the crash site. He rubbed his butt and felt only bones. On the twentieth day, still on the ridgeline, he concluded, "Either I starve to death here, or I get down to the plain and try to steal food there."[92] The next day, he decided to make for the plain at daybreak.

As chance would have it, rain kept Roger awake most of the night and he overslept. He was upset with himself but knew it was too dangerous to proceed. He instead slept for a couple more hours, but soon awakened to the sounds of SAMs being launched from nearby Yen Bai airfield. He quickly turned on his radio and monitored the Guard channel, but heard nothing. He then risked a transmission.

"Any US aircraft—this is Oyster-Zero-One Bravo—over."

Steve Ritchie, flying with DeBellevue that day, thought, "'We don't have an Oyster call sign today,' but my backseater, Chuck DeBellevue, shouted, 'My God, that's Roger Locher!' We answered, and Roger said, 'Hey guys, I've been down here a long time. Any chance of picking me up?'"

"You bet—you bet there is," Steve radioed back.[93]

A rescue force of two HH-53 Super Jolly Green Giant helicopters, four A-1 Skyraiders ("Sandies"), and four F-4s on airborne alert were ordered by King Bird, an airborne C-130 search-and-rescue control ship, to check out the transmissions. The A-1s, propeller-driven aircraft loaded with four 20-mm cannon and 7,000 pounds of bombs, went in first to reconnoiter the area and make sure it was safe for the vulnerable helicopter force.

Given Locher's long absence, there was a strong possibility of a ruse. Every airman left the answers to four personal questions behind with Seventh Air Force intelligence for identification purposes. These questions were relayed to King Bird in real time from headquarters, Seventh Air Force in Saigon by way of the Rescue Coordination Center at Nakhon Phanom AFB in Thailand. Locher answered a question about his mother's maiden name correctly and the Sandies began to come in for a pass. But then Ron Smith, one of the A-1 pilots, suddenly saw a MiG-21. "*Get down! Get down! MiG! MiG!*" he screamed to the Jollies.[94]

The helicopters dove toward the ground just as the MiG-21 flew within 1,000 feet of them. For reasons unknown the MiG never opened fire, but this encounter caused the rescue to be aborted.

Back at Udorn, a lieutenant colonel came over to Captain Schneider's desk and said, "I think you better sit down."[95] He then told her about the radio transmission, and ordered her to start preparing the intel for a major rescue operation. With shaky knees, she listened to the tape, "to see if it was his voice and if he was under duress. We were all under the opinion that it was his natural voice and he did not seem under duress."[96]

"Myself, Woodstock, and a male intel officer from Kansas State then sat down and tried to come up with another unique question that the rescue forces could use to verify Locher's identity. The K-State guy came up with a good one: 'What's Kites?'"[97] A graduate of the sunflower state's university would certainly know of this popular bar in downtown Manhattan, Kansas.

While this young intelligence crew worked in Udorn, General Vogt, the Seventh Air Force commander in Saigon, struggled to decide what to do next. No pilot had ever been rescued from a location as deep in North Vietnam as Locher was, and a proper rescue would require 119 aircraft[98]—approximately the same number of planes used on 10 May to bomb the Paul Doumer bridge and the Yen Vien rail yard—and would force the cancellation of a major strike planned on 2 June against Hanoi. Failure could very well mean the end of General Vogt's career, not to mention the loss of numerous lives and aircraft. "I had to decide whether we should risk the loss of maybe half a dozen airplanes and crews just to get one man out," he recalled. "Finally I said to myself, god damn it, the one thing that keeps our boys motivated is the certain belief that if they go down, we will do absolutely everything we can to get them out. If that is ever in doubt, morale would tumble. This was my major consideration. So I took that on myself. I didn't ask for anybody's permission, I just said, 'Go do it!'"[99]

Vogt's plan called for a major fighter strike against Yen Bai airfield to suppress the North Vietnamese MiGs while the Sandies and Jolly Greens went in-country to snatch Locher. The low-altitude on-scene commander was Captain Ron Smith. Flying Sandy 1, Smith led the force to a prebriefed point just over the mountains to the southwest of Locher's location. Smith and Sandy 2 then continued to the evacuation area.

When Locher came up on the radio, Smith said, "Hey Oyster, I got a question for you and you'd better answer it right. What's Kites?"[100]

"It's a place to drink beer," Locher radioed back.

"What?" shouted Smith.

"It's a place to drink beer."

"You sound like the guy we're looking for."

"You're damn right I am!" Locher shot back.

Locher then revealed his position to the rescue force with a small strobe light. Four F-4s rolled in and dropped loads of bombs on the south end of

Yen Bai, and another four bombed several anti-aircraft batteries in the area. Sandy 1 yelled "Tally-ho!" and two A-1s laid a smoke screen between Roger Locher and the Red River valley. One of the Jolly Greens then hovered 50 feet above Locher and dropped a jungle penetrator down to him. Designed to cut through jungle, the penetrator looked like a torpedo with three fold-out shovels or "spades." Locher sat down on one of these spades and pulled a safety strap over his upper body. The helicopter then drew Locher up on the cable. The whole process to get Locher up to the helicopter's door took only two minutes. A monstrous parajumper (PJ) then hauled Locher in and threw him on the floor of the chopper, then another PJ threw him a coffee can filled with cookies. With tears dripping down his face and a broad grin, Locher began eating the cookies, then, a few moments later, began stuffing some in his radio pouch. "I didn't think we were going to get out of North Vietnam without getting shot down again and I'd be darned if I was going to get shot down twice with nothing to eat."[101]

While Locher munched cookies, Captain Dale Stovall turned the helicopter around and flew over the ridgeline back to Udorn. As this 27-year-old pilot rounded the ridge, he almost ran straight into a railroad. A 14-car-train, its driver seeing the smoke at Yen Bai, had stopped. "Two cars had sandbagged gun positions, similar to what you see in World War Two movies," explains Stovall.[102] Fortunately for him, the gunners were aiming in the wrong direction and could not get their guns turned around in time to take him out. "It was like a kids' parade. We [the Sandies and the two Jollies] went right over them and pressed on at low level across the valley."[103]

Three hours later the flight touched down at Udorn. The A-1s made a low-level victory pass over the field and then landed, followed by the helicopters, which popped red smoke markers to announce their triumphant return. General Vogt himself flew in from Saigon to greet Locher and the rescue crew. Amid the throngs of cheering airmen who watched the thin, pale, bearded Roger Locher emerge from the Jolly stood Captain Patty Schneider. "I hung back when everybody greeted him and then some of my buddies pushed me up to hug him," she said. "I didn't feel like I had a right to hug him because we weren't dating or anything. And then some of my buddies pushed me into the ambulance with him."[104]

Locher didn't know then that Schneider was in love with him. "That's one of the things I sure as hell didn't know about. I guess I started figuring that out, because in her spare time she was hanging out at the hospital, you know, and bringing me crackers, and I gave her some money to go buy a portable radio so I could hear some music because there was nothing going on in the hospital and then I guess we kind of hit it off after that."[105]

The night of the rescue, the flight surgeons allowed him to go to the Officers' Club at 1900 for thirty minutes. The word went out and officers from across the base packed the club. Locher came in a new man, washed and shaved and wearing a Triple Nickel party suit. Designed by local Thai tailors for partying, these suits sported squadron insignia and a few humorous patches such as the famous "Yankee Air Pirate" patch.

Locher's friend Steve Ritchie remembers the evening. "Roger walked through the door to applause that went on for twenty minutes. Hands were shaken. Tears were shed. Camaraderie and love bound us together that morning. Enormous resources and many lives had been risked."[106] Ritchie could exhibit tremendous focus and commitment while chasing MiGs, but no event gave him more satisfaction than the rescue of a fellow American pilot. As one of the Jolly Green pilots put it, "The reason we did so much for those guys was because they were there to have it done for them. We all hoped that if the role was reversed that he would do for us what we were trying to do for him. I think that is about all there is to that."[107]

Paula Flight

While Roger Locher's personal war ended on June 2, Steve Ritchie and Chuck DeBellevue's would continue for many more months. Just two days before Ritchie, with Lawrence Pettit in the backseat, managed to get behind an element of MiG-21s and fire four Sparrows at the trailing MiG. The first one corkscrewed to the right, the second two detonated early, but the last one found its mark.[108] Ritchie now had two kills and was well on his way to becoming America's first Air Force ace in Vietnam.

Rather than spending his off hours relaxing, Ritchie instead spent his time getting to know the support personnel who would prove essential to his future success. After experiencing poor performance from his Sparrow missiles, he spent several days in the missile shop learning the ins and outs of the AIM-7E2 system. Ritchie also spent time in the radar shop and with the load crews. Not only did he learn more about his equipment, he also developed a first-name working relationship with his crews, a relationship strong enough for him to insist that his missiles get a complete check-up after every ten flights. This procedure presented the work crews with hours of extra work, but as Ritchie put it, "they were happy to do the work because they knew what it meant to our success."[109] Steve Ritchie, in short, took a special interest in his crew, and they in turn, worked harder than ever to give him a winning edge.

Another group of individuals that Ritchie got to know were the airborne controllers who flew Disco, the airborne EC-121 based at Korat. Ritchie made a point of visiting these men and getting to know them face to face. He also phoned them and their Navy counterparts on the Red Crown radar ship on the secure telephone the morning before every mission to go over critical details such as names and call signs. He spent his days at Udorn like a quarterback, constantly checking in with all his teammates to make sure that everyone understood the plays. He also stayed away from booze and women during these operational periods. As his teammate Chuck DeBellevue put it, "If you wanted to sit by the pool, you probably weren't flying with us. And if you drank a lot, you definitely weren't flying with us."[110]

Steve Ritchie certainly knew how to play hard, but he could work as hard as his classmate Bob Lodge when necessary. Ritchie would never admit it, but Lodge's death changed him; it not only gave him more responsibility within the wing, it forced him to grow. The Air Force needed an ace in 1972 and he appeared to be its best hope for that distinction; he could not afford to screw up. But he would not transform himself into an ascetic like Lodge to achieve this status. Rather, he would work as hard as possible while flying missions, but would continue to frequent steam baths and enjoy a few beers in the Officers' Club when off duty. Steve Ritchie, in short, understood the importance of creating a sense of balance in life—a critical ingredient of his success that may help explain why he became the Air Force's only pilot ace in the Vietnam war and why his colleague Bob Lodge never made it.

On 8 July, all of Ritchie's hard work paid off. For the first six days of July 1972, bad weather had prevented him from flying, so he was anxious on the eighth to get back in the air and start "swinging the golf clubs." His flight rose at 0300 in the morning to CAP a strike force headed for Hanoi. About 60 miles from Bullseye (Hanoi), one of the chaff escorts* took an Atoll missile in the wing during a hit-and-run MiG attack on the strike force. The F-4 pilot then broke every rule in the book by transmitting on the Guard frequency his position, heading, altitude, and battle damage. Ritchie, leading a flight comprised of junior lieutenants, immediately changed direction

---

*These planes drop strips of tin foil to jam North Vietnamese radar.

and headed towards the crippled aircraft at 5,000 feet. As the flight came within 30 miles of Bullseye, a call suddenly came in from Disco.

On that day, Ritchie's call sign was Paula, but rather than saying, "Paula-one, this is Disco-Two-Three, you have Blue Bandits [MiG-21s] bearing three-five-oh, suggest you come left to a heading of two-nine-five," the controller simply said, "Steve, they're two miles north of you."[111] This controller, having spoken to Ritchie earlier that morning, felt comfortable enough with the pilot to break conventional radio procedures and go with a shortened transmission. The two seconds saved by this action probably earned Ritchie his third MiG kill.

After hearing the transmission, Ritchie "made an immediate left turn to a heading of north, and picked up a MiG-21 at ten o'clock. If I had stayed on an easterly heading just a few more seconds, we probably would not have seen the MiG."[112] The MiG-21 glistened in the sun—a perfect target, or so it seemed. But Ritchie knew that MiGs generally flew in pairs and refused to be baited by the trap. Instead, he blew his wing fuel tanks, went to full afterburner, and passed the MiG head on flying just below Mach 1.[113] Having practiced this maneuver dozens of times at Nellis, he felt confident he had made the right move. "I rolled level, pushed the nose down and waited. Sure enough, the second MiG was about 6,000 feet in trail," ready to pounce upon any pilot stupid enough to take on the lead plane. The North Vietnamese were willing to sacrifice their lead plane to get a shot at the rear quarter of an F-4—a sacrifice the United States Air Force would never make.

As Ritchie passed the trailing MiG, he did a hard 6.5-G slicing turn into the hostile plane. The MiG tried to avoid him by turning right, and ended up on his front quarter—not an optimum position for a Sparrow kill. To get to the rear quarter of the MiG, Ritchie then barrel-rolled left to his five-o'clock position at about 6,000 feet, roughly minimum range for a Sparrow shot. Looking into the small circular gunsight that projected onto his front windscreen, he put the target into the sight, hit the auto-acquisition switch, got an immediate lock-on, and patiently waited four seconds to squeeze the trigger.

"A-thousand-one, A-thousand-two, A-thousand-three, A-thousand-four," he counted while pulling his aircraft in a 4-G turn—the maximum Gs allowed for a successful Sparrow launch. Two quick squeezes of the trigger, and then another 1.5 seconds' wait until the first missile left its well. During that brief delay, over 90 electronic and pneumatic steps had to take place in sequence before the missiles fired. The lead missile exploded in the center of the MiG's fuselage, causing the aircraft to erupt in a massive fireball right in front of Ritchie's windscreen. The second missile passed right through the fireball.

"Steve, I've got one on me!" radioed First Lieutenant Tommy Feezel as Ritchie pulled his F-4E over the top of the fireball. The MiGs and the F-4s were now flying in a huge circle pattern, with the lead MiG now on Feezel's (Paula 4's) tail. No problem. Ritchie selected maximum afterburner and cut right across the circle. The MiG, seeing him, tried to turn down into him. Ritchie, doing 5 Gs and 60 degrees angle off, took a hip shot at the MiG from about 3,000 feet away. "The missile appeared out in front, snaking back and forth like a Sidewinder, and seemed not to guide," he recalls. "All of a sudden the missile pulled every available G [approximately 25], made almost a ninety-degree turn, and hit the MiG dead center in the fuselage at just about missile motor burnout, which accelerated the 500-pound Sparrow to approximately 1,200 miles per hour above launch velocity."[114]

"*Splash two!*" yelled Ritchie. His flight flew two victory rolls (one for each victory) over Udorn that afternoon, and then had a "party that night you would have enjoyed."[115] Other than the Locher rescue, this was the greatest mission of Steve Ritchie's career, and one of the Air Force's few bright moments of the Vietnam War. As Ritchie put it, "Virtually everything went right." Airborne early warning and control came just at the right moment; the missile systems worked perfectly; and his training and preparation prevented him from falling into the same emotional trap that killed Lodge.

———————

Steve Ritchie's last MiG kill took place on August 28, 1972. Though not as spectacular as the Paula 1 kill, the engagement clearly reveals the teamwork and coordination involved in a successful kill—something that Ritchie always emphasized in interviews about his exploits. This interaction can be seen in the radio transmissions between Ritchie (Buick 1a) and DeBellevue (Buick 1b), Captain John Madden (Buick 3), Buick 4, Red Crown (the Navy radar controller on a picket ship in the Tonkin Gulf), and the other F-4 flights in the air that day, Olds and Vegas Flights.

RED CROWN: *Buick, Bandits 240/30 Bullseye.* (MiGs are at 240 degrees and 30 miles from Hanoi.)

RITCHIE TO RED CROWN: *Copy 240 at 30.*

RITCHIE TO DEBELLEVUE [intercom]: *What in the hell are they doing down there?*

DEBELLEVUE [intercom]: *What's our fuel?*

RITCHIE [intercom]: *11.2 (11,200 pounds).*

DEBELLEVUE [intercom]: *Okay.*

DEBELLEVUE [intercom]: *I've got some friendlies and some MiGs. The MiGs are behind the friendlies right now. (Chuck can differentiate between the two types of aircraft because the identification friend or foe transponder (IFF) of the friendly aircraft makes these aircraft appear differently on his radar scope.)*

RITCHIE TO FRIENDLY AIRCRAFT: *Buick shows MiGs 10 miles behind friendlies.*

RITCHIE TO FRIENDLY AIRCRAFT: *Stand by for position.*

OLDS FLIGHT LEADER: *Olds 90 right. (Olds flight is also turning toward the MiGs.)*

RED CROWN: *This is Red Crown. Bandits at 253/37, Bullseye.*

RITCHIE TO RED CROWN: *Copy that.*

RITCHIE [intercom]: *Bandits on the nose.*

DEBELLEVUE [intercom]: *It looks like two of them at least.*

RITCHIE [to other members of his Buick flight]: *Buick Flight, fuel check.*

OLDS FLIGHT LEAD: *Olds, 90 (degrees) left.*

RED CROWN: *This is Red Crown. Bandits 252/51, Bullseye.*

JOHN MADDEN IN BUICK 3, RITCHIE'S WINGMAN: *Buick four, this is three. Can you read me? We've got bogeys off to the left at ten o'clock, way out.*

BUICK 4: *Tally.*

RED CROWN: *This is Red Crown. Bandits 252/57, Bullseye.*

DEBELLEVUE [intercom]: *Roger, I've got 'em.*

RITCHIE [intercom]: *I can't believe we're not getting a SAM shot at us.*

DEBELLEVUE [intercom]: *Me either.*

DEBELLEVUE [intercom]: *Bandits. We're running in.*

DEBELLEVUE [intercom]: *He's at one o'clock right now. (Buick flight is now converging on the MiGs head on.)*

RITCHIE [intercom]: *Keep giving it to me, Chuck.*

DEBELLEVUE *Okay.*

RITCHIE TO THE AIRBORNE USAF RADAR AIRCRAFT, CODE-NAMED DISCO: *Disco, do you have an altitude on them? (Ritchie knows the approximate azimuth of the MiGs from DeBellevue but he needs an altitude, a speed, and a range to complete his fire solution.)*

DEBELLEVUE [intercom]: *Looks like the MiGs are at 160° from us. (Steve now has an exact azimuth.)*

RED CROWN: *This is Red Crown. Bandits 250/67, Bullseye.*

DEBELLEVUE [intercom]: *One o'clock—two of them at least.*

RED CROWN: *Vegas, they are 255/62 Bullseye.*

VEGAS FLIGHT LEAD: *Roger.*

DEBELLEVUE [intercom]: *Two sets look like . . . May be 4 MiGs.*

DISCO: *Vegas, Disco. They are 248 for 53.*

RITCHIE TO DISCO: *Say altitude of MiGs.*

DISCO: *Buick, they are 266 for 32. Heading 080. Speed. 7 (Mach).*

RITCHIE: *Say their altitude.*

DEBELLEVUE [intercom]: *Twenty-two miles dead ahead.*

RITCHIE TO DISCO: *Say altitude please.*

RITCHIE: *Anybody know their altitude?*

DEBELLEVUE [intercom]: *Twenty-five. We're locked. Twenty-five thousand [feet of altitude] fifteen miles dead ahead. (DeBellevue just discovered the altitude of the MiGs with his radar and informed Ritchie that he can now take a shot at any time.)*

RITCHIE [intercom]: *Buick flight, reheat. (Ritchie tells his flight to light their afterburners and climb from 15,000 to 25,000 feet to meet the MiGs.) (Pause.) We want to get a visual first. (There are too many friendly planes in the vicinity to risk a beyond-visual-range shot.)*

DEBELLEVUE [intercom]: *They are dead ahead going right to left. They're about 1130. You're in range. (Pause.) Come left a little. (Pause.) Come left a little. (Pause.) About eleven o'clock. Three and a half miles ahead. Turning left. Three miles, two and a half. They are off the scope. Hurry it up!*

RITCHIE [intercom]: *I've got 'em. I've got 'em, I got 'em! (visual)*

RITCHIE TO BUICK FLIGHT: *Buick's got a tally-ho. (Steve informs the flight that he sees the MiGs).*

DEBELLEVUE [intercom]: *Three miles—three and a half miles, two o'clock. (Ritchie and DeBellevue are now in a hard climbing turn, trying to get behind the MiG. Ritchie fires two Sparrows at this point, which miss.)*

DEBELLEVUE [intercom]: *You got min overtake. Okay, you are out of range.*

RITCHIE [intercom]: *They are at twelve o'clock straight ahead.*

DEBELLEVUE [intercom]: *You're in range. You're in range. Fire. (Ritchie fires two more Sparrows, and the last one finds its mark.)*

RITCHIE [intercom]: *He's conning way high. (The MiG is making a contrail.)*

RITCHIE TO BUICK FLIGHT: *Splash! I got him! Splash!*

DEBELLEVUE [intercom]: *Good show, Steve!*[116]

"I don't think the MiG pilot ever saw us," Steve Ritchie says.[117]

When tail number 463, the plane Ritchie had flown almost exclusively for the past six weeks, touched down his crew chief, Chief Sergeant Reggie Taylor, ran up the ladder to greet him. "I think he was even more excited than I."[118] Taylor had spent hours of extra time trying to ensure that 463 was the best Tree aircraft in the theatre; he was an integral part of the team. Ritchie felt he could not have done it without Taylor's help. That plane now sits on the campus of the Air Force Academy, a symbol of excellence for the United States Air Force.

During the next couple of days, Ritchie received cables from the president, the secretary of defense, the secretary of the Air Force, and numerous officials around the globe. However, the one he most cherished came from Brigadier General Robin Olds, the former Eighth Wing commander and until that moment, the Air Force's top MiG killer of the war. It read:

> Foxtrot Bravo. Absolutely Sierra Hotel, Tiger. I've been pulling for you since May. Thousands of blue-suiters around the world are standing taller—*Robins Olds*.[119]

"That said it all. It was the greatest message I ever received from anyone." This is what motivated a man like Ritchie to excel as a warrior—not the fanfare, not the fame, but acceptance into a unique brotherhood of fighter pilots.

Steve Ritchie, Bob Lodge, Roger Locher, Chuck DeBellevue (who later got two more kills, making him the top ace of the war), and John Markle all belonged to this fraternity. What separated these men from the ordinary pilot who flew a hundred missions with the Nickel and never saw a MiG is not so much technology, training, or even situational awareness, but plain and simple desire. Each of these warriors wanted with everything in his heart to kill MiGs. MiG kills consumed them and became more important than women, drink, food, or sleep. Lodge and Ritchie devoted every waking hour to that goal and made it a personal crusade. Locher got so wrapped up with MiG killing that he failed to notice the advances of his future wife. Lodge did not even associate with women. Ritchie had a gorgeous girlfriend, but ignored her during his peak killing period. For these men, killing absorbed all their psychological, emotional, and even sexual energy. It also hardened them. By 28 August Ritchie and DeBellevue had no trouble sneaking up behind a MiG and literally shooting him in the back; the MiG pilot never knew what hit him. DeBellevue claims he compartmentalized his emotions and could get over the death of a friend with a simple toast at the bar. Locher allowed himself to grieve over Lodge's death only after he knew he would be flying no more missions. He also got annoyed with Patty for grieving over *him* while he was missing. These warriors had a unique ability to block out not only fear, but sadness, melancholy, and a variety of other natural human emotions. This is perhaps why they felt so attached to the technology they flew, because in essence they began to see themselves as nothing but an extension of that technology, as the central processing unit for a complex weapons-delivery system.

An F-105 backseater, Tom Wilson, once said that he became so hardened by the Vietnam experience that it got to the point where he could no longer grieve over the loss of friends. Years later in 1973, while he was shopping at a strip mall in Fort Worth, Texas, an announcement went out over the public-address system that the POWs had been released. Wilson fell to his knees and started to cry. For him, it had taken two years to begin to strip away the emotional armor of war and start to heal emotionally. For other warriors, such healing would never come.

CONCLUSION

We Few, We Happy Few

Most fast-mover pilots were not required by their services to be in Vietnam; nevertheless, some volunteered for two or even three tours. Pilots like J. B. Souder thought that "getting out of the Navy did not do a goddamn thing, but by reenlisting maybe I could help do something to get those guys out of Hanoi." They participated in the war for the sake of their comrades, their units, the service, and to demonstrate their unique skills in an air-combat environment. For J. B., shot down on 27 April 1972, the worst aspect of his predicament was not so much the dread of having to spend the remainder of the war in Hanoi as being "ejected from his squadron." The unit defined an aviator's existence; that's why a good one, such as the 555th squadron in 1972 or the Eighth Wing under Olds, could make even the most oppressive war bearable.

This is not to imply that the war did not frustrate most of the aviators. Robin Olds knew that if the Air Force had had the foresight to put an internal gun in the F-4, the Eighth Wing might have killed many more MiGs than it did. Similarly, J. B. Souder knew that his last battle might have gone the other way if his F-4 had been equipped with a newer pulse-Doppler radar set. With a standard radar, one needs to be at coaltitude or better yet, below altitude, to spot a MiG, but with a Doppler one can pick out a low-flying moving target even through ground clutter. But things often worked out that way in Vietnam. America could produce state-of-the-art technology or intelligence, but often could not employ it effectively. It would take another 19 years for the armed services to develop an effective doctrine to exploit the Vietnam War technology, such as smart bombs, look-down/shoot-down capability, airborne command and control, and beyond-visual-range missiles, to their full potential. In the meantime, opportunities were missed and U.S. planes shot down due primarily to mismanagement—especially at the highest command levels but occasionally even at low levels. Even Robin Olds sometimes failed to employ technology properly, as his many missed missile shots during Operation Bolo demonstrate. It would take a new generation of young officers, like Steve Ritchie and Bob Lodge, to fully harness the awesome capability of the F-4—and even these men had to fight tremendous bureaucratic inertia to bring it all together. It is therefore no surprise that the Vietnam War didn't produce a single ace until 1972 and that three out of five of these aces were weapons-systems operators, well versed in technology, rather than pilots.

Fatigue was another critical factor, affecting even the best pilots and WSOs including John Nichols and Roger Locher. It is no wonder that so many pilots sought emotional release through prostitutes or drink. They needed a release from the war short of leaving their squadrons, because quitting simply was not an option for the majority of aviators. J. B. Souder remembered vividly a confrontation between himself and an antiwar demonstrator outside the gate of Alameda Naval Air Station. "Peace, man," the protester implored. "Yeah, man, peace. No one wants it more than me." But neither J. B. nor most others dropped out and joined the antiwar movement, or even dropped out to run a bar or sell used cars. Instead, they flew and fought on. Many went further and "hung it out" for their units. As the pilot in the bar told Ed Rasimus, "There are a lot of worse things than dying. Living with dishonor is one of them." That's one reason why the majority of aviators continued to resist the enemy even when in captivity: honor and respect for the unit and pride in being officers.

Another reason why some aviators fought hard without complaint is that jet combat, especially against other jets, turned out to provide quite a rush. Men like Robin Olds actually enjoyed the thrill of the hunt and—yes—the kill. Call it the "adrenaline rush," or "hubcap thievery"; most of these men found a degree of pleasure in combat. That's why Ed Rasimus enlisted for a second tour. That's why Bob Lodge and Roger Locher became so drunk with killing that they lost their perspective and got shot down. That's why Roger Sheets could ignite the passions of his Vultures with the simple line, "Gentlemen, *let's go out and kill something!*" That's one reason why, in the final analysis, "Vietnam was the best war we had." A "good war"?

Certainly not, but a war nonetheless. As Robin Olds put it so well, "Remember, for those truly involved in war, civilians and soldiers alike, emotions run deep. You hurt and you hate." Like a powerful drug, combat was difficult for pilots to quit, especially when rotation policies or pilot shortages made it easy for them *not* to do so.

However, it was not simply the addictive effect of combat which led these men to conclude that this war, viewed by most American civilians and military as a tragedy, was one of the most positive experiences of their lives. Very few aviators "gave a damn" about the fate of South Vietnam or the rise of communism in Southeast Asia. In fact, most felt that nothing over there was "worth one American life." But that's not why these men fought. "Shitty as it was," the Vietnam War offered fast movers the best available opportunity to test their unique skills, live up to their reputations as Naval, Air Force, and Marine aviators, and partake in a challenging struggle with a like-minded brotherhood of comrades. Not everyone could do what these men did, nor could just anyone join their special fraternity. The "100 Missions North" patch meant so much to Ed Rasimus because it proudly proclaimed that he had stood the test of combat and performed his duty. It symbolized acceptance into the most elite community of military aviation.

The innermost circle of this club were the aces, and America has not added any pilots to the rolls of this club since 1972. In fact, a recent book by novelist Stephen Coonts referred to Steve Ritchie as America's "last ace."[1] In that piece, Coonts argues that modern air wars are so short and intense that America will probably never again produce a pilot ace. Whether Coonts' assertion is correct or not matters less than the notion of the ace status as the pinnacle of aviation. No aviators receive as much attention or as many accolades as aces. That's why the most important letter Steve Ritchie received after his fifth kill was not the one from President Nixon (though he was respected by Ritchie and most other aviators), but the one from Robin Olds.

War can bolster the reputation of pilots, but not without a price. Steve Ritchie lost his flight leader; John Nichols and Robin Olds, their wingmen. Others, like Charlie Carr, saw their roommates and friends become POWs. No actions embodied the special bond between aviators and their friends (a bond that many argue is stronger than marriage) more than rescue missions. That's why General Vogt stopped the war to rescue a lowly F-4 navigator. Similarly, when aviators did end up in Hanoi, they gladly risked beatings and torture to boost the morale of a fellow American. Neither

Kevin Cheney nor Max Dat (now a U.S. citizen) knew Roger Lerseth personally, but both put themselves in tremendous jeopardy to raise this man's spirits in a time of need. That was part of the fast-mover credo, and it was why these men fought so hard and took such pride in their wartime services. In a senseless war, the knowledge that your fellow aviators will go to almost any length to assist you in your need provided a motivational framework that kept the air war going. As General Vogt emphasized, "Damn it, the one thing that keeps our boys motivated is the certain belief that if they go down, we will do absolutely everything else we can to get them out."

Many historians have stressed that the American armed forces are a people's military and if the people lose faith in a war, so too will our armed forces. The air war over Vietnam offers a different conclusion. An elite group of military professionals like the fast movers will go and fight wherever they are lawfully ordered, regardless of what public opinion polls say. The challenge of war, combined with the pride of enjoying a uniquely high status within the military culture, is all the motivation they need.

ACKNOWLEDGMENTS

Check 6:

A pilot often ends a letter or an e-mail message with the closing, "Check 6." In a combat situation, this means "Look to the rear of the aircraft for MiGs." A skilled wingman always keeps a close eye on the "6" of his lead pilot. While I was writing *Fast Movers,* literally hundreds of pilots checked my 6 to ensure that what resulted was as accurate as possible. I e-mailed nearly every air-to-air combat description to actual pilots (including participants) for fact checking. I also called aviators throughout the production of the manuscript to clarify or expand on a point mentioned in an oral history. In short, I developed an excellent working relationship with the pilots I interviewed for the book, which I believe has led to a better history. However, the interpretations, analysis, and opinions expressed in this book represent those of the author alone.

It would be impossible for me to mention in this short space all the people who assisted me. Beyond the 300 pilots I actually interviewed, I communicated with hundreds more on the phone or by e-mail. A few pilots, though, deserve special mention. Robin Olds, Ed Rasimus, Roger Sheets, Charlie "Vulture" Carr, Phil "Beer Barrel" Schuyler, Bill "Cowboy" Angus, Ted Sienicki, Roger Lerseth, Jim Latham, John "Pirate" Nichols, Richard S. "Steve" Ritchie, Chuck DeBellevue, J. B. "Tomcat" Souder, Patty "P²" Schneider, Roger Locher, Cal Tax, Jerry "Devil" Houston, Tom Wilson, Jerry "Hob Nose" Hoblit, Darrel D. Whitcomb, Mark Berent, and John Markle endured multiple interviews, and searched through their private files to find documentation to support many of the stories they told on tape.

The archivists and librarians at the Air Force Historical Research Center at Maxwell AFB, Alabama, the Air Force History Support Office at Bolling AFB, DC, the National Archives and Records Center in Washington, DC, and the Naval and Marine Corps Historical Centers in the Washington (DC) Navy Yard, provided me with tremendous support in uncovering unique documentation and photographs for this book. Wayne Thompson of the Air Force History Support office also let me "raid" his files for valuable documents on the air war in Southeast Asia and allowed me to read and cite a manuscript copy of his forthcoming official history of the Air Force's war against North Vietnam, *Rebound: The Air War over North Vietnam 1966–1973.*

The following associations aided me in tracking down pilots for interviews: The Red River Valley Fighter Pilot's Association, The Tailhook Association, the Association of Naval Aviation, the Marine Corps Aviation Association, the Phantom's Lair, Marine All Weather Attack, and the Fourth Allied POW Wing.

Special thanks go out to colleagues who took time away from their own books, jobs, or dissertations to read and comment on the manuscript: Allida Black, Daniel Mortensen, Randy Papadopoulos, John Ratliff, Rachel Riedner, Ronald Spector, and Aimee Turner. Aimee Turner also helped with photography research, and Randy Papadopoulos carefully copy edited the manuscript and provided a sounding board for ideas at all stages of the enterprise. I am indeed privileged to have a colleague and friend like him.

The Free Press lived up to its reputation as being one of the finest commercial publishers of serious nonfiction in the United States. Bruce Nichols, the senior editor at the press, did not simply "quarterback" the project, but carefully edited every word I wrote. His thoughtful comments, along with those of his editorial assistant, Daniel Freedberg, helped me to transform *Fast Movers* from simply good writing to good history. Finally, a word of thanks to my agent Don Gastwirth, my colleagues at the Naval Historical Center, my friends, my wife, Darina, and my family—faithful supporters of the project from its outset.

GLOSSARY

7 and 7 Seagram's 7 Crown Whiskey and 7-Up–a popular cocktail in the 1960s and early 1970s.

A-1 The A-1 Skyraider was developed during World War II as a carrier-based dive bomber, and used by the Navy and Air Force in Vietnam as a fighter-bomber and as a rescue escort fighter-bomber or "Sandy." The advantage of the A-1 for Sandy use was its large load capacity of over 10,000 pounds of bombs or mixed ordnance (including rockets and additional cannons or machine guns), and its two 20-mm guns. The A-1 had a maximum speed of 321 mph.

A-4 The McDonnell-Douglas A-4 Skyhawk was a light attack jet powered by one Pratt & Whitney J-52 turbojet. Nicknamed the "scooter" by Navy pilots because of its small size and tremendous maneuverability, the A-4 could achieve a maximum speed of 670 mph. Armament consisted of two 20-mm cannons and 4,000 pounds of bombs.

A-6 Intruder A Navy low-level attack plane capable of delivering nuclear or conventional weapons on targets completely obscured by clouds or darkness. The A-6 had a maximum speed of 648 mph and could carry up to 18,000 pounds of bombs or external fuel tanks on five attachment points.

A-7 The Ling-Temco-Vought A-7 Corsair was a single-seat light attack aircraft. First flown in 1965, the A-7 was powered by an Allison TF-41 turbofan engine and could achieve a top speed of 693 mph. Armament consisted of one 20-mm multi-barreled cannon and up to 15,000 pounds of bombs, rockets, or missiles.

AAA Anti-aircraft artillery.

Ace A pilot or navigator who downs five enemy aircraft in aerial combat.

ACM   Air combat maneuvering.

After burner   Installed downstream from the turbine of a conventional jet engine, a device called an "after burner" can add more than one third to the power plant's normal propulsive thrust, giving added power for takeoff, during combat conditions, or where extra speed is required. This is accomplished by spraying fuel into the tail pipe where its combustion adds mass and velocity to the gases of the jet stream. This after burner is in effect a ram-jet engine, where the speed of the air stream in the tail pipe is well above that needed to make the ram-jet operate. the after burner does not inpose any additional stress on the operation of the turbo jet—a desirable quality since turbo-jet power plants are operating near the critical stress limits of the turbine components.

AIM-4 Falcon   A missile similar but inferior to the AIM-9 Sidewinder. This heat-seeking air-to-air missile was manufactured by Hughes; it was 6.5 feet long and weighed 120 lbs. The Falcon had a range of five miles.

AIM-7 Dogfight Sparrow   A radar-guided air-to-air missile. The 400 pound missile rode the radar beam of an F-4 to its target and carried a 65-pound warhead. The Sparrow had a head-on attack range of 12 miles and a 3-mile range from the rear. Its minimum range was 3,000 feet.

AIM-9 Sidewinder   An air-to-air heat-seeking missile. First developed in 1953 by the U.S. Navy, the Sidewinder has a length of 9 feet 2 inches and weighs 159 pounds. It has a range of two miles and can reach speeds of Mach 2.5.

Air Defense Command   Created in 1951, the Air Defense Command (ADC) was responsible for providing air defense for the United States. In 1954, ADC was renamed Continental Air Defense Command, and in 1957, this command again changed its name to the North American Aerospace Defense Command, better known by its acronym of NORAD.

AK-47   The AK-47 was the basic assault rifle of the North Vietnamese Army and the Viet Cong. Named after their Soviet designer, A. Kalashnikov, most of the AK-47s used in Vietnam were manufactured in China. The AK-47 fires a 7.62 mm bullet in a fully automatic mode, and holds thirty bullets. The high muzzle velocity of the weapon and the tumbling action of its bullets tend to produce large entry and exit wounds, which meant that accuracy was not a crucial issue in its operation and even the most poorly trained soldiers could use the weapon effectively. Because it was a more durable weapon in the tropical climate than the American M-16, it was considered superior to its American counterpart.

Alpha Strike   A maximum strength effort from a Navy carrier. During the Vietnam War, an Alpha strike from an *Essex*-class carrier generally consisted of 30 aircraft of various types.

Atoll   A NATO code name for a Soviet heat-seeking air-to-air missile similar to the Sidewinder. It has infrared guidance, a single-stage solid-propellant engine and a length of 110 inches.

Aviation Cadet Program Established in 1942, the Aviation Cadet Program became the primary commissioning program for Army Air Forces pilots during World War II. The program was designed to fill the wartime demand for pilots by taking enlisted airmen and civilians without college degrees and training them rapidly to be pilots and officers. The program ended in 1945, but reopened again 1947 to fill the service's Cold War demand for pilots; during this late period, applicants needed to have either two years of college or pass an educational equivalency test to get in. Terminated in 1965, Aviation Cadets produced a total of 500,000 pilots during its long history.

AWS Amphibious Warfare School

B-52 A long-range strategic bomber with a top speed of 650 mph, a payload of 70,000 pounds, and a crew of five (an aircraft commander, pilot, radar navigator, navigator, and electronic warfare officer). The B-52 Stratofortress made its first appearance over South Vietnam in 1965. The B-52, however, was not used against North Vietnam until 1972. See **Linebacker.**

"Ball"/"Meatball" A powerful light that was beamed onto a stabilized mirror and shot out over the stern of the ship by a Fresnel lens. The cone of light provided the optimum glide slope for landing aircraft. If a pilot kept his descending plane within the cone of light, he would make a safe landing. To him, the narrowing cone looked like a white spot, or "meatball." Along the top and bottom of the "ball" were rows of green datum lights. If a pilot were too high the "ball" would appear above the datum lights, or below them if he were too low.

Blue Bandits Mig-21s

Blue Chip Seventh Air Force Command Center in Saigon

BN Bomber/Navigator

Bolter When a Navy aircraft fails to catch the arresting cable on a carrier and is forced to fly off the carrier and come around for another approach, it is called a "bolter."

BOQ Bachelor Officers' Quarters

Bright Light Code name for POW rescue operations.

Buffs A nickname for the B-52 bomber. See **B-52.**

Bullseye Hanoi

BuPers U.S. Navy Bureau of Personnel—the personnel directorate of the Navy during the Vietnam War

C-119 A Fairchild twin-piston engine transport first flown in 1944. This "Flying Boxcar" could carry 62 troops or 32,000 pounds of cargo and fly 200 mph.

C-130 The C-130 Hercules was the workhorse transport aircraft during the Vietnam War. First flown in 1954, the C-130 is powered by four Allison T-56 turboprops, and can achieve a maximum level speed of 357 mph. Its crew numbers five, and it can carry either 92 troops or a payload of 35,000 lbs.

C-141   The Lockheed C-141 Starlifter is a transport powered by four turbofan engines, and has a range of 6,140 miles. First flown by the USAF in 1963, the C-141 can carry 154 troops and can fly up to 570 mph.

CAG   Carrier Air Group/Wing commander

Camp Unity   Once the civilian section of Hoa Lo (Hanoi Hilton), Camp Unity was transformed into a POW holding facility after U.S. special forces stormed an empty Son Tay in 1971 and the Vietnamese were compelled to close outlying POW camps and consolidate all POWs in Hanoi area facilities. The seven open bay rooms of Camp Unity each held 40–60 POWs in 20- by 60-foot areas.

CBU-24   A cluster bomb consisting of 500 baseball-sized bomblets

CCA   Carrier Control Approach Officer—the officer who controls the landing pattern during carrier landing operations.

Chickenshit   Petty regulations of the military

Christmas bombings   Pilot nickname for Linebacker II. See **Linebacker.**

COD   Carrier Onboard Delivery Plane. The Navy's COD is the E-2 Greyhound, the transport derivative of the E-2 Hawkeye. The C-2 has a crew of three and can carry up to 28 passengers. It is powered by two Allison T-56 turboprops, and can achieve a maximum speed of 372 mph.

Code of Conduct   The principles that members of the U.S. Armed forces are expected to measure up to in combat or captivity. The code was first promulgated by President Eisenhower in 1955; it is based on time-honored concepts and traditions that date back to the American Revolution. For POWs in the Hanoi Hilton, the most significant article was Article V. It stated that "When questioned, should I become a prisoner of war, I am bound to give only my name, rank, service number, and date of birth. I will evade answering further questions to the utmost of my ability. I will make no oral or written statements disloyal to my country and its allies or harmful to their cause."

Combat Tree   Special equipment that can track enemy aircraft by interpreting signals from a plane's identification friend or foe system. See **IFF.**

Counter   Vietnam slang for a combat sortie. After 100 missions, a pilot was sent home; hence the term "counter."

CTF-75   The cruiser task force that operated on Yankee Station with TF-77. See **TF-77** and **Yankee Station.**

Daisy Cutter   A 750-pound bomb with a fuse extender. The fuse extender caused the bomb to detonate just prior to hitting the ground, thereby increasing its blast radius.

DIA Defense Intelligence Agency

DIANE Digital Integrated Attack and Navigation Equipment. The system allowed the A-6 to attack preselected locations or targets of opportunity without the crew having to look outside the cockpit from launch to recovery. A Bomber/Navigator sat adjacent to the pilot and managed DIANE. Steering Instructions from the Navigator's systems were displayed to the pilot through a Visual Display Terminal (VDT), and all a pilot did in this mode was respond to the steering blip on his VDT. See **A-6 Intruder.**

Disco An EC-121 supporting counter-MiG operations in North Vietnam. See **EC-121.**

DMZ Demilitarized Zone—a 10-kilometer buffer zone along the Song Ben Hai River (on the 17th parallel), which divided North and South Vietnam during the Vietnam War.

EA-6B Electronic-warfare version of the A-6. Its four-man crew included a pilot and three NFOs who operated sensors and jamming equipment. See **A-6 Intruder.**

EC-121 An airborne early-warning version of the Lockheed C-121 Super Constellation. The EC-121 was powered by four Wright R-3350 propeller engines and carried a crew of 26. Its maximum speed was 368 mph, and it featured large radomes above and below its fuselage.

Echelon, in echelon A formation of planes in which the group is disposed to the right or left of the one in front.

ECM Electronic countermeasures: electric signals that jam radars.

Ejection Seat A seat that sits on rails, which can expel a pilot safely from a aircraft flying at high speed.

Essex-class carrier Especially designed 27,000-ton (standard displacement) aircraft carrier. See p. 251, note 29.

EWO Electronic Warfare Operator

F-101 The F-101 Voodoo was originally constructed as a supersonic twin-engine jet fighter, but eventually evolved into a strike aircraft as well. The Voodoo was powered by two Pratt & Whitney J-57 turbojets with **afterburners** (which see) and could reach a maximum level speed of 1,220 mph. Armament consisted of four 20-mm cannon and one Mark 7, one Mark 28, and one Mark 43 nuclear bomb.

F-104 Designed as an air-superiority fighter capable of operating from forward airfields and climbing rapidly from the ground to engage in air-to-air combat, a Lockheed F-104 Starfighter prototype first flew in 1952. The plane was powered by one General Electric J-79 afterburning turbojet and could achieve a maximum level speed of Mach 2.2. Armament consisted of one 20-mm Vulcan cannon and up to 4,000 lbs of weapons, including Sidewinder and Sparrow missiles.

F-105 The Republic F-105 Thunderchief was developed as a single-seat supersonic strike fighter capable of delivering nuclear weapons, but became famous for its role as a conventional fighter-bomber in Vietnam. The F-105 was powered by a Pratt & Whitney J-75 afterburning turbojet and could achieve a maximum level speed of 1,385 mph. Typical armament consisted of one General Electric M-61 Vulcan automatic multibarrel 20-mm gun, an AIM-9 Sidewinder missile, and sixteen 750-lb bombs.

F-111 The General Dynamics F-111 is a two-seat, all-weather fighter-bomber. First flown in 1964, the F-111 has a top speed of 2.5 Mach and can carry up to a total offensive load of 35,000 pounds.

F-4 Phantom The leading all-purpose U.S. fighter of the 1960s and early 1970s. USAF, Navy, and Marine Corps Phantom IIs achieved 277 air-to-air combat victories in Vietnam. The two-engine turbojet could achieve a maximum level speed of 1,500 mph and its armament consisted of four AIM-7 Sparrow semiactive radar homing air-to-air missiles in semirecessed slots in the fuselage belly, plus two to four AIM-9 Sidewinder infrared homing air-to-air missiles, which were carried under the wings on the inboard pylons. A total offensive load of up to 16,000 pounds could be carried on the centerline and four underwing hardpoints.

F-8 The Vought F-8 Crusader was the last Navy fighter developed by the Chance Vought Corporation before it was absorbed into Ling-Temco-Vought. The F-8 was designed to be a supersonic air-superiority fighter for the Navy; it first flew in 1952. Powered by a Pratt & Whitney J-57 Turbojet, the F-8 could achieve a maximum level speed of 1,133 mph. Armament consisted of four 20-mm cannon and up to four Sidewinder missiles or up to 5,000 pounds of bombs.

F-80/P-80 The Lockeed F-80 Shooting Star was the first operational American jet fighter. Designed in just 143 days in 1944, the F-80 was powered by a single Allison J-33A-23 turbojet and had a maximum level speed of 580 mph. Armament consisted of six 50-caliber machine guns plus up to 2,000 pounds of bombs. The F-80 did not see combat in World War II but was used extensively by the Air Force as a fighter-bomber in Korea.

F-86 The North American F-86 Sabrejet was the first swept-wing transsonic jet to be built. The F-86A first flew in 1948 and achieved a maximum speed of 671 mph in level flight. Armament consisted of six 50-caliber machine guns.

F-9 The Grumman F-9F Panther was the Navy's main jet fighter during the Korean War. Made famous by the film *The Bridges at Toko-Ri* (1955), it was powered by a Pratt & Whitney J-48 turbojet, and had a top speed of 579 mph. Armament consisted of four 20-mm cannons.

FAC Forward Air Controller/Forward Air Control aircraft. A person or aircraft that directs other aircraft to targets. In Vietnam, most FACs were slow-moving, propeller-driven aircraft such as the OV-10 Bronco. However in a high-threat zone a fast mover or fast FAC such as an F-4 might be employed in such a role. See **OV-10**.

Fansong   NATO code-name for the acquisition and fire-control radar of North Vietnam's SA-2 Guideline SAM. See **SAM.**

Fast Mover   A term used to describe jet fighters and attack aircraft during the Vietnam War. A slow mover, by comparison, was a propeller-driven plane or a helicopter.

FastFAC   See **FAC.**

Feet Wet   Fighter direction brevity code indicating that a plane has left land ("feet dry") and is now over water.

Finger 4   Standard four-plane Air Force formation, which resembles the four fingers of a hand

Firecan   The NATO code name for a Soviet E-band anti-aircraft-artillery fire-control radar

Flak   (1)Explosive fired from anti-aircraft cannons; (2) An anti-aircraft cannon. The term was originally an acronym of the German word *Fliegerabwehrkanone* or anti-aircraft cannon.

Flameout   The extinguishing of the flame in a jet engine

FNG   Fucking New Guy; A POW captured after the death of Ho Chi Minh on 3 September 1969.

FOG   Fucking Old Guy; A POW captured before the death of Ho Chi Minh on 3 September 1969.

Fox 2   U.S. code for a Sidewinder launch

FW-190   One of the most advanced mass-produced fighters of World War II, the German Focke-Wulf 190 was extremely small, yet it had an extremely powerful, 1,600 hp BMW 901 C engine with a maximum speed of 408 mph. Early FW 190A-1 fighters had four 7.92-mm guns. The A-2 had two MG 151/20 cannons and the A-3 had two 20-mm and two MG-151/20 cannons.

GIB   Guy in the back—a slang term for a WSO or RIO

Gloster Meteor   The first British mass-produced jet fighter, the Meteor was the only Allied jet to see combat in World War II. The aircraft was powered by two Rolls-Royce turbojets and had a maximum level speed of 592 mph. Armament consisted of four Hispano 20-mm cannon.

G-Suit   Chaps that fit around the legs and a stomach bladder. When a pilot pulled Gs, the suit filled with air and prevented blood from pooling in the lower extremities of the body.

Guard   A radio channel reserved for emergency situations

Hanoi Hilton   Hoa Lo Prison in Hanoi

Hard points　attachments on an aircraft for hanging munitions

HC　Helicopter combat-support squadron

Heartbreak Hotel　Eight one-man cells and a bathing cell just off the main court-yard of the Hanoi Hilton. Prisoners were generally held in Heartbreak immediately after their interrogation.

HH-53　The HH-53 Super Jolly Green Giant was a large assault transport heli-copter with a maximum speed of 196 mph and enough cargo space for 38 troops.

Hootch　Shack where pilots lived in Southeast Asia.

IFF　Identification Friend or Foe; an electronic device carried by military aircraft that, when interrogated correctly by a radar, sent back a unique and clearly iden-tifiable return signal.

Igloo White　Air Force sensor string in Laos, activated in December 1967.

Iron Hand　Navy and Air Force code for a SAM suppression mission. See SAM.

JCS　Joint Chiefs of Staff

Jolly/Jollies　See **HH-53.**

KA-3　Tanker version of the Douglas A-3 Skywarrior: a Navy heavy-attack plane. The KA-3 was powered by two Pratt & Whitney J-57 turbojets and could achieve a maximum speed of 610 mph. The plane carried a crew of three, two 20-mm can-nons, and up to 12,000 pounds of fuel or bombs.

KC-135　A Boeing 707 designed to carry 31,000 gallons of fuel for air-to-air refu-eling. The KC-135 Stratotanker had a top speed of 605 mph.

Knot　A rate of speed of one a nautical mile per hour, which equals 1.1516 statute miles per hour.

Linebacker　Two U.S. bombing campaigns, 10 May–23 October 1972 (Line-backer), and 18–29 December 1972 (Linebacker II). Ordered in reaction to North Vietnam's invasion of the South in March 1972, the two campaigns helped persuade the North Vietnamese to conclude a peace agreement with the United States.

Loose deuce　Standard two-plane Navy fighter formation

LSO　Landing Signal Officer; the officer who controlled carrier landings by telling each pilot how well he was flying approach relative to the optimum flight path for a successful carrier landing.

Mach　Named for Ernst Mach (1838–1916), an Austrian physicist, Mach measures the speed of a moving body as a function of the speed of sound. The speed of sound in dry air at 32 degrees Farenheit is about 1,087 feet per second or 741 mph.

MACV　U.S. Military Assistance Command Vietnam

Mather　Air Force Navigator Training Program at Mather AFB, California.

MCAS   Marine Corps Air Station

ME-109   The Bf-109 (designed by Willy Messerschmitt) was the most famous German fighter of World War II. Over 35,000 were built between 1935 and 1945. The plane had a maximum speed of 386 mph, and carried a 20-mm cannon and two 13-mm machine guns. Olds's P-38, by comparison, had a maximum speed of 414 mph and carried one 20-mm cannon and four .50-caliber machine guns.

MERS   Multiple Ejection Bomb System

MIA   Missing In Action

MiG   Named for General Artem Mikoyan and General Mikhail Gurevich, Russian aircraft engineers, the term **MiG** describes aircraft designed and developed by the Mikoyan and Gurevich design bureau. During the Vietnam War, the two MiGs most likely to be encountered by U.S. pilots were the **MiG-17** Fresco, an interceptor armed with one 37-mm and two 23-mm cannon capable of a maximum speed of 711 mph, and the **MiG-21**, an air-superiority fighter armed with a 30-mm cannon and two Atoll heat-seeking missiles. The MiG-21 was capable of speeds in excess of Mach 2.1.

MiG-17   The MiG-17 Fresco was first developed in 1953 by the Soviet Union. It had a top speed of 0.975 Mach and was armed with two 23-mm and one 37-mm cannon.

MiG-19   Known as "the Farmer," the MiG-19 was a Soviet-built supersonic fighter first built in 1955. The MiG-19 had a top speed of 850 mph, and carried three 30-mm cannons plus bombs.

MiG-21   The MiG-21 is an air-superiority fighter first flown in 1955, powered by an afterburning turbojet, that can achieve speeds in excess of Mach 2.1. Armament consists of one twin-barrel 23-mm gun and four wing pylons for Atoll missiles or drop tanks.

MIGCAP   MiG Combat Air Patrol

Military Alphabet   A set of common code words used by the Armed Services to denote letters of the alphabet: Alpha, Bravo, Charlie, Delta, Echo, Foxtrot, etc. With usage, these words can also take on additional meanings. For example, pilots use the alphabet-code words "Sierra Hotel" to mean "Shit Hot."

MK-36   A US Navy 500-pound acoustic mine

MK-52   A US Navy 100-pound magnetic mine

MK-82   A 500-pound general-purpose bomb

MOS   Military Occupational Specialty

NAS   Naval Air Station

National War College (NWC)   An educational institution established in 1946 in Washington, DC, to prepare senior officers (colonels) for high-level policy, command, and staff functions and for the performance of strategic planning functions.

NCO   Noncommissioned officer

New Guy Village   An area located at the southern corner of the Hoa Lo Prison in Hanoi

NFO   Naval Flight Officer. In fighters, the NFO generally acted as a navigator, radar intercept officer, or bombardier.

NVA   North Vietnamese Army

OER   Officer evaluation report

Operation Homecoming   Following the cease-fire agreement of January 1973, U.S. Armed Forces launched this repatriation program, which provided the returning POWs with extensive medical, psychological, and emotional support to ease the transition from captivity to freedom.

Ordnance   In the airpower lexicon the term *ordnance* is commonly applied to aircraft cannon and machine guns, ammunition, bombs, rockets, rocket launchers, and explosives, together with the appropriate repair tools and equipment.

OTS   Officer Training School

OV-10   The North American OV-10 Bronco is a two-seat twin-engine reconnaissance aircraft and FAC. It initially went into production in 1962, and is powered by two Garrett T-76 turboprops. Its maximum speed is 288 mph and its armament consists of four .30-inch machine guns and up to 3,600 pounds of marking rockets, gun pods, or other ordnance.

Oyster   Air Force code for certain flights of F-4s out of Udorn. These codes often changed daily.

P-38   Developed during World War II by Lockheed, the P-38 Lightning is remembered primarily for its service as a long-range escort fighter for Eighth Air Force bombers. It was powered by two 1,475-hp Allison engines and could achieve a maximum level speed of 414 mph. Armament consisted of one 20-mm cannon and four 50-caliber machine guns plus up to 1,600 pounds of bombs.

PAO   Public Affairs Officer

Pathet Lao   Laotian Communist Guerrillas

Pickle   To drop one's bombs.

PI   Photo Interpreter

Pipper   A small hole in the reticle (the cross hairs of the gunsight) of an optical or computing sight.

PJ   Parajumper—a crewman on a HH-53 rescue helicopter. These men were trained to jump out of a helicopter into the open ocean to rescue an injured pilot. See **HH-53.**

PLC   USMC Platoon Leadership Class; an officer-candidate school designed to commission recent college graduates

Plums   A 1967 modification of the Code of Conduct by POWs in the Hanoi Hilton. *Plums* was a code word meaning something like jewels, which denoted "little jewels of knowledge." Plums were rules conceived by the senior American leadership of the Hanoi Hilton that augmented, expanded, or substituted for the Code of Conduct. Under Plums, a pilot was required to take physical abuse and torture before acceding to specific demands, but he was not expected to die or to seriously jeopardize his health and safety. See **Code of Conduct.**

Pocket Money   U.S. Navy operation to mine Haiphong harbor in May 1972.

POL   Petroleum, oil, lubricants

Prairie Fire   Code name for special operations in Laos.

PTSD   Post–traumatic stress disorder

PX   Post Exchange—a general store on a military base

R&R   Rest and relaxation

RA-5C   The reconnaissance version of the North American A-5 Vigilante. The Vigilante carried a crew of two and was powered by two General Electric J-79 turbojets. It could achieve a maximum speed of 1,385 mph and carried electronic equipment in its bomb bay, including side-looking radar, oblique and split image cameras, and ECM equipment; see **ECM.**

RAG   Replacement Air Group; A Navy term for a training wing

Rapid Roger   A program designed by then Air Force Secretary Harold Brown to increase sortie rates in Southeast Asia by having aircraft fly more missions with smaller bombloads. Rapid Roger ran from August 1966 through February 1967.

Red Crown   Code name for the Navy radar controller on a picket ship in the Gulf of Tonkin, or for the ship itself

REMF   Rear Echelon Motherfucker

RF-8   Unarmed photo reconnaissance version of the F-8 Crusader

RHAW   Radar Homing And Warning set; gear that can pick up and home in on enemy radar emissions

RIO   Radar Intercept Officer—the officer who sat in the backseat of the F-4 and operated the radar during an intercept mission

Rolling Thunder   Code name for the U.S. bombing campaigns against North Vietnam from March 1965 to October 1968

ROTC   Reserve Officer Training Corps; a training corps with units established at civilian educational institutions to qualify students for appointment as reserve officers. In the United States, the program began during the Civil War when the Morrill Act (1862) authorized government financial assistance to universities and colleges offering such courses. The Army Air Forces established its program, known as AROTC, in 1946 with almost 9,000 students. During the Vietnam War, 175 schools offered AFROTC; during its peak year of 1966–67, over 70,000 students were enrolled. Enrolment declined to 20,000 in 1973.

Route Package System   An arbitrary geographical division of North Vietnam into six zones for the purpose of strike planning. Most U.S. losses occurred in Route Package 6, the area around Hanoi and Haiphong.

S-2   The Grumman S-2 tracker was a twin-piston-engine antisubmarine warfare plane. First flown in 1952, it had a maximum speed of 253 mph and carried a crew of four and up to 4,810 pounds of torpedoes, depth bombs, rockets, and sonar buoys.

SAC   From 1946 to 1991, the Strategic Air Command (SAC) operated the intercontinental and nuclear strike forces of the U.S. Air Force. During most of this period, SAC was the most influential and important command in the Air Force. SAC controlled the B-52s used in Vietnam.

SAM   Surface-to-air missile. During the Vietnam War, the predominant SAM was the SA-2 Guideline missile: a radar-guided high-altitude missile that could reach Mach 2.5 and packed an 86 pound warhead. In 1972, the North Vietnamese also began using shoulder-fired heat seeking missiles called SA-7 Strellas.

Sandy   A rescue escort fighter-bomber. See **A-1.**

SEA   Southeast Asia.

7 and 7   Seagram's 7 Crown Whiskey and 7-Up–a popular cocktail in the 1960s and early 1970s.

Shrike missile   An air-to-surface antiradar missile carried by SAM suppression aircraft. The Shrike was 10 feet long and had a range of ten miles.

Silver Star   America's third-highest award for gallantry

SNJ   The North American SNJ Texan, known in the Air Force as the T-6, was the Navy's basic propeller-driven trainer throughout the 1950s. Powered by a Pratt & Whitney R-1340-AN-1 engine, it could fly at a top speed of 205 mph.

SOG/MACV-SOG   US Military Assistance Command Vietnam Studies and Observation Group; special forces used for special intelligence missions such as Prairie Fire

Sortie Restrictive term used for purposes of credit to a unit or to a combat crew member: a flight or sally of a single aircraft that, in accordance with the duties of a combat mission, penetrates into airspace where enemy fire is—or may be—encountered

Sparrow See **AIM-7 Dogfight Sparrow**

Splash U.S. code for downing an enemy aircraft.

Sponson A structure projecting from the side of an aircraft to support a gun.

SRO Senior Ranking Officer, in a POW cell

Steel Tiger Code name for U.S. interdiction bombing in southern Laos of the Ho Chi Minh trail, beginning in 1965.

Students for a Democratic Society (SDS) Founded in 1960 by a group of Michigan students, SDS initially espoused a broad agenda concerned with racism, poverty, and social justice. SDS spread to most campuses around the United States and eventually espoused the antiwar cause. In 1968 many members adopted a radical Marxist philosophy, and some members splintered off to form the terrorist organization, Weathermen. SDS sponsored its last major antiwar march on Washington in 1969.

Station or Stanchion Attachment on an aircraft for hanging munitions or fuel

SUU-16 A 20-mm gun pod carried by an F-4

T-33 The trainer version of the F-80 Shooting Star; see **F-80**

T-37 The Cessna T-37 Tweet was the first jet produced strictly as a trainer. The T-37 first flew in 1954; by 1977 Cessna had delivered 1,272 T-37s to the USAF. The T-37 was powered by a Continental J-69 turbojet and could achieve a maximum speed of approximately 500 mph.

T-38 The T-38 Talon is a Northrop supersonic trainer first flown by the USAF in 1959. It has a maximum speed of Mach 1.3.

T-6 See **SNJ.**

TACAN Tactical Air Navigation System; TACANs generally employed fixed radio signals to help guide aircraft.

Talos A surface-to-air and surface-to-surface guided missile built by Bendix for the U.S. Navy. It was 31 feet long and weighed 7,000 pounds, with a range of 65 miles and either a conventional or a nuclear warhead.

Tank Refuel in the air

TARCAP Target Combat Air Patrol—the planes that patrolled the skies over a target for MiGs.

TDY Temporary duty

TF-77 U.S. Navy carrier strike force engaged in combat actions off the coast of North Vietnam

Top Gun Navy Fighter Weapons School at Miramar, California.

Tracer A bullet containing a pyrotechnic mixture that, once ignited by the exploding powder charge in the cartridge, makes the flight of the projectile visible both by day and by night.

Tree *See* **Combat Tree**

Triple Nickel Slang for the USAF's 555th Tactical Fighter Squadron

Turbojet Engine A continuous-combustion-type power unit designed to exert thrust. It consists of an air compressor, a combustion chamber or chambers, and a gas turbine. Air enters the engine from the front and is then compressed, heated by combustion of fuel, expanded through the gas turbine, and ejected at high velocity from the rear.

27 Charlie Carrier A variant of the World War II *Essex*-class carrier design. The SCBC-27C modernization transformed a straight-decked *Essex*-class ship into a more modern angled-deck carrier with steam catapults and a mirror landing system. See **Essex class carrier.**

Ubon The principal Air Force F-4 base in northeast Thailand, near the Mekong River. See also **Udorn.**

Udorn One of the two Air Force F-4 bases in northeast Thailand. Located about 200 miles up the Mekong River from Ubon, Udorn was used early in the war as a base for the reconnaissance version of the F-4, the RF-4, and also for older RF-101s, reconnaissance Voodoos, and F-104 Starfighters. These older planes were replaced in 1967 by more RF-4s and standard-model F-4s. See also **Ubon.**

UPT Undergraduate Pilot Training; the basic flight training that pilots receive in the Air Force before getting their wings.

USAF United States Air Force

VA Identification for a Navy attack squadron.

VC Vietcong.

VDI Visual Display Terminal; See **Diane.**

VF Identification prefix denoting a Navy fighter squadron

VMAT Marine Attack Training Squadron

VMA (AW) Marine All-Weather Attack Squadron.

r Force

widow of a WestPac pilot; (2) A woman married to a
xual relations with other pilots during her husband's

Pacific

asel   An F-105G: a two-seat hunter-killer ground-defense suppression ver-
on of the F-105. The Weasel used Shrike and Standard Arm antiradiation missiles to destroy the radars of SAM and radar-ranging artillery sites.

Wolf FACs   F-4 FACs based at Ubon, Thailand during the Vietnam war. See FAC.

Wolfpack   Eighth Tactical Fighter Wing, during the Vietnam War period

WSO   Weapons Systems Operator—same as **RIO,** which see.

XO   Executive Officer—the second in command in a Navy squadron

Yankee Station   Area off the coast of North Vietnam where U.S. Navy aircraft carriers conducted offensive air operations against North Vietnam. Yankee Station was
located at 17°30'N by 108°30'E in the South China Sea.

Yoke   A control column, especially a dual control column.

Zoo   A former film studio turned prison at Cu Loc on the southern outskirts of
Hanoi.

Zuni rocket   A solid-propellant 5-inch air-to-surface unguided rocket. It has a
range of five miles and can be armed with various munitions, including flares, fragmentation heads, or armor-piercing heads.

NOTES

PROLOGUE

1. Although the offensive destroyed $600 million dollars worth of the North Vietnamese property, the country received $2 billion dollars of economic aid, primarily from the Soviet Union. For more statistics on Rolling Thunder, see Micheal Clodfelter, *Vietnam in Military Statistics: A History of the Indochina Wars, 1772–1991* (Jefferson, NC: McFarland & Company, 1995), pp. 218–223.

2. Michael Clodfelter, *Vietnam in Military Statistics*, p. 222.

3. The Hanoi targets for B-52s were on the outskirts of the city. Stray B-52 bombs did explode within the city, and fighters struck a few targets there.

4. John Warden, cited in Richard T. Reynolds, *Heart of the Storm: The Genesis of the Air Campaign Against Iraq* (Maxwell Air Force Base, AL: Air University Press, 1995), p. 29.

5. Darrel D. Whitcomb, *The Rescue of Bat 21* (Annapolis, MD: Naval Institute Press, 1998), p. 134.

CHAPTER 1

1. For more on Rolling Thunder, see Earl H. Tilford, *Setup: What the Air Force Did in Vietnam and Why* (Maxwell Air Force Base, AL: Air University Press, 1991); Mark Clodfelter, *The Limits of Air Power: The American Bombing of North Vietnam* (New York: Free Press, 1989).

2. Headquarters Pacific Air Force (HQ PACAF), "End of Tour Report (Col. Robin Olds, 8th Tactical Fighter Wing)," 27 November 1967, p. 30.

3. Robert Clinton, interviewed by the author, telephone. 21 October 1997.

4–5. Ralph Wetterhahn, interviewed by the author, 28 September 1997.

6. For a detailed discussion of air-to-air encounters during this period, see HQ PACAF, Directorate, Tactical Evaluation, Contemporary Historical Evaluation of

Current Operations (CHECO) Division, "Air-to-Air Encounters over North Vietnam 1 July 1967–31 December 1968," Marshall L. Michel, III, *Clashes: Air Combat over North Vietnam 1965–1972* (Annapolis, MD: Naval Institute Press, 1997); USAF Southeast Asia Monograph Series, Monograph 2, *Battle for the Skies over North Vietnam* (Washington, DC: U.S. Government Printing Office, 1976).

7. Vance O. Mitchell, *Air Force Officers: Personnel Policy Development, 1944–1974* (Washington, DC: Air Force History and Museums Program, 1996), p. 245.

8. Colonel John T. Miller, "An Analysis of Aircrew Personnel Flying Out-Country Interdiction Missions," Air War College Report No. 3651, p. 41.

9. Mitchell, *Air Force Officers,* p. 244.

10. Cmdr. James B. Souder, USN (Ret.), e-mail correspondence with author, 1 October 1998.

11. Brig. Gen. Robin Olds, USAF (Ret.), U.S. Air Force Corona Ace Oral History Interview K239.0512-1079, interviewed by Lt. Col. John N. Dick, Jr., and Lt. Col. Gordon Nelson, 17 February 1977, p. 110.

The Corona Ace Oral History interviews at Maxwell AFB, Montgomery Alabama, were initiated in late 1976 by Gen. David Jones, Air Force Chief of Staff, and placed under the direction of Lt. Gen. John P. Flynn, Air Force inspector general. The overall purpose of Corona Ace was to conduct an in-depth study of USAF air-to-air combat capability. Its principal goals were to provide a historical perspective as well as to attempt to develop an ace profile for the selection and training of future pilots. About the Robin Olds interview the editors of the project wrote in their preface, "As one of the most open and frank discussions on airpower, the interview covers the people who shaped it as well as its potential for the future. It is one of the best interviews to be found in the Corona Ace collection." Robin Olds himself wrote on the release form at the beginning of the interview, "Do not think ill of me for the language. Fighter pilots talk that way."

12. Tom Buckley, "Robin Olds and His Battle Aces," *Esquire* (October, 1967), p. 119.

13. Mitchell, the former deputy chief of the Air Service, was court-martialed and found guilty of insubordination for accusing senior Navy and Army leaders of "almost treasonable administration of the national defense" after the Navy dirigible *Shenandoah* crashed in a storm, killing its crew of fourteen.

14. Robin Olds, "Forty-Six Years a Fighter Pilot," *American Aviation Historical Society Journal* XIII (Winter 1968), p. 235.

15–17. Robin Olds, interviewed by the author, telephone. 26 March 1997.

18. Mitchell, "Air Force Officers," p. 50.

19. Hub Zemke, "Mayhem—P-38 Style," in Joe Foss and Matthew Brennan, eds., *Top Guns: America's Fighter Aces Tell Their Stories* (New York: Pocket Books, 1991), pp. 140–141.

20. Robin Olds, "From Muritzsee to Rostock," *Daedalus Flyer,* September 1974, p. 44.

21. During this period, strafing a target without bomber support was common during armed reconnaissance missions.

22. John L. Frisbee, "Col. 'Hub' Zemke," *Air Force,* Vol. 78, No. 4 (April 1995).

23. U.S. Air Force Oral History Interview K239.0512-1079, Brigadier General Robin Olds, USAF Ret., Corona Ace, 17 February 1977, interview by Lieutenant Colonel John N. Dick, Jr., and Lieutenant Colonel Gordon Nelson, pp. 50–51.

24. Robin Olds, interviewed by the author 26 March 1997.

25–27. Olds, "From Muritzsee to Rostock," p. 44.

28. A stick that is attached to the ailerons and elevator of the aircraft.

29–31. "From Muritzsee to Rostock," p. 46.

32–33. Robin Olds, interviewed by the author 26 March 1997, telephone.

34. The daughter of an engineer, Ella Raines completed her education at the University of Washington. After stage experience, Raines was signed for films by a production company headed by Charles Boyer and Howard Hawks. When this enterprise failed to bear fruit, in 1943 Raines went with Universal Studios, where she received her best screen role: the inquisitive, extremely adaptable heroine in the 1943 *film noir Phantom Lady.* Impressed by this performance, Paramount producer/director Preston Sturges borrowed Raines from Universal to costar with Eddie Bracken in *Hail the Conquering Hero* (1944). After marrying Robin Olds in February 1947, Raines retired from the acting business. However, she returned in the early 1950s to star in the popular syndicated TV series *Janet Dean, RN,* which she coproduced with Joan Harrison, who had produced *Phantom Lady.* Ella Raines' final film appearance was in the 1956 British effort *Man in the Road.* (Data from Hal Erickson, *AMG All-Movie Guide* [http://allmovie.com/]).

35. *Esquire* (October 1967), p. 119.

36. June G. McNaughton e-mail correspondence with author, 25 June 1999.

37. Once married, Raines put her marriage to Olds ahead of her career, traveling with him to various assignments around the globe. They lived in a damp and draughty castle in England, and a hacienda in Libya where their two girls, Christina and Susan, each had their own burro. (Data from Hal Eriskson, *AMG All-Movie Guide* [http://allmovie.com]).

38. Robin Olds, interviewed by the author 26 March 1997.

39. The first British mass-produced jet fighter, the Meteor was the only Allied jet to see combat in World War II. The aircraft was powered by two Rolls-Royce Derwent 8 turbojets and had a maximum level speed of 592 mph. Its armament consisted of four Hispano 20-mm cannon.

40–41. Robin Olds, interviewed by the author 26 March 1997.

42. The North American F-86 Sabrejet was the first swept-wing transsonic jet to be built. The F-86A first flew in 1948 and achieved a maximum speed of 671 mph in level flight. Its armament consisted of six 50-caliber machine guns.

43. James Salter, *Burning the Days* (New York: Random House, 1997), p. 180.

44. Robin Olds, interviewed by the author 26 March 1997.

45. From 1946 to 1991, the Strategic Air Command (SAC) operated the inter-continental and nuclear strike forces of the U.S. Air Force. During most of this period, SAC was the most influential and important command in the Air Force.

46–47. Robin Olds, interviewed by the author 26 March 1997.

48. The National War College is an educational institution established in 1946 in Washington, DC to prepare senior officers (colonels) for high-level policy, com-mand, and staff functions and to teach them strategic planning.

49. Robin Olds, interviewed by the author 26 March 1997.

50. The F-101 Voodoo was originally constructed as a supersonic twin engine jet fighter, but eventually evolved into a strike aircraft as well. The Voodoo was powered by two Pratt & Whitney J-57 turbojets with afterburners and could reach a maximum level speed of 1,220 mph. Armament consisted of four 20-mm cannon and one Mark 7, one Mark 28, and one Mark 43 nuclear bomb.

51. J. Alfred Phelps, *Chappie: America's First Black Four-Star General* (Novato, CA: Presidio, 1991), p. 205.

52. Marcelle Size Knaack, *Post-World War II Fighters: 1945–1973* (Washington, DC.: Office of Air Force History, 1986), pp. 135–157.

53. Robin Olds, interviewed by the author 26 March 1997.

54. Marshall L. Michel, III, *Clashes: Air Combat Over North Vietnam 1965–1972* (Annapolis, MD: Naval Institute Press, 1997), pp. 14–15.

55. Ted Sienicki, interviewed by the author 17 March 1997, telephone. Sienicki actually flew with the Eighth Wing, but his experiences are similar to those who flew against MiGs with the 432nd Wing.

56. Michel, *Clashes,* pp. 88–89.

57. Ibid., p. 110.

58. Ibid., p. 156.

59. Ibid., p. 110.

60. Ibid., pp. 14–15, 182.

61. Ibid., p. 279; Wayne Thompson, "Rebound: The Air War Over North Vietnam 1966–1973" (Washington, DC: Air Force History and Museum Programs), unpublished manuscript, p. 264.

62. Joseph F. Tuso, *Singing the Vietnam Blues: Songs of the Air Force in Southeast Asia* (College Station, TX: Texas A&M University Press, 1990), p. 82.

63. For additional insight on the connection between killing in war and pro-creation, see Dave Grossman, *On Killing: The Psychological Cost of Learning to Kill in War and Society* (Boston: Little, Brown and Company, 1995), p. 2. Pilot Darrel Whitcomb claims that some pilots in the forward air control community got so aroused during their missions that they would relieve their sexual tension through masturbation during lulls. Author interview with Darrel D. Whitcomb 2 May 1999, telephone.

64. Robert Clinton, e-mail to the author, 2 November 1997.

65. Robin Olds, "She's a Lady," published on the World Wide Web at: http://www-afsc-saia.af.mil/magazine/htdocs/augmag96/robinold.html.

66. Robert Clinton, "Ode to the Phantom," *The Phantom's Lair* (May 1994), p. 5.

67. Barbara Ehrenreich, *Hearts of Men: American Dreams and the Flight from Commitment* (New York: Doubleday, 1984).

68. Col. J. L. Adkinson, "The Playboys!" *Marine Corps Gazette*, Vol. 70, No. 5 (May 1986), pp. 96–102. Although technically the "Playboy" call sign refers to TA-4F forward-air-control planes of the First Marine Air Wing, many F-4s flew with this unit on Playboy missions and therefore consider themselves to be a part of the Playboy family; see Adkinson, p. 102.

69. "Hotshot Charlie Rides Again," *Esquire* (October 1967), pp. 111–116.

70. See Michel, *Clashes*, p. 19.

71. R. Frank Futrell, et al., *Aces and Aerial Victories: The United States Air Force in Southeast Asia 1965–1973* (Washington, DC.: U.S. Government Printing Office, 1976), p. 160.

72. Radar-guided air-to-air missile. The 400-pound missile rode the beam of an F-4 radar to its target and carried a 65-pound warhead. The Sparrow had a head-on attack range of twelve miles and a three-mile range from the rear. Its minimum range was 3,000 feet.

73. U.S. Air Force Corona Ace Oral History Interview K239.0512-1672, Brig. Gen. Robin Olds, 1967–1972, interview by Lt. Col. Mank, 5 June 1979, p. 19.

74. Robin Olds, interviewed by the author 26 March 1997.

75–76. Elements of Olds' famous "New Guy" speech can be found in Ralph Wetterhahn, "Change of Command," *Air & Space* (August/September, 1997), p. 66; Brig. Gen. Robin Olds, USAF (Ret.), U.S. Air Force Oral History Interview K239.0512-1079, p. 36; Robin Olds, interviewed by the author 26 March 1997.

77. Brig. Gen. Robin Olds, USAF (Ret.), U.S. Air Force Corona Ace Oral History Interview K239.0512-1672, p. 16.

78. Three of the F-4Cs came from the Eighth Wing (tail numbers 63-7643, 63-7642, and 62-4331). Number F1-05D 62-4331 came from the 388th Wing, and F-105D 60-502 came from the 355th. See Rob Young, "US Aircraft Losses to MiGs in Southeast Asia, 1965–1972" (Wright-Patterson AFB, OH: National Air Intelligence Center).

79. John Stone, interviewed by author, 30 Sep 1997, telephone.

80. Michel, *Clashes*, p. 73.

81. Brig. Gen. Robin Olds, USAF (Ret.), U.S. Air Force Oral History Interview K239.0512-1079, pp. 49–50: Robin Olds, interviewed by the author 26 March 1997.

82. Futrell. et al., *Aces and Aerial Victories*, p. 37.

83. Robert Clinton, interviewed by the author 21 October 1997.

84. Jerry Scutts, *Wolfpack: Hunting MiGs Over Vietnam* (Osceola, WI: Motorbooks International, 1988), p. 39.

85. Weapons Systems Evaluation Group, WSEG Report 116, Air-to-Air Encounters in Southeast Asia, Volume 1: Account of F-4 and F-8 Events Prior to March 1967, October 1967, Institute for Defense Analysis, p. 419; Ralph Wetterhahn, interviewed by the author 28 September 1997.

86. Olds, cited in Futrell et al., *Aces and Aerial Victories*, p. 39.

87. Michel, *Clashes*, p. 74.

88. Brig. Gen. Robin Olds, USAF (Ret.), U.S. Air Force Corona Ace Oral History Interview K239.0512-1079, pp. 55–56.

89. Duncan Craighead, "Robin Olds," *Air Force and Space Digest* (from Robin Olds' personal files, no date), p. 23.

90. Robin's backseaters for his four Vietnam War kills were:
    02 January 1967: 1st Lt. Charles Clifton
    04 May 1967: 1st Lt. William Lafever
    20 May 1967 (2 kills): 1st Lt. Stephen Croker

91–92. Robin Olds, interviewed by the author 26 March 1997.

CHAPTER 2

1. U.S. Air Force Historical Support Office, Table 15: "Fate of Crew on Aircraft Lost in Combat By Aircraft Type and Country," p. 61.

2. The bombing phases described here were the result of the Johnson administration's reluctance to authorize new targets. The Air Force proposed hitting all important targets quickly at the outset.

3. Micheal Clodfelter, *Vietnam in Military Statistics: A History of the Indochina Wars, 1772–1991* (Jefferson, NC: McFarland, 1992), pp. 218–223.

4. Ed Rasimus, unpublished memoir.

5. Ed Rasimus, interviewed by the author, Washington, D.C., 6 May 1997.

6. Overall, only nine of the 360 graduates of the Air Force's eight pilot training schools were selected for 105s in 1965.

7. U.S. Air Force Historical Support Office, Table 15: "Fate of Crew on Aircraft Lost in Combat by Aircraft Type and Country," p. 61.

8. Ed Rasimus, interviewed by the author 6 May 1997; Ed Rasimus, unpublished memoir.

9. Jim Gormley, interviewed by the author 5 April 1997.

10. Ronald G. Bliss, interviewed at the USAF Academy in Colorado Springs on 17 October 1991. Bliss is a former F-105 pilot and a POW shot down on 4 Sep 66. Lt. Col. Richard Copock, USAF (Ret.), 1991, pp. 41–42.

11. Brig. Gen. Ken Bell, USAF (Ret.), *100 Missions North: A Fighter Pilot's Story of the Vietnam War* (Washington: Brassey's, 1993), pp. 8–9.

12. While the F-105 could carry up to sixteen 750-pound bombs, it generally only attacked targets on North Vietnam with 6 due to the large amount of fuel required to fly to those targets.

13. Marshall L. Michel, III, *Clashes: Air Combat Over North Vietnam, 1965–1972* (Annapolis, MD: Naval Institute Press, 1997), pp. 10–11.

14. Jack Broughton, *Thud Ridge* (New York: Lippincott, 1969), p. 37.

15–16. Ed Rasimus, interviewed by the author 19 January 1997.

17. Which home in on the electronic emissions generated by SAM radars.

18. Jack Broughton, *Going Downtown: The War Against Hanoi and Washington* (New York: Pocket Books, 1988), pp. 107–108.

19. Bell, *100 missions North*, p. 229.

20–21. Ibid., p. 24.

22. Jim Gormley, interviewed by the author 5 April 1997.

23. Ed Rasimus, interviewed by the author 6 May 1997.

24. John T. Miller, "An Analysis of Aircrew Personnel Flying Out-Country Interdiction Missions," Air War College Report 3651, April 1968, pp. 34–35.

25. Dick Guild, interviewed by the author 12 November 1997.

26. Cal Tax, combat diary of his 100-mission tour at Takhli, June–October 1967.

27. Jim Gormley, interviewed by the author 5 April 1997.

28. Cal Tax, diary, 7 October 1967.

29. Ibid., 13 October 1967.

30. Ibid., 16 September 1967.

31. Dick Guild, interviewed by the author, telephone. 12 November 1997.

32. Jerry Hoblit, quoted in Broughton, *Going Downtown*, p. x.

33. Dave Groark, cited in ibid., p. xvi.

34. Jerry Hoblit, interviewed by the author 5 May 1997. Hoblit mentioned that he learned this saying from one of his tactical officers at West Point, Major George S. Patton IV.

35–36. Tom Wilson, interviewed by the author, 20 May 1997, telephone.

37. Jack Broughton, *Going Downtown*, p. 176.

38. Jerry Hoblit, quoted Broughton, *Going Downtown*, p. 176.

39–40. Tom Wilson, interviewed by the author, 20 May 1997.

41. Bell, *100 Missions North*, p. xiii.

42–45. Ed Rasimus, interviewed by the author 6 May 1997.

CHAPTER 3

1. William Harris, quoted by Roger Sheets when interviewed by the author, 9 February 1998.

2. Admiral Jesse Greer, quoted by Roger Sheets when interviewed by the author 9 February 1998.

3. Roger "Blinky" Sheets, interviewed by the author 9 February 1998.

4. William "Charlie" Carr, Jr., interviewed by the author 26 January 1998.

5. Ralph Brubaker, interviewed by the author 25 February 1998, telephone.

6. Joe Michaels, *A-6 Intruder* (Carrollton, TX: Squadron/Signal Publications, 1993), p. 7.

7. Roger Sheets, interviewed by the author 9 February 1998.

8. William "Charlie" Carr, Jr., interviewed by the author 26 January 1998.

9. Roger Sheets, interviewed by the author 9 February 1998.

10. Low-drag bombs, or "snake eyes" as they were called, had fins that opened up and retarded the speed of the bombs when dropped. The advantage of snake-eye

bombs is that they could be dropped from low altitude without damaging the bomber. A low- altitude delivery, in turn, allowed for increased bombing accuracy—an important consideration in close-air-support operations.

11. Roger "Blinky" Sheets, interviewed by the author 9 February 1998.

12. William "Charlie" Carr, Jr., interviewed by the author 26 January 1998.

13. Frederick the Great, quoted in Charles M. Westenhoff, *Military Air Power: The CADRE Digest of Air Power Opinions and Thoughts* (Maxwell AFB, AL: Air University Press, 1990), p. 150.

14. See S. L. A. Marshall, *Men Against Fire: The Problem of Battle Command in Future War* (Gloucester, MA: Peter Smith, 1975).

15–17. Roger "Blinky" Sheets, interviewed by the author 9 February 1998.

18. Although scholars and veterans continue to argue that the 4 August attack never happened, the Department of the Navy, based on classified data, still maintains that this attack took place.

19. Everett Alvarez, Jr., and Anthony S. Pitch, *Chained Eagle* (New York: Donald I. Fine, Inc., 1989), p. 12.

20. In addition to working as a CCA, Sheets also helped plan the retaliatory raids for the alleged Tonkin attacks, including the one on the naval base at Hon Gai harbor on 5 August.

21–22. Roger Sheets, interviewed by the author 9 February 1998.

23. Each Navy squadron has four department heads who serve under the XO and CO—Operations (third in command), Maintenance (fourth), Administration (fifth). By comparison, Air Force squadrons do not have XOs. In a USAF unit, the Operations Officer is second in command.

24–28. Roger "Blinky" Sheets, interviewed by the author 9 February 1998.

29. William Angus, interviewed by the author 3 February 1998.

30. Roger "Blinky" Sheets, interviewed by the author 9 February 1998.

31. Wayne Thompson, "Rebound: The Air War Over North Vietnam 1966–1973," unpublished manuscript (June 1997), p. 250. Manuscript on file at archives of Air Force History, and Museum Programs, Washington, DC.

32–42. William "Charlie" Carr, Jr., interviewed by the author 26 January 1998.

43. Jerry B. Houston, interviewed by the author 29 March 1997; David Cortright, *Soldiers in Revolt: The American Military Today* (New York: Anchor, 1975), p. 112.

44. Cortright, *Soldiers in Revolt*, p. 112.

45. Interviewed by the author 3 February 1998.

46. Jerry B. Houston, interviewed by the author 29 March 1997.

47. William "Charlie" Carr, Jr., interviewed by the author 26 January 1998.

48. Memorandum from Lt. Col. B. R. Stanley, Commander of Marine All Weather Attack Squadron 224, Marine Aircraft Group 14, 2d Marine Aircraft Wing, Fleet Marine Force, Atlantic, to Commandant of the Marine Corps, subject: Command Chronology, period 1 January 1971 to 30 June 1971.

49. William Angus, interviewed by the author 3 February 1998.

50. William Harris, quoted by Thomas Sprouse, when interviewed by the author, 24 February 1998.

51. Ralph Brubaker, interviewed by the author, 25 February 1998.

52. General Tom Miller, quoted by Ralph Brubaker, when interviewed by the author, 25 February 1998.

53. Ralph Brubaker, interviewed by the author 25 February 1998.

54. Roger "Blinky" Sheets, interviewed by the author 9 February 1998; Robert K. Wilcox, *Scream of Eagles* (New York: Wiley, 1990), pp. 240–241.

55. Wilcox, *Scream of Eagles*, p. 240.

56–57. Roger Sheets, interviewed by the author 9 February 1998.

58. William "Charlie" Carr, Jr., interviewed by the author 26 January 1998.

59. Wilcox, *Scream of Eagles*, p. 242.

60. Roger "Blinky" Sheets, interviewed by the author 9 February 1998.

61. Top Gun was established by the Navy in 1969 to teach fighter pilots advanced air-combat maneuvers; Wilcox, *Scream of Eagles*, p. 242.

62. William "Charlie" Carr, Jr., interviewed by the author 26 January 1998.

63. Jerry B. Houston, interviewed by the author 29 March 1997.

64. William "Charlie" Carr, Jr., interviewed by the author 26 January 1998.

65. Jerry B. Houston, interviewed by the author 29 March 1997.

66. Jerry B. Houston, quoted in Wilcox, *Scream of Eagles*, p. 244.

67. Jerry B. Houston, interviewed by the author 29 March 1997.

68. William "Charlie" Carr, Jr., interviewed by the author 26 January 1998.

69. John Prados, *The Hidden History of the Vietnam War* (Chicago: Ivan R. Dee, 1995), pp. 261–274; David Reed, "Mission: Mine Haiphong!" *Reader's Digest* (February 1973), pp. 76–81.

70–72. John Prados, *Hidden History*, pp. 261–274.

73. William "Charlie" Carr, Jr., interviewed by the author 26 January 1998.

74. *Operation End Sweep: A History of Minesweeping Operations in North Vietnam*, Edited by Edward J. Marolda, (Washington, DC: Naval Historical Center, 1993), pp. 42, 102.

75. William "Charlie" Carr, Jr., interviewed by the author 26 January 1998.

76–77. Roger "Blinky" Sheets, interviewed by the author 9 February 1998.

78. President Richard M. Nixon, speech quoted in Jeffrey Ethell and Alfred Price, *One Day in a Long War* (New York: Random House, 1989), p. 16.

79. Charles D. Melson and Curtis G. Arnold, *U.S. Marines in Vietnam: The War that Would Not End, 1971–1973* (Washington, DC: History and Museums Division, Headquarters, U.S. Marine Corps, 1991), p. 177.

80. Walter J. Boyne, "Linebacker II," *Air Force Magazine*, November 1997, pp. 56–57.

81. This $25-million epic recreates the events that led to the Japanese attack on the American naval base at Pearl Harbor during World War II, and contains spectacular scenes of the bombing of that base.

82–84. William "Charlie" Carr, Jr., interviewed by the author 26 January 1998.

85. William Angus, interviewed by the author 3 February 1998.

86–88. William "Charlie" Carr, Jr., interviewed by the author 26 January 1998.

89–90. Ralph Brubaker, interviewed by the author 25 February 1998.

91–99. Phil Schuyler, interviewed by the author 4 February 1998, telephone.

100. Ralph Brubaker, interviewed by the author 25 February 1998.

101. William "Charlie" Carr, Jr., interviewed by the author 26 January 1998.

102–103. William Angus, interviewed by the author 3 February 1998.

104. Thomas Sprouse, interviewed by the author 24 February 1998.

105–106. William Angus, interviewed by the author 3 February 1998.

107. Thomas Sprouse, interviewed by the author 24 February 1998.

108. Melson and Arnold, *U.S. Marines in Vietnam*, p. 177.

109. James Holloway, quoted by "Blinky" Roger Sheets when interviewed by the author, 9 February 1998.

CHAPTER 4

1. William Angus, interviewed by the author 3 February 1998, telephone.

2. E-mail from James B. Souder to author, Sunday, August 16, 1998 9:19 AM; Jim Stockdale and Sybil Stockdale, *In Love and War: The Story of a Family's Ordeal and Sacrifice During the Vietnam Years* (New York: Harper & Row, 1984), p. 252; Stuart I. Rochester, *Honor Bound: The History of American Prisoners of War in Southeast Asia, 1961–1973* (Washington, DC: Historical Office of the Office of the Secretary of Defense, 1998), pp. 533–534.

3. Wayne Thompson, "Rebound: The Air War Over North Vietnam 1966–1973," unpublished manuscript (June 1997), p. 206. On file at office of Air Force History and Museum Programs, Washington, DC.

4–6. William Angus, interviewed by the author 3 February 1998.

7. Author interview with J. B. Souder, 17 July 1998.

8. Stockdale and Stockdale, *In Love and War,* pp. 459–460.

9. Geoffrey Norman, *Bouncing Back: How a Heroic Band of POWs Survived Vietnam* (Boston: Houghton Mifflin, 1990), p. 33.

10–12. Stockdale and Stockdale, *In Love and War,* p. 172.

13. Soon after his repatriation in 1973, Commander James Stockdale filed a formal indictment against Wilber and Miller for collaboration and mutiny. However, the Department of the Navy decided not to prosecute. The two retired with administrative letters of censure and lasting disgrace. See Rochester, *Honor Bound,* p. 568.

14. William Angus, interviewed by the author 3 February 1998.

15–43. Ted Sienicki, interviewed by the author 17 March 1997, telephone.

44. Rochester, *Honor Bound,* p. 55.

45. Kittinger and Captain William Schwertfeger, USAF were the only known FNGs to be tortured with ropes; Author conversation with Commander James Souder, 22 February 1999; Author e-mail correspondence with Major Theodore Sienicki, USAF Ret., 23 February 1999.

46. Author e-mail correspondence with Major Theodore Sienicki, USAF Ret., 23 February 1999.

47. Author interview with 1LT Ted Sienicki, USAF, 3 March 1997.

48. E-mail correspondence between author and CMDR C. Ronald Polfer, 11 February 1999.

49. Author interview with 1LT Ted Sienicki, USAF, 3 March 1997.

50. E-mail correspondence between author and CMDR C. Ronald Polfer, 11 February 1999.

51. Author interview with 1LT Ted Sienicki, USAF, 3 March 1997.

52. Sienicki would later receive a poor fitness report from Colonel Kittinger for this and other acts of defiance; author interview with 1LT Ted Sienicki, USAF, 3 March 1997.

53. E-mail correspondence From Ted Sienicki to author, 15 February 1999.

54. E-mail correspondence between author and CMDR C. Ronald Polfer, 11 February 1999.

55–57. E-mail correspondence from James B. Souder to author, 17 February 1999.

58. E-mail correspondence from Ted Sienicki to author, 15 February 1999.

59. E-mail correspondence between author and CMDR C. Ronald Polfer, 11 February 1999; author interview with 1LT Ted Sienicki, USAF, 3 March 1997.

60–61. Ted Sienicki, interviewed by the author 17 March 1997.

62–65. J. B. Souder, interviewed by the author 17 July 1998.

66–69. Ted Sienicki, interviewed by the author 17 March 1997.

70–74. Roger Lerseth, interviewed by the author 16 January 1998, telephone.

75–87. Roger Lerseth, unpublished manuscript, 9 February 1998. Draft completed on 9 Feb 98 by Lerseth

88. Roger Lerseth, interviewed by the author 16 January 1998.

89. Roger Lerseth, unpublished manuscript, 9 February 1998.

90. Roger Lerseth, interviewed by the author 16 January 1998.

91–92. Roger Lerseth, unpublished manuscript, 9 February 1998.

93–102. Roger Lerseth, interviewed by the author 16 January 1998.

103. Kevin Cheney, interviewed by the author 28 May 1998.

104. Roger Lerseth, interviewed by the author 16 January 1998.

105. Kevin Cheney, interviewed by the author 28 May 1998.

106–112. Roger Lerseth interviewed by the author 16 January 1998.

113. James D. Latham, interviewed by the author 30 March 1998.

114. Sue Latham, interviewed by the author 31 March 1998.

115. Michael J. H. Taylor, ed., *Jane's Encyclopedia of Aviation*, rev.'ed. (New York: Crescent Books, 1989), p. 767. For two well-written memoirs by former Vietnam War OV-10 pilots, see J. M. Moriarty, *Ground Attack Vietnam: The Marines Who Controlled the Skies* (New York: Ivy Books, 1993) and Tom Yarborough, *Danang Diary* (New York: St. Martin's, 1990).

116. Headquarters United States Air Force, Historical Support Office, "Fate of Crew on Aircraft Lost in Combat by Aircraft Type and Country, 1 Jan 62–31 Dec 72"; Document held by the Air Force History Support Office, Washington, DC.

117. The field is now called Eglin Air Force Auxillary Field 9.

118. The code-name for these FACs was "Nail."

119. For more on the Air Force's interdiction programs in Laos during Latham's tenure there, see Eduard Mark, *Aerial Interdiction in Three Wars* (Washington, DC: Center for Air Force History, 1994), pp. 327–365.

120. James D. Latham, interviewed by the author 30 March 1998.

121. John L. Plaster, *SOG: The Secret Wars of America's Commandos in Vietnam* (New York: Simon & Schuster, 1997), pp. 339–340.

122–123. James D. Latham, interviewed by the author 30 March 1998.

124. Richard Bates, interviewed by the author 12 January 1998.

125–126. Frederick Blesse, *Check Six: A Fighter Pilot Looks Back* (Mesa, AZ: Champlin Fighter Museum Press, 1987), p. 144.

127–128. Mark E. Berent, "A Group Called Wolf," *Air Force Magazine* (February 1971), p. 90.

129. Sue Latham, interviewed by the author 31 March 1998.

130. James D. Latham, interviewed by the author 30 March 1998.

131–132. Richard Bates, interviewed by the author 12 January 1998.

133. According to Richard Bates, it was "probably a 57-mm round. However, I was told that the North Vietnamese dragged in some SA-6s and there is some speculation that it was an SA-6 that hit us. There was no logic for SA-6s in our RHAW (radar homing and warning) gear at that time." Richard Bates, interviewed by the author 12 January 1998.

134–152. James D. Latham, interviewed by the author 30 March 1998.

153–155. Richard Bates, interviewed by the author 12 January 1998.

156. James D. Latham, interviewed by the author 30 March 1998.

157. Richard Bates, interviewed by the author 12 January 1998.

158. In general, there were 801 Vietnam War POWs as listed by the Defense Department. This included 36 who escaped and 765 who were released. There were 660 military men captured (532 were released, 28 escaped), and 141 civilian/foreign nationals (133 released and 8 escaped). Some were released early for propaganda purposes. 591 were released in Operation Homecoming in Feb/Mar/Apr of 1973. Source: Fourth Allied POW Wing.

159. Stockdale and Stockdale, *In Love and War,* p. 435.

160. Roger Lerseth, interviewed by the author 16 January 1998.

161. William Angus, interviewed by the author 3 February 1998.

CHAPTER 5

1. Marshall L. Michel, III, *Clashes: Air Combat Over North Vietnam 1965–1972* (Annapolis, MD: Naval Institute Press, 1997), p. 161; Barrett Tillman, *MiG Master,* 2nd ed. (Annapolis, MD: Naval Institute Press, 1990), pp. 114–117.

2. For an overview and clinical definition of PTSD, see Matthew J. Friedman, "Post-Traumatic Stress Disorder: An Overview," National Center for Posttraumatic Stress Disorder, http:// www.dartmouth.edu/dms/ptsd/overview.

3–8. John "Pirate" Nichols, interviewed by the author 23 March 1997.

9. For additional information on the training of naval aviators in the 1950s, see Deputy Chief of Naval Operations [Air Warfare] and Commander, Naval Air Systems Command, *Naval Aviation Training* (Washington, DC: 1987).

10–16. John Nichols, interviewed by the author 23 March 1997.

17. Tillman, *MiG Master,* pp. 40–41.

18. Tillman, *MiG Master,* pp. 22–24.

19. John B. Nichols, III, and Barrett Tillman, *On Yankee Station: The Naval Air War in Vietnam* (Annapolis, MD: Naval Institute Press, 1987), p. 72.

20–27. John B. Nichols, III, interviewed by the author, 23 March 1997.

28. By the end of the Vietnam War, the *Shangri-La* was showing so many signs of age that sailors began calling it the "Shitty Shang."

29. The *Essex* CV-9 was to be the prototype of an especially designed 27,000-ton (standard displacement) aircraft carrier, considerably larger than the *Enterprise* (CV-6) and smaller than the *Saratoga* (CV-3). These were to become known as the Essex class carriers, although this classification was dropped in the 50's. They were as follows: *Essex* (CVA-9), *Yorktown* (CVA-10), *Intrepid* (CVA-11), *Hornet* (CVA-12), *Franklin* (CVA-13), *Ticonderoga* (CVA-14), *Randolph* (CVA-15), *Lexington* (CVA-16), *Bunker Hill* (CVA-17), *Wasp* (CVA-18), *Hancock* (CVA-19), *Bennington* (CVA-20), *Bon Homme Richard* (CVA-31), *Leyte* (CVA-32), *Kearsarge* (CVA-33), *Oriskany* (CVA-34), *Antietam* (CVA-36). Several characteristics marked the Essex class carriers upon their introduction to the Fleet. The pyramidal island structure, for instance, rose cleanly from the starboard side, topped by a short stack and a light tripod mast. The port elevator was also a distinguishing feature, along with the two inboard elevators. Overall lengths varied within this class; they were either 872 feet long or 888. Generally, there were accommodations aboard each for 360 officers and 3088 enlisted men. Source: Scot MacDonald, "Evolution of Aircraft Carriers: The Early Attack Carriers," *Naval Aviation News,* November 1962, 44–48.

30. Paul T. Gillcrist, *Feet Wet: Reflections of a Carrier Pilot* (New York: Pocket Books, 1990), pp. 156–157.

31. Ibid., pp. 160–161.

32. Ibid., pp. 162–163.

33. Ibid., pp. 163–164.

34. Paul T. Gillcrist, quoted by John "Pirate" Nicholas when interviewed by the author 23 March 1997.

35–41. John "Pirate" Nichols, interviewed by the author 23 March 1997.

42–48. Paul T. Gillcrist, *Crusader! Last of the Gunfighters* (Atglen, PA: Schiffer Military/Aviation History, 1995), pp. 109–112.

49. Richard W. Schaffert, interviewed by the author 29 April 1998.

50–51. Gillcrist, *Crusader,* p. 83.

52–54. Gillcrist, *Crusader,* p. 87.

55. John B. "Pirate" Nichols, III, interviewed by the author 22 May 1998.

56. John B. "Pirate" Nichols, III, interviewed by the author 23 March 1997.

57. Memorandum from Commanding Officer, Fighter Squadron 191 to Chief of Naval Operations (OP-05A5G); Subject: OPNAV Report 5750-1 (Command History); 1 February 1967; John "Pirate" Nichols, III, interviewed by the author 23 March 1997.

58. John "Pirate" Nichols, interviewed by the author 22 May 1998.

59. Memorandum from Commanding Officer, Fighter Squadron 191 to Chief of Naval Operations (OP-05A5G); Subject: OPNAV Report 5750-1 (Command History); 1 February 1967.

60. John B. "Pirate" Nichols, III, interviewed by the author 23 March 1997.

61–65. John Nichols, and Barrett Tillman, "On Your Wing," *Proceedings* (September 1994), p. 64.

66. Although this version of the even differs from Estocin's Medal of Honor citation, it is corroborated by an interview with John Nichols and *Ticonderoga* (CVA-14) Report No. 01180, "Mission Data Page for Event No. 52G: 208 Estocin, 111 Nichols," 26 April 1967; Mission Intel Debrief Collection (MIDS), Naval Historical Center, Washington, DC. The erroneous Medal of Honor Citation reads:[le]2

*Estocin, Michael J.

Rank and organization. Captain (then Lt. Cmdr.), U.S. Navy, Attack Squadron 192, USS *Ticonderoga* (CVA-14). Place and date: Haiphong, North Vietnam, 20 and 26 April 1967. Entered service at: Akron Ohio, 20 July 1954. Born: 27 April 1931, Turtle Creek, Pa. Citation. For conspicuous gallantry and intrepidity at the risk of his life above and beyond the call of duty on 20 and 26 April 1967 as a pilot in Attack Squadron 192, embarked in USS *Ticonderoga* (CVA-14). Leading a 3-plane group of aircraft in support of a coordinated strike against two thermal power plants in Haiphong, North Vietnam, on 20 April 1967, Capt. Estocin provided continuous warnings to the strike group leaders of the surface-to-air missile (SAM) threats, and personally neutralized 3 SAM sites. Although his aircraft was severely damaged by an exploding missile, he reentered the target area and relentlessly prosecuted a SHRIKE attack in the face of intense anti-aircraft fire. With less than 5 minutes of fuel remaining he departed the target area and commenced in-flight refueling which continued for over 100 miles. Three miles aft of *Ticonderoga,* and without enough fuel for a second approach, he disengaged from the tanker and executed a precise approach to a fiery arrested landing. On 26 April 1967, in support of a coordinated strike against the vital fuel facilities in Haiphong, he led an attack on a threatening SAM site, during which his aircraft was seriously damaged by an exploding SAM; nevertheless, he regained control of his burning aircraft and courageously launched his SHRIKE missiles before departing the area. By his inspiring courage and unswerving devotion to duty in the face of grave personal danger, Captain Estocin upheld the highest traditions of the U.S. Naval Service.

67–68. Nichols and Tillman, "On Your Wing," pp. 67–68.

69. Matthew J. Friedman, "Post-Traumatic Stress Disorder: An Overview," National Center for Posttraumatic Stress Disorder, http://www.dartmouth.edu/dms/ptsd/overview.html

70. This finding was again confirmed by the author in June 1998 when reviewing the recently declassified Mission Intelligence Debrief (MID) for that mission at the Naval Historical Center in Washington, DC.

71. Nichols and Tillman, "On Your Wing," p. 68.

72–73. Memorandum from Commanding Officer, Fighter Squadron 191 to Chief of Naval Operations (OP-05A5G); Subject: OPNAV Report 5750-1 (Command History); 24 March 1969.

74. Nichols and Tillman, *On Yankee Station,* p. 39.

75. Ibid., p. 36.

76. Tillman, *MiG Master,* p. 158.

77. John Nichols, interviewed by the author 23 March 1997.

78. John Nichols, quoted in Tillman, *MiG Master,* p. 159.

79–80. John B. "Pirate" Nichols, interviewed by the author 23 March 1997.

81. Philip Robert Craven, interviewed by the author 22 April 1998.

82–84. John Nichols, III, interviewed by the author 23 March 1997.

85. Foster "Tooter" Teague, cited in Robert K. Wilcox, *Scream of Eagles: The Creation of Top Gun and the U.S. Air Victory in Vietnam* (New York: Wiley, 1990), p. 137.

86. Ron "Mugs" McKeown, quoted in Wilcox, *Scream of Eagles,* p. 139.

87. Foster "Tooter" Teague, quoted in ibid., p. 137.

88–94. John B. "Pirate" Nichols, interviewed by the author 23 March 1997.

95–96. John B. Nichols, III, quoted in Nichols and Tillman, *On Yankee Station,* p. 47.

97–98. John B. "Pirate" Nichols, interviewed by the author 23 March 1997.

CHAPTER 6

1. Chief of staff, USS *Hancock* quoted in John B. Nichols, III, and Barrett Tillman, *On Yankee Station: The Naval Air War Over Vietnam* (Annapolis, MD: Naval Institute Press, 1987), p. 84.

2. John Nichols, interviewed by the author 23 March 1997.

3. Chief of staff, USS *Hancock* quoted in Nichols and Tillman, *On Yankee Station,* p. 86.

4–5. John B. Nichols, interviewed by the author 23 March 1997, telephone.

6. Robert F. Futrell et al., *Aces and Aerial Victories: The United States Air Force in Southeast Asia 1965–1973* (Washington, DC: U.S. Government Printing Office, 1976), p. 117.

7. U.S. Air Force Academy Yearbook, 1964. US Air Force Academy Library.

8. Roger Locher, interviewed by the author, 8 July 1997.

9. Ralph Wetterhahn, interviewed by the author, 28 September 1997.

10. Richard S. "Steve" Ritchie, interviewed by the author, 8 June 1997, Telephone.

11. Robert Lodge, cited in Futrell et al., *Aces and Aerial Victories*, p. 85.

12. Roger Locher, interviewed by the author

13. Sources: Roger Locher, Patty Locher, and Charles DeBellevue.

14. Ritchie claims that he enjoyed wearing Cologne because the squadron room often smelled like a locker room. There was lots of sweaty life support equipment, etc. Richard S. "Steve" Ritchie, interview with the author, 25 April, 1999, telephone.

15. Brigadier General Robin Olds, USAF (Ret.), USAF Oral History Corona Ace Program, Interview K239.0512–1079, 17 February 1977, p. 118.

16–18. Richard S. "Steve," Ritchie, interviewed by the author, 8 June 1997

19. For example, although he is an avid sport shooter, Ritchie refuses to hunt and kill live animals. Interview with author, 25 April 1999, telephone.

20. Captain Richard S. Ritchie, interviewed by Major Lyn R. Officer and Hugh N. Ahmann, USAF Corona Ace Oral History Program, Interview #K239.0512–630, 11 Oct 72 and 30 Oct 72, Maxwell AFB, AL, p. 46.

21–23. Captain Richard S. Ritchie, US Air Force Corona Ace Oral History Program, Interview K239.0512–1078, USAF Historical Research Center, 16 February 1977, pp. 122–123.

24. Dave Grossman, *On Killing: The Psychological Cost of Learning to Kill in War and Society* (Boston: Little, Brown and Company, 1995), p. 3.

25. Grossman, *On Killing,* pp. 183–184.

26. Charles DeBellevue interviewed by the author, 15 August 1997, telephone.

27. John Markle, interviewed by the author, 15 August 1997, telephone.

28. Roger Locher, interviewed by the author, 8 July 1997.

29. Marshall L. Michel, III, *Clashes: Air Combat Over North Vietnam 1965–1972* (Annapolis, MD: Naval Institute Press, 1997), pp. 348–350.

30. Michel, *Clashes,* p. 216.

31. USAF Fighter Weapons School Report, Project Red Baron III: *Air-to-Air Encounters in Southeast Asia,* Vol. II, Pt. 1 (June 1974), p. 104.

32–33. Roger Locher, interviewed by the author, 8 July 1997, telephone.

34. Patty Locher, interviewed by the author,

35. Vance O. Mitchell, "Air Force Officers: Personnel Policy Development, 1944–1974" (Washington, DC: Air Force History and Museums Program, 1996), p. 318.

36. Michel, *Clashes,* p. 397.

37–41. Patty Locher, interviewed by the author, 13 June 1997, telephone.

42. Steve Ritchie also claimed that a therapeutic massage helped to relax him after a long mission. According to Ritchie, a pilot could get an ice cold Singha beer

and a sports massage for $3. For an extra $2 the massage girl would throw in a hand job, but that was generally as far as things went—hence the "steam and cream" nickname. Steve, however, claims he was loyal to his Thai girlfriend and did not indulge in the "extras." Ritchard S. "Steve" Ritchie, interview with author, 26 April 1999.

43–47. Patty Locher Interview ed by the author, 13 June 1997, telephone.

48. Charles DeBellevue, interviewed by the author, telephone.

49. Michel, *Clashes*, p. 251.

50–52. Charles DeBellevue, interviewed by the author, 12 August 1997.

53. Rob Young, "How to Fly and Fight . . . Again: The Story of Capt. Roger C. Locher," unpublished manuscript on file at National Air Intelligence Center, Dayton, OH (1996), p. 4; USAF Southeast Asia Monograph Series, Monograph 2, *The Battle for the Skies over North Vietnam* (Washington, DC: U.S. Government Printing Office, 1976), p. 149.

54. Roger Locher, interviewed by the author, 8 July 1997

55. Roger Locher, e-mail to the author, 5 August 1997.

56. Ibid. Moreover, Steve Ritchie mentioned that Lodge "stated, without going into *that* much detail on *that* mission, previously [8 May] that he did not want to be shot down and captured because he was privy to too much information. He knew too much, and he was not going to be captured. Now, most of us didn't believe him, we did not believe that he would go in with the airplane. Here's what he told us: 'If your airplane is on fire, burning, don't bail out immediately, because the airplane is *probably* not going to blow up.' We knew of no time when an F-4 was on fire that it blew up. What Lodge instructed all of his flights, and was a part of his teaching, was to fly the airplane, even if it was on fire, toward a safe bail-out area as long as you could until it quit flying. In other words, when the fire burned through the control system and the airplane quit flying you would, obviously, have to bail out. He said, 'Now, I'm not going to bail out. I'm never going to bail out because I'm not going to be captured. I'm not telling *you* not to bail out, what I'm telling you to do is fly the airplane until it quits flying.'" Richard S. "Steve" Ritchie, interviewed by the author, p. 31.

57. Roger Locher, e-mail to the author, 5 August 1997.

58. Charles DeBellevue, interviewed by the author, 12 August 1997

59. John Markle, interviewed by the author, 15 August 1997

60. On March 30, 1972, the North Vietnamese launched the Easter offensive, a major coordinated attack against targets along the border with South Vietnam. Twelve North Vietnamese Army divisions and over 500 tanks would eventually participate the campaign. To halt the drive, President Nixon relied heavily on airpower. He ordered the restrictions put in place by President Johnson in November 1968 against bombing targets in North Vietnam to be removed, beginning on 16 April 1972. On 10 May, President Nixon implemented Linebacker, a bold new air campaign designed to cut off the invasion forces from their supplies and achieve "peace with honor" at the negotiating table: an American withdrawal that did not involve

an imminent Communist take-over of the South and the prompt release of all American POWs. The campaign, named after a position in Nixon's favorite sport, quickly escalated bombing levels back to where they were at the height of the air war in 1967–1968.

61. Young, "How to Fly and Fight . . . Again," p. 4.

62. Jeffrey Ethell and Alfred Price, *One Day in a Long War: May 10, 1972, North Vietnam* (New York: Random House, 1989), pp. 55–56.

63. Ethell and Price, *One Day*, p. 56; USAF Southeast Asia Monograph Series, *The Battle for the Skies over North Vietnam*, pp. 160–161.

64. Roger Locher, quoted in Futrell et al., *Aces and Aerial Victories*, p. 92.

65. John Markle, interviewed by the author, 15 August 1997.

66. John Markle, quoted in Futrell et al., *Aces and Aerial Victories*, p. 93.

67. John Markle, quoted in Ethell and Price, *One Day*, p. 58.

68. Captain Richard S. Ritchie, USAF Corona Ace Oral History Program, USAF Interview #K239.0512–630, 11 Oct 1972 and 30 Oct 1972, p. 51.

69. USAF Fighter Weapons School Report, Project Red Baron III: Air-to-Air Encounters in Southeast Asia, Vol. II, Pt 1, June 1974, p. 101.

70. Roger Locher, quoted in Ethell, and Price, *One Day*, pp. 58–59.

71. Charles DeBellevue, interviewed by the author, 12 August 1997

72. Roger Locher as cited in Ethell, p. 59. quoted in Ethell and Price, *One Day*, p. 59.

73. Red Baron III, Vol. II, Pt. 1, p. 101.

74. PACAF Intelligence Index of USAF Personnel MIA/PW Southeast Asia, Headquarters PACAF, 31 July 1969, pp. 8–40.

75. In an F-4, the WSO can eject independently of the pilot; Roger Locher, quoted in Ethell and Price, *One Day*, p. 60.

76. Roger Locher, interviewed by the author, 8 July 1997.

77. Tommy Feezel, quoted in Ethell and Price, *One Day*, p. 61.

78. Roger Locher, e-mail, to author, 5 August 1997.

79. Captain Richard S. Ritchie, USAF Corona Ace Oral History Program, Interview #K239.0512–630, p. 52.

80. Charles DeBellevue, interviewed by the author, 12 August 1997.

81. Captain Richard S. Ritchie, USAF Corona Ace Oral History Program, Interview #K239.0512–630, p. 51.

82. Charles DeBellevue, interviewed by the author, 12 August 1997.

83. Patty Locher, quoted in Ethell and Price, *One Day*, p. 153.

84–85. Roger Locher, interviewed by the author,

86. Roger Locher, Joseph Blank, "Shot Down in North Vietnam!" *The Reader's Digest* (April 1973), p. 82.

87. Roger Locher, interviewed by the author, 8 July 1997.

88. Roger Locher, quoted in Blank, "Shot Down," p. 82.

89. Roger Locher, quoted in Ethell and Price, *One Day*, p. 152.

90–91. Roger Locher, interviewed by the author.

92. Roger Locher, quoted in Blank, "Shot Down," p. 83.

93. Richard S. "Steve" Ritchie, "Leadership that Inspires Excellence," unpublished essay, p. 3.

94. Ron Smith, as quoted in Ethell and Price, *One Day,* p. 158.

95. Patty Locher, interviewed by the author, 13 June 1997.

96. Patty Locher, quoted in Ethell and Price, *One Day,* p. 159.

97. Patty Locher, interviewed by the author, June 1997.

98. The strike force consisted of rescue helicopters; back-up rescue helicopters; fighters and ground attack planes to protect the helicopters; support planes such as tankers, SAM suppression; electronic warfare, and command and control aircraft; aircraft to suppress the MiGs at Yen Bai airfield; aircraft to engage in diversionary strikes; support aircraft for the Yen Bai raid and diversionary strikes; and aircraft and helicopters to rescue any of the rescue forces, support aircraft, or diversionary aircraft shot down.

99. Gen. John W. Vogt, Jr., quoted in Ethell and Price, *One Day,* p. 159.

100. Capt. Ron Smith, quoted in Ethell and Price, *One Day,* p. 161.

101. Roger Locher, interviewed by the author, 13 June 1997.

102–103. Dale Stovall, quoted in Ethell and Price, *One Day,* p. 162.

104. Patty Locher, interviewed by the author, 13 June 1997.

105. Roger Locher, interviewed by the author, 8 July 1997.

106. Richard S. "Steve" Ritchie, "Leadership that Inspires Excellence," p. 4.

107. See Darrel D. Whitcomb, *The Rescue of Bat 21* (Annapolis, MD; Naval Institute Press, 1998), p. 153.

108. Richard S. "Steve" Ritchie, quoted in Futrell et al., *Aces and Aerial Victories,* p. 96.

109. U.S. Air Force Reserve, "Interview with an Ace," (Washington, DC: U.S. Government Printing Office, 1995), p. 4.

110. Charles DeBellevue, interviewed by the author, 12 August 1997.

111–112. Steve Ritchie, interviewed by the author, 8 Junuary 1997.

113. These planes drop Strips of tim foil to jam North Vietnamese radar.

114. U.S. Air Force Reserve, "Interview with an Ace," p. 2.

115. Steve Ritchie, interviewed by the author.

116. Transcript reprinted from Futrell et al., *Aces and Aerial Victories,* pp. 19–22, 8 June 1997.

117–118. Richard S. "Steve" Ritchie, quoted in Futrell et al. *Aces and Aerial Victories,* p. 103.

119. Richard S. "Steve" Ritchie, interviewed by the author, 8 June 1997.

CONCLUSION

1. See Stephen Coonts, *War in the Air: True Accounts of the 20th Century's Most Dramatic Air Battles by the Men Who Fought Them* (New York: Pocket Books, 1997).

INDEX

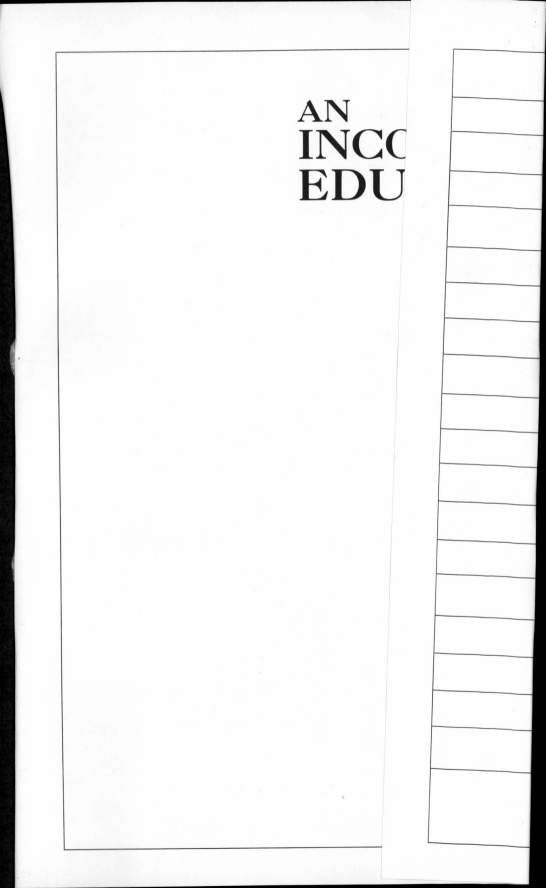

AN
INCO
EDU

AN INCOMPLETE EDUCATION

Judy Jones & William Wilson

BALLANTINE BOOKS

NEW YORK

Portions of this book originally appeared in *Esquire*.

Grateful acknowledgment is made to the following for permission to reprint previously published
material:

City Lights Books, Inc.: excerpt from the poem "The Day Lady Died" by Frank O'Hara.
Copyright © 1964 by Frank O'Hara. Reprinted by permission of City Lights Books, Inc.

Farrar, Straus & Giroux, Inc.: excerpt from the poem "For the Union Dead" from *For the Union
Dead* by Robert Lowell. Copyright © 1960, 1964 by Robert Lowell. UK rights administered by
Faber & Faber, Ltd. Reprinted by permission of the publishers.

Henry Holt and Company, Inc. and Jonathan Cape, Ltd.: excerpts from the poems "Nothing
Gold Can Stay" and "Directive" by Robert Frost from *The Poetry of Robert Frost*, edited by
Edward Connery Lathem. Copyright 1923, 1947, © 1969 by Holt, Rinehart and Winston, Inc.
Copyright 1951 by Robert Frost. Copyright © 1975 by Lesley Frost Ballantine. Reprinted by
permission of the publishers and the Estate of Robert Frost.

Harper & Row Publishers, Inc.: excerpt from the poem "Daddy" from *The Collected Poems of
Sylvia Plath*, edited by Ted Hughes. Copyright © 1963 by Ted Hughes. Reprinted by permission
of Harper & Row Publishers, Inc.

Page 659 constitutes a continuation of the copyright page.

LIBRARY OF CONGRESS CATALOGING-IN-PUBLICATION DATA

Jones, Judy, 1946–
An incomplete education.

Includes index.
1. Handbooks, vade-mecums, etc.   I. Wilson, William, 1948–   .   II. Title.
AG105.J64   1987   031'.02   86-91572
ISBN 0-345-29570-6

Text design by Beth Tondreau
Photo editor: Cheryl Moch
Manufactured in the United States of America

20   19   18   17   16   15

CONTENTS